CHRISTIAN DOCTRINE

CHRISTIAN DOCTRINE

W. T. CONNER, B.D., Ph.D., D.D.

Professor of Systematic Theology in the Southwestern Baptist
Theological Seminary, Seminary Hill, Texas; author of
The Epistles of John, The Resurrection of Jesus,
Revelation and God, and other books

BROADMAN PRESS
NASHVILLE, TENNESSEE

Copyright, 1937
Broadman Press
Nashville, Tennessee

4217-01
ISBN: 0-8054-1701-X

Printed in the United States of America

THIS BOOK IS GRATEFULLY DEDICATED TO
THE MEMORY OF MY THREE TEACHERS IN
THEOLOGY
CALVIN GOODSPEED, A. H. STRONG
AND E. Y. MULLINS

CONTENTS

CONTENTS

PREFACE

This book is a revision of my former book, *A System of Christian Doctrine*. The revision is in the nature of an abbreviation and simplification. I have added, however, two chapters on the church and the ordinances. These two chapters are reproduced, by permission of the publisher, from my book, *Gospel Doctrines*.

I have had in mind a double purpose in the preparation of this book. One is its use as a text for a course in Christian Doctrine in colleges. I find a considerable interest in the matter among Bible teachers in colleges and a seeming need for such a book. In some cases where time is limited, such teachers might find it expedient or necessary to omit certain portions of the book. Each teacher, of course, would exercise his own judgment as to what portion of the book he would omit. I would suggest, however, that in some cases he might find it advisable, in case of limited time, to begin with chapter VII and give a course on the doctrine of salvation and the Christian life. In some cases he might find it advisable to give two courses, using chapters I-VI for the first and the rest of the book for the other.

Such a study of Christian Doctrine in college, as is here contemplated, would undoubtedly prove of value to laymen and women and also to ministerial students whether they later attended a theological seminary or not. In case they attended a theological seminary, such a study would be a helpful preparation for a more extended course in systematic theology. In case they were deprived of the privilege of a seminary course, such a study of doctrine in college would be all the more necessary for them.

In preparing this book, however, I had in mind the general reader. There are hundreds of preachers and other Christian workers in our churches who need a brief treatment of Christian Doctrine. The reading of such a book ought to quicken for them both mind and heart. It ought to deepen their devotion and quicken their activity in the cause of Christ. It ought also to prepare them for further study in this field. The author hopes that the book may be widely useful in these two respects —as a text for a brief course in Christian Doctrine and for general reading.

I am greatly indebted to Rev. S. A. Newman, instructor in the department of Systematic Theology in the Southwestern Seminary, for help in preparing the manuscript and in making the indexes. I am also indebted to Misses Marie Tatum and Wilmoth Woods for efficient service in preparing the manuscript.

W. T. CONNER.

Seminary Hill, Texas.

INTRODUCTION

THE NATURE AND NEED OF CHRISTIAN DOCTRINE

I. NATURE

    1. Definition
    2. Purpose

II. NEED

    1. Demanded by man's nature
    2. Teaching emphasized in the New Testament
    3. Christian life based on truth
    4. Knowledge of truth necessary to propagate the gospel
    5. Knowledge of truth necessary to defend the gospel

INTRODUCTION

THE NATURE AND NEED OF CHRISTIAN DOCTRINE

In this introductory chapter we will make a preliminary survey of our subject. Certain questions naturally arise in approaching any study: such as, What is the nature of the study? What is the need for it? These questions we will consider in this introductory study.

I. The nature of our study

1. *Definition*

Christian Doctrine is that line of study that undertakes to set out the teachings of the Christian religion. It is the organized exposition of the main doctrines of Christianity. It is the setting out in more or less complete and systematic form of the ideas necessary to an understanding of the Christian religion.

2. *Purpose*

The purpose of a treatment of Christian Doctrine is not primarily to prove that Christianity is true, but rather to set out what Christians believe about their religion. This means that we assume the Christian point of view and undertake to make clear to our minds and to others the nature and meaning of Christianity. We try to discover and state what the Christian view is with reference to the main facts and phases of Christianity. It is, then, the interpretation of Christianity as a Christian sees it. It is an effort to make intelligible the facts of Christianity.

II. The need for Christian Doctrine

Many people today have little patience with any kind of definite doctrinal teaching in religion. This aversion to religious doctrine is not confined to those who are altogether indifferent or hostile to religion. Even many religious people are unfriendly toward any kind of definite doctrinal teaching. They wish to confine religion to the realm of feeling or friendly good will, or make it a matter of practical social activity. There has been much discussion as to whether religion is properly a matter of feeling, or belief, or activity. As a matter of fact, it is all three. Without the element of feeling, religion has little motive power; without doctrinal belief, the element of intelligence is lacking; without practical activity, it is vapid and empty.

Now we maintain that the element of doctrine in Christianity is necessary for the following reasons:

1. *The nature of man necessitates doctrine*

As indicated above, the true ideal of religion involves the whole of man's nature. When religion ministers to only one aspect of man's being, then religion becomes one-sided and perverted and develops one-sided and perverted people. Men cannot expect to exercise their intelligence in all other phases of life's activities and then stifle their intellects when it comes to religion. Men will think about religion; and when a man thinks about religion, what he thinks is his religious doctrine. The man who is unfriendly to religious doctrine has thought to some extent about religion and often tells us with great vehemence what his thoughts are. That gives us his religious doctrine or doctrines. So, as a matter of fact, there can be no such thing as religion without some element of doctrine.

2. *New Testament Christianity put large emphasis on teaching*

About forty-five times in our Four Gospels, Jesus is called a teacher, and about the same number of times he is said to have taught.[1] Paul and the other apostles and New Testament leaders were teachers. The same thing is true of the Old Testament prophets. This fact —that Old and New Testament religion placed great emphasis on teaching—is so evident that it need not be argued further. Those who believe that the New Testament should be our guide will probably agree that teaching or doctrine is necessary in Christianity. Teaching or doctrine was essential in New Testament Christianity. We hold it is necessary yet.

[1] See Williams, C. B., *The Function of Teaching in Christianity*, pp. 253 ff.

New Testament Christianity was a religion of truth. It put emphasis on truth. Christianity always has claimed to be a form of truth. If Christianity is not a form of truth, then Christians have always been deluded as to the nature of their religion.

Paul tells us what he preached as the gospel. It was that Christ died for our sins according to the Scriptures; that he was buried; and that he was raised from the dead according to the Scriptures (1 Cor. 15: 3, 4). The gospel, then, consists of certain facts, but not just the bare facts (if there could be such a thing), but also of the meaning of those facts. The meaning of these facts carries with it the conclusion that the gospel is one of truth, of significance. Christianity does not consist of unintelligible facts, nor of mere sentiment. It is based on facts, but facts of very definite significance for us and for our spiritual lives.

3. *A knowledge of the truth is necessary in the Christian life*

The Christian life is a life of faith. One becomes a Christian by an act of faith. By grace through faith are we saved (Eph. 2: 8). And whatever else faith may be, it claims to be a recognition of truth and an act of trust based on that knowledge. It is an act of venture based on the promise of the gospel. Faith is based on the Word of the gospel. The gospel is good news—good news of something that God offers to men in Christ Jesus. Faith is the acceptance of that offer.

A knowledge of the truth is necessary to the growth of Christian character.

By faith we enter the Christian life; by faith we grow in the Christian life. Faith is an act of trust based on the promise of the gospel, and by feeding on the Word of the gospel, faith grows. Without a developing knowledge of the truth, there can be little or no growth in the Christian life. One's spiritual life is as dependent on a knowledge of the truth for development as his physical life is on food.

4. *A knowledge of the truth is necessary to propagate the gospel*

One of the fundamental impulses of the Christian life is the impulse to propagate the gospel. It was pointed out above that becoming a Christian was a rational and voluntary act based on a knowledge of the gospel. The one propagating the gospel, then, must be able to give to the one whom he would bring into the Christian life an intelligent conception of what it means to be a Christian. Becoming a Christian is not just a blind plunge in the dark. The propagator of the gospel, therefore, must have an intelligent grasp of the meaning of the gospel and he must be able to give an intelligent statement of the same.

5. A knowledge of the truth is necessary to a defense of the gospel

Sometimes the gospel must be defended. But one cannot defend that which has no meaning. A religion without doctrine would be a religion without meaning. Such a religion could be neither propagated nor defended.

In the New Testament, especially toward the latter part, we find Paul and others vigorously defending the gospel against those who would deny or pervert it. Paul spent much of his life and energy opposing the Judaizers, and Paul and John both vigorously defended the gospel against the Gnostics. To do so they had to state the gospel in terms of definite meaning.

The element of doctrine in Christianity, then, is necessary. To talk about religion without doctrine is to talk nonsense. Of course, this is not to say that doctrine is all that there is in religion. It is possible to over-emphasize the place of doctrine. We need to remember, also, that doctrine does not exist for its own sake; it is not something to be held in the mind and thought about only. It is a program of activity. The whole New Testament emphasizes the fact that to hear the Word is not enough; it must be put into action. Doctrine is not a system of ideas to be contemplated only; it is a call to life and activity. One must not only hear the Word; he must also do it. But, we repeat, doctrine is necessary or our activity is blind and purposeless.

MAN'S CAPACITY FOR GOD

CHAPTER I

MAN'S CAPACITY FOR GOD

CHAPTER I

MAN'S CAPACITY FOR GOD

If man is to live a religious life that is worthy of the name, he must know God, he must enter into fellowship with God. This will necessarily involve two things: revelation on God's part and a capacity on man's part to know God; or, to use the more significant expression, he must be capable of fellowship with God. The question of revelation will be discussed later. In this chapter we want to look at the question of man's capacity for knowing God or having fellowship with God.

We must keep in mind, however, that these two questions in reality belong together, that they are two phases of one question, not in reality separate questions. The question as to whether man is capable of fellowship with God cannot be settled apart from the question of revelation, no more than the question as to whether man can see could be settled apart from objects of vision. Of course, man could not see unless there were objects of vision, nor could there be objects of vision unless man had the power to see. Each involves the other. The same thing is true with reference to revelation and man's capacity for fellowship with God. Sometimes men have discussed man's capacity to know God as if such a capacity in man could be something apart from revelation on God's part. Or they have discussed revelation as if there could be such a thing as revelation apart from a capacity on man's part to receive such a revelation. But all such abstractions miss the point. Man has no capacity to know God except as God reveals himself, nor could God reveal himself to a being who had no capacity to know him. Each implies the other.

[17]

Nor is this to be taken to mean that in religion God and man stand on a plane of equality with each other. This is not true. God always takes the initiative and acts creatively. Man recognizes God as sovereign and acts responsively. Yet man must have a capacity to respond to the creative and redemptive power of God. In other words, there must be something more in man than there is in things or animals; else he could not be religious. If there were not found in man a capacity not found in things or animals, God could not bring him into fellowship with himself.

I. The biblical view of man

1. *Man more than a physical organism*

It is evident from experience and observation on the one hand and the teaching of the Scriptures on the other that man is more than a physical being. His body came from the dust of the ground; but God breathed into his nostrils the breath of life and man became a living soul (Gen. 2: 7). God made man in his own image (Gen. 1: 26, 27). This evidently refers to man's spiritual nature, not to his body. This divine image may be reflected in the fact that man walks upright,[1] but the essence of it lies in something deeper, something not visible to the physical eye. Man, then, is more than a physical being. There is an unseen or non-material phase to his life.

2. *Man a spiritual personality*

What the Bible means by man's being created in the divine image may be expressed by saying that man is a spiritual person. Perhaps it would be better to say that he has the capacity for becoming such a person. The greatest thing about man is not what he is, but it is what he is capable of becoming.

It might be well to look at man's capacities, those that are involved in his personality. What are the powers possessed by man that make him capable of growing into

---

[1]See Strong, A. H., *Systematic Theology*, Vol. II, p. 523.

a spiritual personality—not powers fully developed but
rather capacities or potentialities?

(1) One is intelligence.

The power to think, to know, marks man off from
things and animals. Animals have a rudimentary form
of intelligence, but in this respect they cannot be put in
the same class with man. Man has the power to reason,
to reflect, to investigate, to come to conclusions, to guide
his life by his thoughts and conclusions. This the lower
animals cannot do. Man has not only the power of consciousness; he has also the power of self-consciousness.
He has the power to objectify self, to make self an object of thought, to know oneself in relation to the world
in which we live and in relation to other selves. No dog
or horse or ape ever shows any sign of such a capacity.

(2) Another capacity that belongs to man by virtue
of his spiritual personality is the power of will.

Man has the power to choose, to form ideals, to direct
his energies toward the realization of his ideals. Some
men hold that man has no freedom, that he is wholly
determined by heredity and environment. Others have
held that his freedom is practically unlimited, that he
can do anything he chooses. Neither of these positions
is true. Man is free, but his freedom is limited. He is
partly determined by heredity and environment. By
his heredity and environment, very serious limitations
are placed on him, but to some extent he can rise above
these. We might say, rather, that within certain bounda-
ries marked by these, man is self-directive. He is not
wholly the slave of either heredity or environment.
Within the range of his heredity and environment, he
has power of choice and self-determination. He has the
power of choice sufficient to make him a responsible
moral agent.

This freedom is enhanced when man comes into conscious fellowship with God in Christ. The New Testament emphasizes this freedom of the sons of God—those
who are reborn by faith in Christ. This is a freedom

that gives him a victory in principle over himself and the world. Man as possessed by the Spirit of God is truly a regal being in his power over the hostile forces of nature and of sin. And even by nature there is an inherent power of choice in him that makes him a "subject of gospel address," a power that belongs to no being in the realm of nature below him.

(3) There belongs to man also the power of rational affection.

Lower animals have the power of instinctive affection. In the animal world, the mother will sacrifice herself for the good of her young. But in human life, this power of sacrifice rises to the level of rational quality. That is, a person may, and sometimes does, rise to the level of deliberate sacrifice for the good of others. This is exhibited in the family relation—parent for child or child for parent. Or such sacrifice may be manifested on the part of friend for friend, patriot for his country, or in many other human relations.

Again, this power is seen at its best only where man has been purified from sin and drawn into fellowship with God in Christ. The supreme demonstration of such love was in the Cross of Christ; and Christ alone has the power to inspire such love in the hearts of men so that it becomes the consuming and controlling passion of life.

(4) As a spiritual personality, man also has a moral nature.

This means that he has a sense of right and wrong, that he can distinguish right from wrong, and that he judges himself and others with reference to right and wrong.

The sense of right and wrong is inherent in man; it is a part of his moral constitution. Without this he would not be human; he would be only a beast. Man possesses this sense of right and wrong by virtue of the fact that he is human. By the sense of right and wrong we mean the feeling (or intuition) that there is such a thing as right and wrong and that we are obligated to do the right and avoid the wrong. This sense of right and wrong cannot be originated in either the individual or the race by experience. So far as this author can see, it comes to both the race and the individual by a creative act of God. Nor can this sense of right and wrong be interpreted in terms of any other kind of experience. It cannot be reduced to the pleasurable or the utilitarian. The feeling that a thing is right and that it is pleasant or useful are two different types of experience altogether. The feeling that an act or course of conduct is right is not a feeling of expediency. It partakes of the nature of a "categorical imperative." We feel that we are *bound* to do the right whether it is pleasurable or expedient or not. We *may* seek the pleasurable or expedient; we *must* pursue the right. Moral obligation is something imposed. We do not place the obligation on ourselves. Sometimes we would give the world if we could throw it off. It is placed on us by the system of things to which we belong—as the Christian believes by God. This feeling of moral obligation may be increased and clarified, or it may be dulled by experience; but clearly from its nature it is not originated by or in experience.

II. Personal powers necessary to a Christian life

We would like now to point out that these powers or capacities of man as a spiritual person are essential to his religious life. We believe this could be made evident with reference to any type of religion worth considering, but we will consider it from the standpoint of the gospel of Christ. Since it is Christian Doctrine that we are considering, not religion in general, let us see how these powers are essential to man's fellowship with God in Christ. This is so evident, however, if we keep in mind the teachings of the New Testament, that no extensive discussion is necessary.

The gospel of the New Testament was a message that each man must hear and accept for himself. It addressed itself to man as an intelligent being and appealed to his mind and will. One did not enjoy its benefits by virtue of being a Jew, nor by virtue of being a member of a particular family. Jesus was a divider. He divided families (Matt. 10: 21, 35, 36). Men aligned themselves for and against him. He appealed to the wills of men. They must choose to follow him.

Moreover, he summed up God's requirements for man in love—love to God and man (Mark 12: 30, 31). This love that God calls for is not natural affection; it is rational good will. And the sons of God are expected to have this rational good will toward all men—enemies as well as friends. In this way only can we be the true sons of God (Matt. 5: 43ff.).

Only, then, as an intelligent and free being, with power to know and choose, can man respond to and accept the gospel of Christ. Only as a being with a moral nature capable of knowing right from wrong with capacity to love God and man, can he live the life required by the gospel.

III. Man's thirst for God

There is something in man that will not be satisfied with the seen and the temporal. Something in him cries out for the spiritual and the eternal. Man thirsts for God. In the midst of the visible and the transient, he reaches out after the invisible and the abiding. The Psalmist voices this universal cry of the human heart when he says: "As the hart panteth after the water brooks, so panteth my soul after thee, O God" (Psalm 42: 1). Wherever men have been found they have had some form of religion. If there are any exceptions to this statement, they are so insignificant as to be negligible. All men of all races and climes have cried out for God.

Another noteworthy fact is that this craving of the human spirit is met in Christ. He is the light of the world (John 9: 5). He is the bread of life (John 6: 35).

He is the way, the truth, and the life (John 14: 6). He is to the soul what light is to the material world. He is to man's spirit what bread is to his body. He satisfies the deepest yearnings of the human spirit.

Thus we see that man was made for the gospel, and the gospel was made for man. They fit each other as the glove fits the hand. Each was designed for the other. Man's nature was made for God, and apart from God man misses his true destiny.

REVELATION

CHAPTER II

REVELATION

I. THE MEANING OF REVELATION

1. Definition
2. Phases of this definition
   (1) It is God's act
   (2) It is God that is revealed
   (3) It comes to us through Christ
   (4) It makes possible fellowship with God

II. THE MEDIUM OF REVELATION

1. Jesus' consciousness of God
2. Jesus' teaching concerning God
3. Jesus' character and life
4. Jesus' claims concerning his relations to God
   (1) That God sent him into the world
   (2) That he had a special and intimate knowledge of God
   (3) That he is the sole mediator of such knowledge of God
5. Jesus' redemptive work
6. Revelation through nature
   (1) Is insufficient for man's religious needs
   (2) Is essential

III. THE BIBLE AND REVELATION

1. The Four Gospels present the heart of the gospel
2. The Acts records the work of the gospel
3. The Epistles interpret the meaning of the gospel
4. Revelation forecasts the triumph of the gospel
5. The Bible is centered in Christ
6. The Bible is a record of a progressive revelation
7. The Bible is God's message given through human agency
8. The Bible is authoritative

CHAPTER II

REVELATION

As set forth in the last chapter, religion, if it is to have any reality worth while, must be a matter of fellowship between God and man. But such fellowship is dependent on two things: revelation on God's part, and a capacity on man's part for fellowship with God. This corresponds to the fact that in all knowledge two factors are necessary: an object of knowledge, and the activity of the knowing mind. Religion is a reciprocal relationship between God and man in which God discloses himself to man and man responds to God's revelation of himself.

All religions hold the idea that somehow God (or the gods) reveals himself to man. The idea of revelation of some kind and in some way is organic to the idea of religion. It is very doubtful, to say the least of it, if there could be religion worthy of the name that was not thought of as being dependent on revelation.

In the last chapter we considered man's capacity for God. Now we wish to examine the idea of revelation—in particular, the Christian doctrine of revelation.

I. The meaning of revelation

First of all, let us consider the meaning of revelation. What is revelation?

1. *Definition*

Revelation in the Christian sense is that self-disclosure of God in Christ which makes it possible for man to know God and to live a life of fellowship with him.

2. *Phases of this definition*

We might with profit dwell on some phases of this definition and thus bring out more clearly some things in the meaning of revelation.

(1) Notice that revelation is God's act.

Sometimes men have spoken of man's knowledge of God as being a kind of joint activity on the part of God,—of man-revelation on God's part and discovery on man's part. This can be very easily put in such a way as to be false. Man's knowledge of God is a revelation on God's part. It is man's discovery in the sense that it is something new in his experience. He comes to know something that he did not know before. It breaks in on his consciousness as a new experience. It is new, not only in the sense that he now knows something that he did not know before, but also in the sense that it is a new *kind* of experience. Man does not discover God in the same sense or in the same way that he discovers truth in the realm of science or philosophy or other fields of human learning.

We do not mean to say either that God reveals himself to man apart from man's seeking. Man seeks God and God responds to man's seeking by imparting a knowledge of himself.

But we do mean to say that, when man comes into a conscious fellowship with God, he knows in his heart that his seeking did not produce that fellowship. He is conscious that God produced this knowledge of himself in man's heart. This means a further thing—namely: that man's very seeking after God is itself the work of God. As seen in the previous chapter, man must have the capacity to respond to God. But in that connection we need to remember two things: One is that this capacity is itself the gift of God; the other is that God himself stirs up, guides, and directs man's aspirations toward himself. Thus man's capacity to know God, his feeling out after God, his awakening to a sense of God's presence—all this is God's work. Revelation is thus God's work from beginning to end. He does not reveal himself apart from man's response but he brings about that response itself.

(2) Not only is revelation God's act; it is God that is revealed. Revelation is a self-disclosure. God discloses himself. Doctor Mullins reminds us that revelation is primarily an impartation of God himself rather than of truth about God.[1]

There is today a decided movement back to the idea that God rather than man constitutes the center of religion. And God is the center in Christianity, not only in the sense that God acts, but also in the sense that God acts to make himself known. The content of revelation is God-centered. God is the substance of revelation.

(3) Another thing involved in our definition is that revelation comes to us through Christ. Christ is such an embodiment of God that he could say: "He that hath seen me hath seen the Father" (John 14: 9). This point will be developed later in this chapter.

(4) Revelation is such a disclosure on God's part as to make possible a life of fellowship with God. Revelation is a making of God known. But it is not designed primarily to give us a theory of God and the universe. This is not its purpose. Its purpose is such a disclosure of God as to give man a knowledge of God designed to bring man into fellowship with God. This definition gives us the general idea of revelation in Christianity. In the following discussion some phases of this matter will be developed more fully.

II. The medium of revelation

One of the main factors in the Christian Doctrine of revelation is that Christ is the medium of revelation.

1. *Jesus' consciousness of God*

One of the most noteworthy things about Jesus—a fact at once obvious and significant—is that he was a religious man. The whole of life was lived in view of God and was consecrated to him. Every duty was duty to God. There was no sphere of life in which God was

---

[1]*The Christian Religion in Its Doctrinal Expression*, p. 141.

not recognized. There was no element in life that was secular, nothing that was common or unclean. God was recognized as the Source of every blessing and as the Master of destiny for this world and the world to come.

His life was one of unclouded fellowship with God. He was distinguished not only by the fact that he was a man whose whole life was religious, but also by the further fact that his communion with God was unbroken. It was his meat and drink to do the will of God. The consciousness of God was to him the breath of life. Never did he betray the least consciousness of disharmony or lack of fellowship with God. The earliest recorded saying we have from him was, "Knew ye not that I must be in my Father's house?" (Luke 2: 49) while with his expiring breath he said, "Father, into thy hands I commend my spirit" (Luke 23: 46). His whole life was one of obedience to God. Rather than deny the Father's will, he drank the bitter cup of suffering and death on the Cross.

2. *Jesus' teaching concerning God*

Another factor in Jesus' revelation of God was his teaching concerning God. Jesus was a religious teacher, and central in his teaching was his doctrine of God. It is generally held by all classes of students of the New Testament that Jesus' teaching concerning God is the highest the world has ever seen. He is a God of perfect wisdom and power. There is no doubt about the personality of God in the conception of Jesus. To him God was no abstract principle or impersonal power or pantheistic absolute. He was a person of perfect righteousness and love. He is good to the evil as well as to the good; he sends the rain on the unjust as well as on the just (Matt. 5: 43-48). This goodness to the evil is the chief element in his perfect character, the one that should be imitated by men if they would be true sons of the Father. His character can be summed up in the name Father. He is interested in all that concerns his children on earth. The very hairs of their head are all numbered. Not a

sparrow falls to the ground without his notice (Matt.
10: 29, 30). His people can trust him to supply their
every need (Matt. 6: 25ff.). He knows beforehand what
they need and they can therefore pray to him with confidence that he will supply their need (Matt. 6: 6-8). He
does not give evil things but good, in answer to the
prayers of his people (Matt. 7: 7-11). His mercy is
extended to sinners and he will gladly receive them when
they repent and come to him (Luke 15). We are not
to interpret this to mean, however, that the sterner qualities are absent from the character of God as taught by
Jesus. He warns men to fear him who is able to destroy
both soul and body in hell (Matt. 10: 28). The man
who has the spirit of hatred toward his brother or the
spirit of unforgiveness, and manifests this spirit in hasty
and unbrotherly language, is in danger of the judgment
and the hell of fire (Matt. 5: 21-26).

3. *Jesus' character and life*

Another thing that enters as an important factor into
Jesus' revelation of God is his spotless character and life
of service to God and to man. Jesus was the perfect embodiment and representation of his own teaching. He
was all that he taught. He held up before men the perfect character of God as the ideal toward which they
were to strive (Matt. 5: 48). No disciple of Jesus has
ever been able to reach that high ideal. But what about
Jesus? With him the story is different. He was the
embodiment in human form of the holy life of God. No
man could have a higher aspiration in the realm of character than to desire to be like him. He so lived among
men that to be like him became the passion of the noblest
souls who knew him.

This perfect character of Jesus was the exponent in
human form of the holy character of God. When Jesus
was accused of eating with publicans and sinners, his
answer was to admit the charge and then to give three
parables to show that God loved sinners, held them as of
practically infinite value and stood ready to forgive the

penitent prodigal (Luke 15). What was this but to say that his love for sinners and outcasts was the love of God? And sinners from that day to this have so taken it and by coming to Christ have found the forgiving love of God. Jesus said that he cast out demons in the power of God (Matt. 12: 22ff.). His works of healing and blessing men were the method by which the benevolence of God manifested itself toward sinful and needy humanity. The works of Jesus were the works of the Father and were a manifestation of his unity with the Father (John 14: 10, 11).

4. Jesus' claims concerning his relations to God

In connection with the teaching of Jesus concerning God and the character of Jesus as the embodiment of the moral life of God, it will be well to look at the claims of Jesus concerning his relations with God. Here there are three distinct, but related, claims on the part of Jesus.

(1) One is that God sent him into the world. Jesus lived his life under the sense of a divine mission. His one desire was to do the work for which God sent him into the world. He was distinctly conscious that he came forth from God on a mission; to the accomplishment of this mission he gave his life (John 4: 34; 5: 30; 6: 38).

(2) Jesus also laid claim to a special and intimate knowledge of God, a knowledge of God that did not belong to any other. He says, "Neither doth any know the Father, save the Son" (Matt. 11: 27). Jesus here lays claim to a direct and immediate knowledge of God that other men did not have. Again, speaking of the Father, he says, "I know him; because I am from him, and he sent me" (John 7: 29). Talking about himself as the good shepherd, Jesus says that he knows his sheep, "even as the Father knoweth me, and I know the Father" (John 10: 15). This knowledge of God that Jesus claims is knowledge that grows out of direct spiritual communion between the Father and the Son.

(3) Jesus furthermore claims to be the sole mediator of such a knowledge to men. No one knows the

Father, save the Son, "and he to whomsoever the Son willeth to reveal him" (Matt. 11: 27). Here is the astonishing claim that all other men are dependent on him for a knowledge of God. His own knowledge of God is direct and immediate; that of other men is mediated by him. In this realm all things have been committed to him of the Father. He is the Lord of this realm. Other men are dependent on him. God reveals himself to other men only through the Son.

5. *Jesus' redemptive work*

An essential element in Jesus' revelation of God is the redemptive work accomplished by Jesus on behalf of man. He says that the Son of man came to seek and to save that which was lost (Luke 19: 10). His was a redemptive mission. He was a Saviour as signified by the name Jesus (Matt. 1: 21). What we are here concerned about is to show that the work of Jesus in redeeming man is a revelation of God.

The central thing about Christ in the New Testament is that he is Saviour from sin. He gave himself, even unto the death of the Cross that men might be saved.

As an integral part of the redemptive work of Jesus and the culmination of it, the Resurrection of Jesus was the work of God. Peter told the people on the day of Pentecost that this Jesus, whom they had crucified, God raised from the dead and exalted to his right hand, the position of supreme authority and power (Acts 2: 32, 33). It is not simply the Jesus who lived among men on earth and died on the Cross that reveals God to men; it is this same Jesus who also rose from the dead and ascended to glory. One who denies that Jesus thus conquered death and was enthroned at the right hand of God is entirely consistent in denying that through him we get a unique and unparalleled knowledge of God.

We might sum up the point that in Jesus we have a historical and objective revelation of God in the language of the Fourth Gospel. "No man hath seen God at any time; the only begotten Son, who is in the bosom of the

Father, he hath declared him" (John 1: 18). Here the writer says that God whom men had never been able to bring within the range of their vision had been brought within their knowledge by the only begotten Son. He has stated in the first verse of the chapter that the eternal Word was with God and was God himself. Then he says all things have come to be through him (verse 3). This Word he tells us became flesh and tabernacled among us and men beheld his glory, glory as of the only begotten from the Father (verse 14). This eternal Word is the revelation of the Father.

The New Testament idea of revelation is that Jesus Christ, by the life that he lived, by the words that he spoke, by the deeds of mercy that he performed, especially by his death and resurrection, and by the divine life that he communicates to men, reveals God. He reveals God, not in the sense that he pulls a curtain so that men may behold God at a distance, but in the sense that he brings God into the life of men. He brings men into fellowship with God.

A further word needs to be said here about what is meant when we say that Christ is the medium of revelation. We do not mean that the revelation is something, apart from him, that comes to us through him. He is that revelation. He is the substance as well as the medium of revelation. The revelation is identified with him. In him men know God.

6. Revelation through nature

When we say that Christ is the medium of revelation, we do not mean to deny that nature and man constitute a means of revelation. Such would not be true.

The Bible clearly recognizes that nature (and man) is a medium of revelation. The biblical writers regard nature as the work of God and hence as expressing something of God's wisdom and power. The heavens declare the glory of God (Psalm 19: 1). In substance this is the testimony of the whole Bible. Jesus regards nature as the sphere of God's operation and as the means of expressing his will. Paul teaches that nature and man reveal God (Rom., chapters 1 and 2).

Moreover, history and human experience bear testimony to the fact that nature has always spoken to man of something beyond itself. Man's consciousness has always been a religious consciousness. He has everywhere believed in a Power above and beyond the world that spoke to him through the world around him and the voice of his own soul within.

In regard to this revelation of God through nature, two things might be emphasized:

(1) One is that this revelation through nature (including man) is not sufficient for man's religious needs. This revelation brings man no clear voice telling him of a God of mercy that saves from sin. That comes only in Christ. Nowhere else in all the world except in Christ do we get a gospel of salvation from sin. Hence the only revelation that can be spoken of as the Christian revelation is the one that comes in the gospel of Christ. No other revelation can be equated with that of the gospel.

(2) But this does not mean that the revelation that comes through nature and man is worthless.

The Bible everywhere presupposes such a revelation and builds on it. In the Bible, God addresses man as a being who has a naturally religious consciousness. It is taken for granted that man has a consciousness of God and can know God. Hence, while the revelation of God through nature is not sufficient, it is essential. Without man's religious consciousness the revelation of God in the Bible and in Christ would have been impossible.

III. The Bible and revelation

Christ is God's revelation to man. The only begotten Son has declared the Father (John 1: 18). He is the substance of revelation. The record of this revelation—the literary means of its transmission to us—is the Bible. Revelation produced the Bible. Or, to limit our view to the New Testament for the present, revelation produced the New Testament. God gave Christ as the expression of his will for mankind. Out of this self-disclosure on God's part grew our New Testament.

1. *The heart of the Bible is the Four Gospels*

The center of the Bible is the Four Gospels that give us the account of the birth, the life, the teaching, the death, resurrection, and ascension of Jesus. If the Gospels were taken out of the Bible, this Book would be de-hearted. The whole Book would be largely without meaning. The Bible is a body of literature that finds its unity and meaning in him; and if the account of his life on earth were taken out of the literature, we could no longer speak of it as a Book, for its unity would be gone. He is the key to what goes before, and all that comes after him goes back to him.

2. *The Book of Acts records the work of the gospel*

The Book of Acts contains the story begun in the Gospels. (Cf. Acts 1: 1.) It gives us to understand that he is a superhistoric Christ. He lived in history; but in his death and resurrection he rose above history and acts on history from above. His is a "perpendicular gospel in a horizontal world." From above he pours a stream of new life into the depleted moral and spiritual forces of the world. That is the world's only hope.

The first great demonstration of this we have on the day of Pentecost. Pentecost was the releasing of the re-demptive power of Calvary. The risen Christ sent the Spirit upon his people to make them to do the work which he (Christ) had commissioned them to do (Acts 1: 8; 2: 33).

Thus in the Book of Acts we have an outline of Christ's redemptive plan (Acts 1: 8), and the inauguration of the movement to carry out this plan. We have the record of how the gospel was released from its narrow Jewish racial limitations and how it becomes in principle a worldwide gospel.

3. *The Epistles interpret the meaning of the gospel*

The Epistles of the New Testament are mostly tracts written by Paul and others of the Apostolic group or those closely related to this group. These Epistles explain the principles of the new religion, correct errors that were appearing in the churches, and apply the principles of this new religion to various questions of personal, domestic, community, and church life. But everything goes back to Christ and what he had done for men and what he means for human life.

4. *The Book of Revelation forecasts the triumph of the gospel*

The Book of Revelation sets out something of a forecast of the final triumph of the Kingdom of God on earth. It represents the fierce conflict that was going on in John's day between the risen Christ and the forces of evil—mainly false religion and corrupt civil forces. It was written to reassure the sorely tried Christians of that day that victory was finally and surely coming. It was a victory which Christ was to win by his Spirit working through his churches. It represents the final triumph of the movement that we see inaugurated in Acts.

5. *The Bible centered in Christ*

Thus we see that Christ constitutes the heart and the center of the New Testament. But what about the Old Testament? In one word we can put it: The Old Testament was a preparation for Christ and his coming.

God chose Abraham and his descendants as his people in a peculiar sense—not for their sakes only but for the sake of the world (Gen. 12: 1-3). With this race God dealt in such a way as to give them a knowledge of himself possessed by no other people. By his providential dealing, by his judgments on their sins, his long-suffering patience, his gentleness and his mercy, by the institutions of worship, by raising up leaders for them, and especially by revealing himself to and through the prophets, he prepared the way for Christ and his saving work. In these ways he deepened their sense of God and their need of him; he sharpened their sense of sin over against the holiness of God; he prepared the way for the inauguration of a spiritual religion and its introduction in the Roman Empire. He gave this religion such a footing that the forces of evil could not uproot it.

Specific references from the New Testament are not needed to corroborate this view. It is the view of Jesus and of all the writers of the New Testament. And it throws a flood of light back on the Old Testament and God's dealings there with his chosen people.

6. *The Bible a record of a progressive revelation*

The Bible is thus the record of a progressive revelation that came to its culmination in Christ.

That revelation as recorded in the Bible is progressive few men today would deny. Yet it has not been always clearly grasped. The author of the Book of Hebrews shows in the first verse of his Epistle that he understood this principle. So did Jesus. He came to fill full a revelation that was incomplete (Matt. 5: 17ff.). So teaches Paul. He says that Christ came in the fulness of time (Gal. 4: 4). A revelation historically conditioned could hardly be otherwise than progressive. We can see this in the doctrine of God in the Bible. In the first part of the Old Testament emphasis is laid upon God's power. His moral qualities are not disregarded, but they do not receive the emphasis that we find later on in the Psalms and the Prophets. And we do not come to the climax of the biblical view of God until we get to the revelation of God in Christ as recorded in the New Testament.

But why the long delay in bringing revelation to a climax? Because the giving of a revelation on God's part is morally and spiritually conditioned on man's part. There were moral, social, political, and spiritual conditions involved. These conditions must mature before God's final revelation could be given. God does not hurry. He waits until things are right to accomplish his purpose.

This must not be interpreted to mean that revelation is only a naturalistic evolution, or that it could be given only as things of themselves developed so that it could be given. One part of the giving of the revelation was the creation on God's part of such conditions as would make it possible for man to receive the revelation. God can give only as man receives; but man's receptivity is God's creation. But in creating this receptivity, or in other words bringing about the conditions necessary to the reception of a revelation, he is limited by the conditions with which he deals.

Jesus recognized this principle as applied to moral questions in what he said about divorce (Matt. 19: 3-12). If one looks upon the teachings of the Bible as all being on the same moral and spiritual plane, these difficulties are insoluble. On the basis of a progressive revelation, such questions as the wholesale destruction of enemies at God's command will then be relieved, if not solved. Such a question cannot be solved simply by referring it to the sovereignty of God. Even a sovereign God must do right. But when we understand that the men God was using to carry out his purpose were men of very low moral ideals as compared with a later age, and remember that the nations to be destroyed were so morally and spiritually corrupt that their complete extermination was probably the best thing for the world, then the question is not so difficult. Does not God yet use the nations to scourge one another? And do not the innocent yet suffer on account of the sins of others? Or, take the matter of the imprecatory psalms. The Psalmist seemed to think it would be a pious thing to destroy the infant children of his enemies (Psalm 137: 8, 9). Should a Christian feel that way toward his enemies today? Certainly not. But any man should be measured by the moral standards of his day, not by those of a later day. Besides, if God could not use imperfect men, how long would he have to wait before finding a man he could use? He manifests his wisdom by the use of imperfect men, especially if they are upright in heart and have their faces set in the right direction.

When it comes to a practical use of the Bible, no man believes that all parts of it are of equal value. No one would put some genealogical table in the Old Testament on the same level with John 3: 16. Yet this would not mean that the genealogical table did not have its place. My finger nail is not of as much vital importance to my body as my heart. Yet it is a part of my body and I would not needlessly cut it off. If a man should start out to trim his body down to the essential organs and cut off all members that he could live without, he would remind us of some of the "shorter Bibles."

7. *The Bible, then, is God's message given through human agency*

The Bible did not grow up out of man's life, but it came from God to meet the needs of man's life.

Is the Bible a human book or a divine book? It is both. It was written by men inspired of God. Its message came from God, but he used the biblical writers to communicate that message to man. And in recording that message each man was free. He did not lose his individuality. Man was as free and as truly himself as if God had had nothing to do with the giving of the message and putting it into written form. Each writer has his own style and peculiar method of thought. He tells things in his own way.

One of the greatest causes of trouble concerning the Bible has been the assumption in men's minds, often unconsciously held, that the human and divine elements were mutually antagonistic and exclusive. This assumption has wrought pernicious results in many places; for example, in the doctrine of the Person of Christ, in the doctrine of salvation by grace as related to man's freedom, regeneration and faith, preservation and perseverance, and so on. In regard to the Bible, men have often assumed that, if God inspired men to write the Bible, then man must cease to be himself, could not think his own thoughts, write in his own style, tell things from his own viewpoint—in fact, that man must become a passive, if not an unconscious, instrument in the hands of God—not realizing that it is only in God that man comes to his true self in the proper use of his powers.

The moral and spiritual grandeur of the Bible comes from divine inspiration. From the beginning there is a moral and spiritual grandeur about the Bible that we do not find in any other body of literature. In this respect, it is in a class by itself. This quality belongs to it by virtue of the fact that it is God-inspired. It has the life of God in its message. This quality of the revelation does not come from man; it comes from God. Yet it is not foreign to man's life as a cinder in the eye is foreign to it. It rather is like light to the eye; it is that for which the eye was made and without which it cannot perform its proper function.

The Bible, then, is God-inbreathed (2 Tim. 3: 16, 17; 2 Peter 1: 21). It is God's message to a lost world. It has in it the vitality of God. Here man finds God. Perhaps it would be truer to say that in it God finds man. It is this that gives it its power over the lives of men. It is this that gives the Christian man his confidence with reference to the Bible in relation to the future religious history of mankind. The place of the Bible in the lives of men in the future will be determined primarily by what the Bible does for the religious lives of men and not by what critics decide about the origin and date of its books. As long as men find God in its message, so long will they love it and live by its teachings.

8. The Bible is authoritative

It is authoritative as the voice of God is authoritative to the soul of man. It finds man, searches him, makes him realize his need of spiritual help. If God speaks to man, he must speak in the tones of authority. He is not simply offering to man advice on spiritual matters which man may accept or reject as a matter of indifference.

He speaks about man's sin, his salvation and destiny, in tones that are authoritative. There is a moral imperative in the message. Men talk today of a democratic God as if God were one of the common herd and as if his voice had no more authority than that of any other member of the mob. The Bible knows no such God. The God of the Bible is a God of holiness who speaks to man by way of command.

The authority of the Bible does not interfere with the freedom of man. But here we come to an objection. The objection is that an external authority of this kind would interfere with man's freedom, with his moral and spiritual autonomy. It is objected that submission to any external authority is subversive of the freedom of man and hence of his highest development. This is a mistaken notion. There is no conflict between submission to proper authority and freedom. In fact, the only way man can realize his true freedom is by submission to rightful authority. Refusal to submit to rightful authority is not freedom. This is spiritual anarchy.

Yet much, if not most, of the objection to the authority of the Bible is based on this mistaken notion with reference to the relation of authority to freedom.

Let us see if this general statement can be made clearer. One thing that will help us is to remember that the authority of the Bible is the authority of Christ. This follows from what has been said about the relation of the Bible and Christ. We do not have two authorities, one, the authority of Christ; the other, the authority of the Bible; but one. Christ speaks to us through the Bible. Authority is ultimately personal in its nature. Our ultimate authority in Christianity is the authority of Christ as the revelation of God. The Bible is the medium through which his will is made known to us. As the revelation of the mind and will of Christ, the Bible is authoritative. But the authority of Christ does not enslave, it liberates. Paul gloried in his liberty as a Christian; yet he called himself the slave of Christ.

By submission to the spiritual authority of Christ man finds his spiritual freedom.

The authority of the Bible, then, is the authority of the grace of God as mediated to us in Christ, the grace that delivers from the guilt and bondage of sin. As Paul shows in Romans 6, there are only two possible masters for man, either sin or Christ. When Christ, as the mediator of the grace of God, delivers us from sin he brings us under captivity to himself. The authority, then, that masters us as Christians is the authority of God's holy love in Christ Jesus. It is a bondage that brings under bondage to itself, but it is a willing bondage of love. Grace captures our hearts and sets us free from the bondage of sin.

THE PERSON OF CHRIST

CHAPTER III

THE PERSON OF CHRIST

I. JESUS AS MAN

    1. The fact of his humanity

    2. His growth as a man

    3. The sinlessness of Jesus

II. JESUS AS SUPERNATURAL

    1. The Virgin Birth

    2. Miracles

    3. The Resurrection

    4. Jesus and the Old Testament

III. JESUS AS SAVIOUR

IV. JESUS AS LORD

V. JESUS AS DIVINE

    1. Some passages examined

    2. The attitude of faith toward him

VI. JESUS GLORIFIED

CHAPTER III

THE PERSON OF CHRIST

We have considered Christ as the revelation of God.
We need now to consider the Christian teaching in regard
to the Person of Christ. Of course, the two things are
directly and vitally related. What Christ is as the revelation of God is a vital element in the doctrine of his
Person and will largely determine what we shall think
of him in other respects. On the other hand, our doctrine
of the Person of Christ will necessarily determine largely
what we think of him as the revelation of God. This
is one of the fundamental questions of Christian theology
and one that has held the attention of thinkers in this
realm from New Testament days to the present.

I. Jesus as man

The favorite designation used by Jesus for himself
was the term, "Son of man." Whatever else this may
mean, it implies that he is human, that he is one with
mankind.

1. *The fact of his humanity*

It seems strange that anybody should ever have ques-
tioned the genuine humanity of Jesus. Theoretically,
very few have ever done so. This was done, however,
by the Docetics who held that the body of Jesus was
not real; that he was not real man, but only God appearing in human form. This, while a fatal heresy,
shows, on the other hand, how firmly the conviction of
the deity of Christ had laid hold on the minds of Christians in early Christian history. Throughout Christian
history, many theologians have so emphasized the deity
of Christ, and assumed such a chasm between God and
man, that they have practically nullified the human life

of Jesus. This is a fundamentally wrong procedure. We should begin with the facts of the life of Jesus as recorded in the New Testament. If we do, we should not argue toward a human life for Jesus; we will rather begin with that as a datum, and that will be our starting point rather than our stopping place. Nobody who takes the New Testament seriously will ever question the humanity of Jesus. The New Testament emphatically protests against a Docetic tendency that was appearing before the close of the New Testament age (John 1: 14; 1 John 1: 1-3; 4: 2, 3; Col. 2: 20-23).

The New Testament tells us how Jesus was born, had family connections, lived in his home at Nazareth, was subject to his parents, rejoiced, was tempted, craved human sympathy, prayed, was obedient to God, had a body, mind, soul, suffered, died, and rose again. John's Gospel and First Epistle are usually looked upon as setting forth the deity of Christ. This is true, but notice also how they emphasize his humanity. The Gospel tells that he became flesh and dwelt among us, that he was tired, thirsty, hungry; while the Epistle begins by emphasizing the fact that the writer with others had seen, heard, beheld, handled the Word of Life (John 1: 18; 4: 6ff.; 1 John 1: 1-3).

While Paul has little to say about the earthly life of Jesus, he does speak of his having been born of a woman (Gal. 4: 4), of his being a man (1 Tim. 2: 5), of his death and resurrection (1 Cor. 15: 3, 4), of his being the head of a new spiritual humanity as the last Adam (1 Cor. 15: 22; Romans 5: 12ff.).

The Book of Hebrews lays special emphasis on the humanity of Jesus. He laid hold on humanity or took our nature, because it was man he came to save (2: 14). He can be touched with the feeling of our infirmity because he has been tempted in all points like as we are, yet without sin (4: 15). He made his prayer to God with strong crying and tears (5: 7). He feared and learned obedience though he was a Son (5: 8).

Everywhere the New Testament presents Jesus as a man. This is so obvious that it is not necessary to dwell on it further.

2. *His growth as a man*

As a man Jesus was subject to the law of growth and development. Luke tells us that he grew in wisdom and stature (or age) and in favor with God and men (Luke 2: 52). Here seems to be a normal human growth. There is mental development—he grew in wisdom. There is physical development—he grew in stature. There is religious development—he grew in favor (or grace) with God. There is social development—he grew in favor with men.

We see him as a boy in the Temple at twelve years of age eager to learn. He was both hearing the rabbis and inquiring as an eager learner (Luke 2: 46).

The author of the Book of Hebrews indicates that there was a moral development on the part of Jesus. He learned obedience by the things that he suffered (5: 8). He was made perfect through sufferings (2: 10).

We do not have much data to enable us to form any very definite idea of the development of the religious life and consciousness of Jesus. We see something later on of his religious habits. He had the custom of attending the synagogue worship in Nazareth (Luke 4: 16). We know that he was a man of prayer (Mark 1: 35; Luke 11: 1, et al). He knew the Old Testament Scriptures (Luke 4: 17, et al).

We are not to think of the moral and religious development of Jesus as taking place without struggle and effort on his part. In this case it would not have been moral. It would have been sub-moral development on a plane of being below the moral and personal. His temptations and struggles were real. His battles with sin and evil were no sham battles. We sometimes make the mistake of thinking that there can be no temptation unless there is something base and ignoble in our lives to which temptation can appeal. But this is a mistake. This will be discussed more fully later on.

3. *The sinlessness of Jesus*

Jesus was tempted; but in all his temptations he was victorious.

He was sinless. He challenged his enemies to convict him of sin (John 8: 46). He forgave sins (Mark 2: 5; Luke 7: 48). He said that his blood was shed for the remission of sins (Matt. 26: 28). He had a consciousness of undimmed fellowship with God (Matt. 11: 27; John 11: 42; 14: 6-11).

Another thing of great significance: Jesus taught that all men should confess their sins and pray for forgiveness (Matt. 6: 12; Luke 11: 4). He denounced those who claimed to be righteous above others. Yet he himself never confessed sin, never prayed for forgiveness, never manifested the least consciousness of sin. What shall we say of one who taught that all other men should confess their sins while not confessing sin on his own part? Will we not have to say that he is either sinless or that he is such a moral pervert that he does not know his own moral condition? One who, if a sinner, was so blinded by moral darkness and self-conceit as not to know his own spiritual condition and needs would certainly be no proper guide for others in spiritual matters.

Paul, Peter, the Book of Hebrews, and John all manifest a belief in the sinlessness of Jesus. Paul says that God made him who knew no sin to be sin on our behalf (2 Cor. 5: 21). Peter says that he died the righteous for the unrighteous (1 Peter 3: 18). The Book of Hebrews says that he was tempted in all points like as we are, yet without sin (Heb. 4: 15. Cf. 7: 26-28). John says that when a Christian sins, he has an Advocate with the Father, Jesus Christ, the righteous (1 John 2: 1). The New Testament as a whole represents Jesus as being without sin.

Moreover, Jesus is presented in the New Testament as our perfect ideal, our example to be followed. He challenged men to follow him and allowed for no excuses. He demanded of men that they put him and his cause first (See Matt. 10: 34ff., et al, and also further in this chapter under Lordship). Paul asks others to follow him as he follows Christ (1 Cor. 11: 1. Cf. 4: 16; Phil. 4: 17; 4: 9). By no means did Paul regard himself as being the embodiment of the ultimate ideal. Christ embodied that ideal and Paul was to be imitated only as he incarnated the spirit of Christ. Paul asked men to follow him only because he could say: "To me to live is Christ" (Phil. 1: 21). John says that we ought to walk even as he walked (1 John 2: 6), and Peter holds up his example for us to imitate, especially in the matter of innocent suffering for evil-doers (1 Peter 2: 19ff.; 3: 14ff.).

II. Jesus as supernatural

There has been a fierce battle raging around the Person of Christ through all the centuries from the New Testament age down to the present. Modern Unitarianism has regarded Jesus as a man only. It has tended more and more to exclude anything like the superhuman from his Person.

But if Jesus was sinless, as above stated, that already brings an element into his Person that marks him as different from all other men. He thus transcends ordinary human life. Moreover, if he is sinless, that fact needs explanation. We cannot have such a fact, if it is a fact, suspended in the air. It cannot be left unrelated. It must be grounded in something deeper than itself. Sinlessness is not a quality of human life as we know it on this earth. This already suggests, if it does not demand, that we regard him as more than a man.

1. *The Virgin Birth*

Matthew and Luke represent that Jesus was born of Mary without a human father. According to their account, he was begotten by the Holy Spirit. There seems to be enough difference between these two to show that they are independent accounts. Neither writer has borrowed from the other.

The fact that the other New Testament writers do not mention the Virgin Birth is no proof that it did not take place. Possibly the other writers did not know about it, or if they did know about it, did not see fit to mention it. We can understand that such a topic would naturally be handled with great reserve among the early disciples. Hence it may not have been known outside a small circle of friends of the family, and if the other New Testament writers did know about it, naturally such a topic would not be a matter of common conversation and men would not write about it unnecessarily.

Some set the accounts aside as of no religious value. But such an origin of the earthly life of Jesus would fit into the account of such a life as he lived. If his life had been such as other men lived, then it would be natural to expect such an origin as belongs to the lives of other men. But the Virgin Birth fits into the account of the sinless life. Luke 1: 35 indicates that there was a connection between the holiness of Jesus and the fact that Mary was overshadowed by the power of the Most High. Would not his origin in such an act of the Holy Spirit help us to understand how, of all men, his is the only exception to the fact that men live under the dominion of sin?

2. Miracles

Another prominent feature of this account of the life of Jesus is his miracles. Jesus is pre-eminently a miracle worker. If we take the miraculous element out of the Gospel records, the records will be so torn to shreds that we will have nothing reliable left. The miraculous element is so deeply embedded in the Gospel narrative that it is impossible to remove this element and leave anything of value in the accounts. The effort to get back to a non-miraculous Christ has signally failed. No matter how minutely the Gospel records are analyzed, the character of the Christ we get in every layer of the deposit is essentially the same. The Jesus who is only a religious and ethical teacher, with the miraculous element left out of his life, has never been found except in the imagination of some critics who superimpose their views on the Gospel records. On any sane criticism of the Gospel records, the miraculous element in the life of Christ remains.

3. *The Resurrection*

The Gospel accounts tell us that on the morning of the third day some women went to the tomb and found it empty. An angel announced to them that Jesus was risen (Matt. 28: 1-8 and parallels). Jesus himself appeared to them (Matt. 28: 9, 10; John 20: 19ff.). He appeared to Peter (1 Cor. 15: 5). He also appeared to two of them on the way to Emmaus (Luke 24: 14ff.). He also appeared to all the eleven except Thomas (Luke 24: 36ff.; John 20: 19ff.). Later he appeared to the eleven, Thomas being present (John 20: 26ff.). He appeared to the eleven in Galilee (Matt. 28: 16ff.).

Paul tells us that Jesus appeared to James, to Peter, to himself, to more than five hundred at one time (1 Cor. 15: 5ff.). Notice that Paul puts his own vision of Christ in the same category as his appearance to James and Peter. He seems to class it as an objective appearance, not simply a subjective vision. Notice also that he says that of the five hundred to whom he appeared, more than half were living at the time he wrote.

It is evident from the Gospel accounts that the disciples did not expect Jesus to rise from the dead (Luke 24: 11, 21ff.; John 20: 24, 25; Matt. 28: 17). It is sometimes said that they expected him to rise, but the whole New Testament account shows that they had no such expectation. When Jesus was crucified, all their hopes were gone; they gave up in despair. They would not believe until they had overwhelming evidence. Such evidence they had (Acts 1: 3). It was no mere apparition that convinced them that Jesus was alive.

It is generally admitted that the disciples believed that Jesus rose from the dead. The idea that they stole the body of Jesus away and reported that he had risen has now been generally abandoned. How came the disciples to believe that Jesus rose? Their own prepossessions were all in the other direction. There was nothing in the social situation to produce such a belief on their part. Everything was against their believing except the evidence. If they came to believe it, it must have been because there was evidence that was fully convincing. They were men of ordinary intelligence who knew how to use their senses. The evidence is that they saw Jesus, heard him, touched him, had social intercourse with him. They record the teachings which Jesus gave them during this period. There is no way to account for the belief of the disciples that Jesus rose except on the supposition that he did rise.

Their belief that Jesus had risen brought over them a great change. They were transformed from a band of discouraged, downcast men into a company of joyous, militant, aggressive propagandists. Did a mistaken belief in the Resurrection of Jesus, based on some kind of an apparition, work this transformation in the disciples?

When they went out to preach, they preached Jesus as risen from the dead. This message proved to be a message of power. How could such a message win in such a situation? Was it a message of truth or was it simply a mistaken notion of theirs? Why should a false report that Jesus had risen from the dead work such a transformation in them and through them in others?

Then there is the testimony of Paul. What was it that wrought the change in Paul? What changed Saul the persecutor of the church to Paul the greatest Christian and advocate of Christianity the world has yet seen? Paul says that the thing that changed him was the appearance to him of the risen Christ. He says that he saw Christ. Was Paul mistaken? What convinced Paul that Jesus was alive? Remember that Paul's testimony comes to us in epistles that practically all critics admit were written by him before 60 A.D. All the evidence favors the view that Jesus rose from the dead.

4. Jesus and the Old Testament

Jesus and all the New Testament writers regarded him as the Old Testament Messiah and as the fulfilment of Old Testament religion. This statement is too obvious to require proof. Jesus was condemned to death, not on the testimony of his enemies, but on his own confession that he was the Christ, the Son of God. This Jesus testified on oath (Matt. 26: 63-66; Mark 14: 60-64). He was on trial before the Sanhedrin; and on the ground that he thus committed blasphemy they condemned him to death.

As the long-looked-for Messiah, he was regarded as the fulfilment of the whole Old Testament order of things. This could hardly be true of one who was a man only. One thing is clear: the New Testament regards Jesus as a supernatural being.

III. Jesus as Saviour

The center of the New Testament doctrine of Christ is the experience of the New Testament Christians of his saving power and their realization of his spiritual lordship in their lives. The motive lying back of their exaltation of him was a religious and practical motive, not a speculative one. As a matter of fact, they do not seem to be conscious that they are dealing with a problem of thought; they are recording what they know from experience. They are telling what they have seen and heard. They do not argue; they bear witness.

The Gospels present Jesus as Saviour. The angel announced to Joseph that he should be called Jesus, because he should save his people from their sins (Matt. 1: 21). An angel also announced to the shepherds that there was born to them a Saviour, Christ the Lord (Luke 2: 11). Jesus said that the Son of man was come to seek and to save that which was lost (Luke 19: 10). He came not to be ministered unto, but to minister and to give his life a ransom for many (Mark 10: 45). His blood was shed for many for the remission of sins (Matt. 26: 28).

In the Fourth Gospel he is the Lamb of God that bears away the sin of the world (1: 29). The Son of man was to be lifted on the Cross that whosoever believes on him should not perish, but have everlasting life (3: 14, 15). God gave his only begotten Son that whosoever believes in him should have everlasting life (3: 16). He that believes on him is not condemned (3: 18). He that believes on the Son has everlasting life (3: 36). To know God and Jesus Christ whom he sent is eternal life (17: 3). The purpose of the writer was that men should believe on him as the Christ and by believing in him have eternal life (20: 31).

In Acts he is presented as the only Saviour. There is no other name given under heaven whereby men must be saved (4: 12). Peter tells Cornelius and his household that all the prophets bear witness to him that through his name every one that believes shall receive remission of sins (10: 43). Paul preaches that by him every one that believes is justified from all things from which men could not be justified by the law of Moses (13: 39). When the jailer asked what to do to be saved, Paul and Silas said: "Believe on the Lord Jesus, and thou shalt be saved" (16: 31).

Paul tells us in Romans 1: 16 that the gospel is the power of God unto salvation to every one that believes, to the Jew first and also to the Greek. We can find what he means by the gospel by turning to 1 Corinthians 15: 1ff. He says there that he preached the gospel, and when he tells what he preached, it was that Christ died for our sins, according to the Scriptures, that he was buried and that on the third day he rose, according to the Scriptures. He devotes a good part of the Letter to the Romans and the one to the Galatians to showing how the sinner is justified by faith in Christ. To those who are in Christ there is no condemnation (Romans 8: 1). For the one who is in Christ there is a new creation (2 Cor. 5: 17).

The realization of Christ's saving power is a matter of spiritual experience. Flesh and blood did not reveal to Peter the Messiahship of Jesus, but the Father in heaven (Matt. 16: 17). Faith is the condition of salvation and faith is the power of spiritual appreciation. One of Paul's favorite expressions is "in Christ." It is in union with him that we are justified, regenerated, given eternal life.

IV. Jesus as Lord

Jesus is also Lord. He is Lord by virtue of the fact that he is Saviour. His saving a man gives him a moral mastery of that man's life. In fact, a man is not saved unless God in Christ masters him.

In the Synoptic Gospels, Christ makes claims that no other man ever made. If men are to be his disciples, they must deny themselves, take up the Cross and follow him (Mark 8: 34). One needs to count the cost before becoming a disciple, for he may afterward find the conditions more than he can meet. He must forsake all, if he would be a disciple (Luke 14: 33). He told the rich young ruler that he must sell all and give to the poor, then follow him (Luke 18: 22). One must not look back, must not return to bury the dead, nor go back to tell his loved ones good-bye (Luke 9: 59-62). One must hate father, mother, brothers, sisters, houses, lands—yes, his own life, to be a disciple of Jesus (Luke 14: 26.) His mother, brothers, sisters are those who do the will of God (Mark 3: 35). One must be converted and become as a little child (Matt. 18: 3), must take his yoke and learn of him (Matt. 11: 29). One who obeys his teachings builds on the solid rock, while the one who does not practice what Jesus teaches builds on a foundation of sand (Matt. 7: 24-27). Jesus claims to have a knowledge of God that no other has and to be the only mediator of that knowledge to men. He mediates that knowledge to whom he wills (Matt. 11: 27).

He claims to be the arbiter of the destinies of men. His gospel is to be preached to all men (Matt. 26: 13). He is to return in glory and power and judge the nations, separating the righteous from the wicked (Matt. 25: 31ff.).

These claims would be preposterous on the part of any man, however great a man, unless he were more than man. He demands that men put him first, ahead of family, friends, worldly prosperity, or life itself.

In the Acts the ascended Jesus is regarded as both Lord and Christ (2: 36). He is at the right hand of God and Stephen prays to him (7: 60).

In the Fourth Gospel he is the only begotten Son of God. All judgment is committed to him (5: 22). He is the resurrection and the life (11: 25). Faith in him brings eternal life (3: 36). All should honor the Son as they honor the Father (5: 23).

Paul regards him as Lord in the absolute sense of the word. He is the one and only Lord (1 Cor. 12: 5). In his resurrection he is instated in a position of power corresponding with his divine nature (Rom. 1: 4). He is the last Adam, the head of a new spiritual humanity (1 Cor. 15: 45-49). He is given a name which is above every name, that in the name of Jesus every knee shall bow and every tongue shall confess that Jesus is Lord to the glory of the Father (Phil. 2: 9-11).

This is the attitude of all the New Testament writers toward Christ. This comes out especially in the Book of Revelation. When John sees him in his glory, in the first chapter, he falls at his feet as one dead. He is recognized as King of kings and Lord of lords (19: 16). There is a protest in the book against the worship of angels but none against the worship of Christ.

The recognition of the Lordship of Jesus is a matter of spiritual discernment. Paul says that no man can call Jesus Lord except in the Holy Spirit (1 Cor. 12: 3). That

is to say that the recognition of the lordship of Jesus
is a matter of faith. By faith we accept him as Lord of
our lives. The act of faith is an act in which we trust
him as Saviour and at the same time submit to him as
Lord.

V. Jesus as Divine

From the time of the New Testament, Christian people have worshiped and reverenced Jesus Christ as divine.

1. *An examination of some particular passages*

Let us look back over the New Testament teaching
with reference to this matter. All that has been said
about his lordship and much else said previously will
bear on this point. The fact that Jesus made such demands as he did is an indication that in his own mind
he was more than human. His claim of unquestioning
obedience and unfaltering loyalty from his disciples looks
peculiar for one who was only a man. Then what shall
we say of his claim that he would judge the world? Also
he claimed to have power to forgive sins (Mark 2: 5).
In the judgment men were to be condemned or approved
according as they had had the right attitude toward him
as represented in his people (Matt. 25: 34ff.). What is
there about him that gives him such a vital and universal relation to men that for one to minister to them
is to minister to him, and to fail to minister to them is
to fail to minister to him? These are some of the indications in the Synoptic Gospels.

If we take now the Fourth Gospel, the evidence is still
clearer. In the prologue (1: 1-18) he is spoken of as
being from the beginning; as being with (face to face
with) God; and as being God. He is eternal, is personally distinct from God and yet is God in nature. The
expression, *"Theos en ho logos"* (the Word was God), is
as accurate an expression as the author could have used
for saying that the Word was absolute deity in his na-

ture, while being personally distinct from God. The author says that all things came to be through him and apart from him nothing came to be that has come to be. Here it is affirmed that he was the mediating agent in creation. It is not said that he was the absolute source of creation but rather the one through whom creation took place. But the author certainly thinks of him as being divine if he ascribes to him a creative function. He is universally the light of men. He lights every man that comes into the world. Here Christ is thought of as sustaining a universal relation to men. All light is his; all truth is his—the light of nature, of reason, of conscience. This one thus described became flesh and dwelt among men. Men saw his glory, glory as of the only begotten from the Father, full of grace and truth. The author sets this one who is full of grace and truth over against Moses. The law was given by Moses; grace and truth came by Jesus Christ.

This writer evidently thinks, then, of Christ as pre-temporal in his being; as divine in his nature; as creative in his relation to the universe; as sustaining universal relations to men; as coming in the flesh and manifesting the glory of God.

Another important passage is in 5: 17-29. Jesus is in a controversy with the Jews about healing a man on the sabbath. In verse 17 he says, "My Father worketh even until now, and I work." The Jews sought to kill him because they said he blasphemed in making himself equal with God. They must have understood Jesus, then, to make himself the Son of God in a unique sense. If Jesus did not mean to claim deity, why did he not allay their anger by telling them that they had misunderstood his claim? But instead of this he goes on with a defense of the claim. He claims to have power to give life to men (verse 21). All judgment has been given to the Son (verse 22). All should honor the Son even as they honor the Father, and one who does not honor the Son does not honor the Father (verse 23). He then re-affirms his power to give life now to the spiritually dead (verse 25). He has authority to execute judgment because he is a son of man (verse 27). In the future he will raise all the dead physically (verse 28). Surely the author of this passage meant to ascribe absolute deity to Christ, for divine functions are claimed by him, and he is to be honored as men honor the Father. No Jew would ever have thus spoken of any one unless he had thought of that one as absolutely divine.

In another controversy with the Jews, in 8: 58, Jesus said: "Before Abraham was born, I am." Again they took up stones to stone him. He has just said that Abraham saw his day and rejoiced. They said Jesus was not yet fifty years old; had he, then, seen Abraham? In answer to this statement Jesus seems to affirm that he transcends time, that he is eternal. Possibly he uses on purpose the title for Jehovah in the Old Testament (Exodus 3: 14). The Jews seemed to catch the significance of it and took the statement to mean blasphemy.

In John 20: 28, Thomas addressed Jesus as "My Lord and my God." Whatever else might be said about this statement, the significant thing is that Jesus accepted the designation. If Thomas was wrong in using such a term, why did not Jesus correct him? His acceptance of this form of address is his virtual endorsement of it.

In Paul's writings there is abundant evidence that he thought of Christ as divine. The most natural interpretation of Romans 9: 5 is that he there calls him God. This is the interpretation given by Sanday and others. He says that Christ is from the fathers as concerning the flesh; that is, on the human side of his being; while on the higher side of his being he is over all, God blessed forever. We have a similar conception in Romans 1: 4. He says there that, as concerning the flesh, on the human side of his being, he was born of the seed of David; but, according to the spirit of holiness, or spiritual side of his being, he was determined (margin R. V.), marked off, or instated in a position of power by the resurrection from the dead. That is, by the resurrection from the dead Jesus came into a position of power that belonged to him by virtue of his possessing the spirit of holiness or divine nature. It is possible that Paul means to call Christ God in Titus 2: 13, but this is more uncertain.

One of Paul's outstanding passages on Christology is Philippians 2: 5-11. Paul says that Christ pre-existed in the form of God and on an equality with God. By "form of God" he evidently does not mean a mere form or state of being as distinguished from the substance or reality belonging to it. For he goes on to say that Christ took on "form of a servant," being made in the likeness of men. Evidently he does not mean by this that Christ was human only in form or appearance. He means that he became a real man in nature and life. So he means by "form of God" that he was God in nature or essence of his being as well as in appearance or form. By "being on an equality with God" he means that in some real sense he was equal with the Father. In verses 9-11 he speaks of the exaltation of Christ as a moral reward for his voluntary humiliation and death. What he says shows that he thinks of Christ as coming into a position of absolute lordship and sovereignty in relation to the whole human race. When he comes now into this position of authority and power he brings with him his glorified humanity. This exaltation comes to him because of his redemptive suffering culminating in his death. His position of sovereignty is now his achievement.

Another outstanding Christological passage in Paul's writings is Colossians 1: 15ff. Here he says Christ is the image of the invisible God; that is, he is such a reproduction or likeness of the God who is within himself invisible to men that this God becomes manifested or known to men. This Christ is the first-born of all creation. He occupies the position of authority and power in God's creation, subject only to the Father himself, just as the first-born son occupied such a position in the oriental household. Paul says that all things, without exception, were created in him and through him. God creates, but he creates in and through the Son, as he saves in and through the Son.

God has no relations with the world, either creative or redemptive, except through Christ as the agent of his outgoing energy and power. Paul agrees with John's statement (John 1: 3) in making Christ, not the absolute source, but the mediating agent, of creation. All things, he says, were created unto him. He is the goal as well as the agent of creation. It was with reference to him that all things were made. Creation finds its rationale, its ground plan, in him. He is before all things and in him all things consist. Not only is Christ the goal towards which creation moves, he is back of creation as its ground and support. All things hold together or consist in him. Then Paul turns to his more distinctly redemptive functions as distinguished from the cosmic. Two or three statements need attention. It was God's purpose that in all things he should have the pre-eminence. He is to be above all creation. According to verse 20, his reconciling work, accomplished through the blood of the Cross, is in some sense universal, including things in heaven as well as things on earth.

It is difficult to see how one can read these statements of Paul and deny that Paul held, in the highest and most absolute sense, to the deity of Christ. (Cf. also Heb., chapter 1; in fact, the whole New Testament. The Apocalypse is especially clear in its language on this point.)

Paul and John represent Christ as existing before he lived on earth. John says that he was in the beginning with God (John 1: 1). He represents Jesus as saying: "Before Abraham was born, I am," (John 8: 58) and, "Father, glorify thou me . . . with the glory which I had with thee before the world was" (John 17: 5). Paul says that he existed in the form of God and on an equality with God (Phil. 2: 6). Peter's statements in 1 Peter 1: 11, 20 are best interpreted to mean pre-existence.

Now these writers probably did not begin with the idea of the pre-existence and go from that to the earthly life. They probably began with the glorified Christ as they knew him in their own experiences and went from that to the idea of his pre-existence. His eternal existence was necessary to explain his redeeming power.

Certainly they did not conceive of this pre-existence simply as an ideal pre-existence; that is, that Christ pre-existed in the mind and purpose of God. This evidently was not Paul's thought, for he says that this pre-existent Christ emptied himself, in becoming man, by the act of his own will, which would have been impossible had he been thinking of him as pre-existing only in the mind and purpose of God. With this agrees John's statement in John 1: 14 when he says that the Word became flesh. The Christ of the New Testament is not a man deified by his zealous disciples, but the eternal Son of God who voluntarily became man to redeem lost humanity.

2. *The attitude of faith toward him*

This question of the deity of Christ in the New Testament, however, does not depend on the exegesis of particular passages so much as on the whole spiritual attitude of the early Christians toward Christ. They were Jews. Strict and uncompromising monotheism had been ground into their thinking from their earliest days. It was a part of the national and religious atmosphere in which they had been born and bred. Yet their whole attitude toward Christ is one that could not be described by any other term than idolatry if Christ is not divine. They trusted, worshiped, served him as men can only trust, worship, and serve God. And what is true of them is true of thousands of men and women in every generation from the New Testament age down to the present and of millions of those now living. What is that attitude? It can be summed up in the word "faith." Christ is the object of faith in the New Testament. This is true in every one of its books from the Synoptic Gospels on.

Faith is trust in Jesus as Saviour from sin. That trust is unconditional and unreserved abandonment of the soul to Christ. It is such trust as one can rightly exercise only toward God. Sin is against God. God only can forgive sins. In this the critics of Jesus were right (Mark 2: 7). Yet Jesus claimed to forgive sins (Mark 2: 5). If Christ claimed to forgive sins, he was either divine or a blasphemer. To trust Christ for salvation is to trust him as God. The Son of man came to seek and to save the lost. But only God can save. Christ and God are one in saving. A man believes in Christ for salvation, or he believes in God revealed in Christ. The two statements mean the same thing. Faith in Christ and faith in God are one faith, not two. God is in Christ reconciling the world unto himself (2 Cor. 5: 19). The work of Christ in saving, then, is the work of God.

It is also surrender to him as Lord. Saviourhood and lordship in Christ are inseparable. New Testament faith involves a recognition of and surrender to the lordship of Jesus. Faith is not only the receiving of Christ, it is the giving of self to Christ. This attitude is an attitude in principle of complete self-abandonment to another.

VI. Jesus Glorified

Following the Resurrection, the New Testament represents Jesus as ascending. He led his disciples out from Jerusalem to the Mount of Olives and there in view of his disciples ascended up into heaven (Luke 24: 50, 51; Acts 1: 9). But he did not cease to be real to the disciples. He now became to them a spiritual reality rather than a corporeal presence. They think of him now as seated at the right hand of the Majesty on High (Acts 2: 33ff.; 7: 56; Heb. 1: 3; Cf. 1 Cor. 15: 25ff.). The whole New Testament after the Gospels is written from the standpoint of the exalted Christ. The writers do not so much look back to the historic Jesus as they look up to the glorified Christ.

Let us look at some specific New Testament passages on this matter. One is a statement from Matthew in which Jesus is represented as saying, "All authority hath been given unto me in heaven and on earth" (Matt. 28: 18). After giving to his disciples the Great Commission on this basis (notice the "therefore" of verse 19), he says again, "And lo, I am with you always, even unto the end of the world" (Matt. 28: 20). This is a post-resurrection statement of Jesus. Notice the universal sweep of the authority here claimed as given him. It is authority that came to be his. Evidently it is authority given to him in the Resurrection. It represents his supreme victory over sin and death. Then he promises his spiritual omnipresence with his people as they carry out his command. In a pre-resurrection statement he promises to be in their midst whenever two or three are gathered in his name (Matt. 18: 20). Evidently Jesus is looking forward to his post-resurrection state and relation to his disciples in this promise.

Another significant statement is found in Acts 2: 36. Peter says, "Let all the house of Israel therefore know assuredly, that God hath made him both Lord and Christ, this Jesus whom ye crucified." Peter is here explaining to his hearers the significance of what has just taken place on the day of Pentecost. He explains that the Holy Spirit has been poured out by the risen and exalted Christ. In fulfilment of Psalm 110: 1, God has raised Jesus from the dead and exalted him to a position of authority and power at his right hand. Jesus who has been thus exalted, having received from the Father the promised Holy Spirit, has poured forth this which they now see and hear. Then he says that the significance of the whole thing, so far as Jesus is concerned, is that God has made this Jesus whom they have crucified both Lord and Christ. God did this in the resurrection and ascension. This is evidenced by the coming of the Holy Spirit.

God has exalted him. God has clothed him with universal authority and power. This power is spiritual in its nature, as shown by the outpouring of the Holy Spirit. It is moral, not physical or military, in character. This is guaranteed in the fact that it is the same Jesus whom they had known and who had died rather than allow his disciples to use force in defending him or rather than call upon supernatural spiritual power as represented in the angels to defend him.

The Book of Acts was perhaps written to set forth the activity of this exalted Christ. Luke's first treatise was about what Jesus began to do and teach, implying that this one is about what Jesus continues to do and teach (Acts 1: 1). The program of the risen Christ is set forth in Acts 1: 8. The rest of the book is to show how the evangelistic and missionary activity of the early disciples was the carrying out of this program as the ascended Christ worked by his Spirit through his people. From Pentecost on in the New Testament we see the presence and activity of the glorified Jesus. By his Spirit he is present with his people and works in and through them to establish his kingdom on earth.

Paul, in Romans 1: 4, doubtless means the same thing as Peter does in Acts 2: 36. Not simply, as the translations would indicate, that Jesus by the Resurrection was declared or demonstrated to be the Son of God; but rather that God in the Resurrection instated Jesus in a position of power that was in accordance with his higher spiritual nature (according to the spirit of holiness). During his earthly life his higher nature was limited, cramped, one might say, in a state or condition of humiliation into which he voluntarily came for man's redemption. The Resurrection was his release; it was his emancipation day. The limits were removed. The everlasting doors were lifted up and the King of Glory marched to his throne.

Essentially the same view is involved in what Paul says in 1 Corinthians 15: 20-28. Christ is the first fruits from the dead. Having risen from the dead, he now reigns at the right hand of God. There he will remain until he has abolished all rule and authority and power. That is, every rival or opposing power in the universe will be subdued. The climax of this conquering reign will come when Christ comes again to raise the bodies of his people from the dead. All things will then have been subdued by Christ excepting God alone, who has subjected all things unto Christ.

Perhaps the most outstanding passage in the New Testament on this question is Philippians 2: 9-11. Here Paul says that God highly exalted Christ, and gave unto him the name which is above every name. He has the supreme place in the universe of God. Every knee is to bow to him, of things in heaven, on earth, and under the earth. Every tongue shall confess that he is Lord to the glory of God the Father. The absolute lordship comes to Christ as a moral reward for his voluntary humiliation and death. Because he emptied himself, God exalted him.

In the Book of Revelation John records his vision of the glorified Christ in the first chapter (verses 10-20). He appears in his majesty and power. His feet that had been pierced are now feet of burnished brass. The strength of the sun is in his countenance. He holds the messengers of the churches in his hands and walks in majesty among the churches. A sharp, two-edged sword proceeds out of his mouth. The Son of God goes forth to war. The Book of Revelation gives us a view of the war that he conducts against darkness and sin. That war never ceases until sin is vanquished and righteousness and truth rule in God's world.

It would be interesting to notice how this thought of the exalted Christ is treated in the Book of Hebrews and other places in the New Testament. But these passages are sufficient to show that the thought is fundamental in the thought of the New Testament writers. Christianity is not a religion that looks back simply to the historical Christ. It looks up to the glorified Christ and worships him.

In his glorification he rose above the limitations of time and space. He came back into the state of glory that he had with the Father before the world was (John 17: 5). His limitations of knowledge and power were removed. He is now spiritually omnipresent (Matt. 18: 20; 28: 20). His spiritual power and omnipresence can be tested out in experience, and have been myriads of times. Every time a sinner turns to him in penitence and finds in him the forgiveness of sins, moral transformation, victory over the power of sin, he realizes the moral omnipotence of Jesus. There is done for him only that which God can do. Again, he is the unseen but universal Companion of his people. As they go out to proclaim the good news of salvation in his name and to extend his kingdom in the world, they realize his presence with them in fulfilment of his promise; and in that presence they find their joy and inspiration in his service.

THE DOCTRINE OF GOD

CHAPTER IV

THE DOCTRINE OF GOD

I. THE PERSONALITY AND SPIRITUALITY OF GOD
  1. Is God a person?
    (1) Definition
    (2) Reasons for holding
      a. Personality in God necessary to explain personality in man
      b. Denial of personality in God takes the meaning out of religion
      c. The Old Testament conception is personal
      d. The revelation in Christ guarantees the personality of God
      e. Christian experience implies personality
  2. God is Spirit
    (1) Definition
    (2) Reasons for holding
    (3) Difficulties
  3. Relation of personality and spirituality

II. THE ABSOLUTENESS OF GOD
  1. Meaning of the term
  2. Some immediate inferences
    (1) Self-existence
    (2) Unity and supremacy
  3. Relation to the world order
    (1) His presence in the world order
    (2) His knowledge of the world order
      a. Not limited by time
      b. Not limited by space
      c. Not the result of inference
      d. Foreknows man's free acts
      e. Knows events as related to all other events
      f. All truth and intelligence grounded in God
    (3) His power over the world order

III. THE MORAL NATURE OF GOD
  1. Holiness
      (1) Ethical transcendence
      (2) Justice
      (3) Grace
  2. Righteousness
      (1) Definition
      (2) Relation to man
          a. Demands righteousness in man
          b. Condemns sin in man
          c. Moves God to save man
  3. Love
      (1) Nature and meaning
          a. Intelligent
          b. Benevolent
          c. Righteous
          d. Self-giving
          e. Demanding man's love
      (2) Love the nature of God
          a. Not accidental or incidental
          b. Creation an act of love
          c. Related to the doctrine of the Trinity

IV. GOD AND THE WORLD
  1. God created the world
  2. God preserves the world
  3. God transcends the world, is immanent in it

CHAPTER IV

THE DOCTRINE OF GOD

The fundamental conception in any religion is its conception of God. As we have seen, God reveals himself in various ways to man, but supremely in Jesus Christ. We wish now to look more specifically at the nature of God as he is revealed to us in Christ.

I. The personality and spirituality of God

If we would get a true conception of God, there are two ideas that we must get a firm grasp on: the personality and spirituality of God. These ideas are so closely related that we consider them together.

1. *Is God a person?*

(1) What is meant by personality? It is usually said that a person is a being who has the powers of self-consciousness and self-determination. Perhaps this is hardly inclusive enough. Let us add to this another mark and say that the marks of personality are three: intelligence, particularly in the form of self-consciousness; self-determination; and moral consciousness.

Intelligence is a mark of personality. A person is one who knows the world around him and particularly who knows himself in relation to that world and to other persons. It is the power to say, "I am I" as over against all other forms of reality in the world. It is the power to know oneself as the abiding subject of all one's various experiences and to distinguish oneself from those experiences. I am not my sensibilities or feelings or thoughts; I am more than any or all of these together. Back of the changing experiences is the abiding self.

Another mark of personality is self-determination. A person may be influenced from without, but the determining factor in shaping life and destiny is from within.

Others may influence us; we determine ourselves. This means that a person has the power of looking ahead and of choosing one's own course. After having chosen an end, one has the power of directing one's energies and efforts to the accomplishment of the chosen end.

A third mark, therefore, of personality is moral consciousness; that is, a person is conscious of the distinction between right and wrong, and of obligation to do the right and avoid the wrong. A being with the power of self-consciousness would not be a person in the full sense of the term without moral consciousness. In fact, it is doubtful if self-consciousness and self-determination come to their most distinctive form except in relation to the idea of right and wrong. A non-moral person would be little if anything more than a thinking machine.

The question of the personality of God reduces itself, then, to the question: Is God self-conscious intelligence; is he self-determining; does he know and have regard to moral distinctions? There is only one answer to this question—an unhesitating affirmative. God is the only being who has perfect self-consciousness. He is, therefore, the only perfect personality. Man is only partially self-conscious. He knows and understands himself only to a small degree. He is only to a limited extent self-determining. His power of self-determination is limited by the world around him, by his own nature and limited powers. His freedom is only a partial freedom. His moral consciousness is very imperfect. His conceptions of right and wrong are often blurred and indistinct. His sense of moral obligation is many times dulled. In view of these facts, some one has said that man is a candidate for personality rather than a person. His personality is, or should be at least,. a developing personality. God's personality is eternally complete. He knows himself perfectly in relation to all things that are; he is competely self-determining—he depends, in the last analysis, on nothing outside himself for what he is and does; his moral consciousness is perfect, for his own moral nature is the ground of the distinction between right and wrong and the ground of all moral obligation in himself and in others.

(2) What reasons do we have for holding to the personality of God?

a. In the first place, personality in God is necessary to account for personality in man. If God is impersonal, then the personality of man has no explanation; the stream rises higher than its source. But if God is a person, we can account for man's personality as being the creation of God who has made man in his own image. But if God is not a person, man's personal qualities are without explanation.

Moreover, any system of thought that denies personality in God will ultimately, as a logical necessity, make man's personal life to be only a bubble appearing for a moment on the surface of the sea of being and then reabsorbed in the sea. Personality in God and in man stand or fall together. There is no place for any permanent personal values in a world which is impersonally grounded.

b. In the second place, if God is not a person, all meaning is taken out of the religious life of man. Religion is one of the most characteristic things about man's life. To do away with the personality of God in our thought of him is not to explain religion but to explain it away. Religion is carried on in personal terms. If God is not a person, then the most essential ideas and activities of the religious life are without meaning. What would sin, repentance, faith, prayer mean except in relation to a personal God? Sin is against a person. Repentance is toward a person. Faith is trust in a person. Prayer is communion with a person. Religion is only a superstition and a sham if God is not a person.

c. The Old Testament conception of God is clearly personal. He feels, speaks, thinks. To the prophets he was the sovereign ruler of the world.

d. But the final guarantee of the personality of God is found in the revelation of God in Christ. Christ thinks of God as a Person. To Jesus God was the loving Father who watches over his children with tender care. He rules the world in love. Not a sparrow falls to the ground without his notice.

The qualities emphasized in Christ's revelation of God are personal qualities. They are supremely love and righteousness. The coming of Christ and his death for mankind are the revelation of the love of God. The dominant qualities in the character of Jesus are the supreme attributes of God. Jesus is himself the embodiment of the life of God. The Christian revelation is founded on the idea of the personality of God.

e. Moreover, in Christian experience when the Christian repents toward God and exercises faith in Christ, he gets a personal response. He experiences the forgiveness of sins, moral transformation, the remaking of his own personality in the moral image of Christ. He has personal communion with the living God as revealed in Christ. This experience of fellowship with God leaves no more doubt in his mind about the personality of God than he has about the personality of his closest earthly friend.

2. *God is Spirit*

(1) Meaning of the statement. By this is meant that the essence of his being is spirit rather than matter. There is no material element in his being. He is not matter. He is not dependent on matter. He has no body. The only way that we can form a positive conception of the spirituality of God, one that will have concrete content, is to construe the life of God in terms of our own inner experience. We must think of God in terms of mental and moral energy and life rather than in material concepts.

(2) Reasons for holding. The Bible everywhere teaches that God is a spiritual being. The clearest expression is that of Jesus when he said, "God is a Spirit" (John 4: 24). This probably should not be translated God is a spirit, that is, an individual spiritual being, but

rather God is spirit, that is, spirit forms the essence of his being. The lesson that he is teaching about spiritual worship would agree better with this translation. There is no article in the Greek and it can be translated either way.

Our fellowship with God as a matter of inner spiritual experience would also lead us to believe that God is a spiritual being. We cannot see God, nor reach him through any other form of sense perception. But we can come into fellowship with God through faith. Through this spiritual experience we know God as an invisible, spiritual power operative within us.

(3) Difficulties. There are two difficulties. One is that the Bible talks about the hands, eyes, mouth, of God. We must, of course, understand these as expressions adapted to our human understanding. God could be revealed to us in no other terms than human terms.

The other difficulty is only another phase of this. It is the difficulty of conceiving God without reference to form or material concepts. This difficulty is met in Christ. No man has ever seen God; the only begotten Son who is in the bosom of the Father he has declared him (John 1: 18). He has made God tangible and real to the thoughts and experiences of men (1 John 1: 1). He is the image of the invisible God (Col. 1: 15; Heb. 1: 3). The history of idolatry is a testimony to man's need of a tangible revelation of the invisible God.

The revelation of God in Christ serves the purpose, then, of revealing God as pure spirit and at the same time making him real to men.

3. *Relation of personality and spirituality*

These two ideas of personality and spirituality are closely related. Some people have difficulty in thinking of personality apart from physical form or space relations. But when we come to see what is involved in personality, we realize that the essence of personality is spiritual, not physical or material. Perhaps it would not be wrong, then, to say that God can be perfect personality because the essence of his being is spiritual rather than material. He transcends the limitations of our finite personalities, for one reason, because he is not limited by, nor dependent on, a body. Other conditions than this may be necessary to constitute the perfection of his personality, but it is difficult to see how he could be perfect in personal life if he were dependent on a body.

We might say, then, that the essence of God's being is spirit, while the form it takes is personal—personal as over against any lower form of being as impersonal.

II. The absoluteness of God

God is perfect in his moral qualities; he is also perfect in every respect in which we can think of him. He is unlimited in wisdom and power. This applies to what is usually spoken of as the natural attributes as well as to the moral nature or character of God. We might sum up God's perfection in his "natural attributes" in the word absoluteness.

1. *Meaning of the term*

This term denotes an idea that we cannot dispense with in our thought of God. The infinity of God means about the same thing. By the absoluteness of God is meant that he is not dependent on anything outside himself; by his infinity we denote the unlimited fulness and perfection of his being.

The term absolute has sometimes been used in the sense of the unrelated. God is not absolute in the sense of the unrelated, but in the sense that his relations to the universe are not necessary from his side. God is not dependent on the world; the world is dependent on God. God can exist without the world; the world cannot exist without God. All his relations to the world are relations that he wills. They are not imposed on him from without, but by his free act. All his relations to the world, such as creation, preservation, and redemption, are relations into which he chose to enter.

This is the difference between the conception of God's absoluteness or infinity in Christian theism and in pantheism. In pantheism God is related to the world by way of necessity; his relations to it are not the result of choice on his part. Consequently, God is as dependent on the world as the world is on him. God and the world are only different aspects of the same reality. On the other hand, some forms of agnosticism speak of an Absolute back of the phenomenal world, but hold that because of its absoluteness it cannot be known by man. This method of thought removes the Absolute so far away from man that he cannot be known. Pantheism brings God so near the phenomenal world that God is lost in that world. He becomes identified with its forces and processes. Pantheism makes God and the world so much alike that it blots out the distinction between God and the world; agnosticism says that they are so unlike that we cannot learn anything about the Absolute through nature. In either case, the world with its forces and processes is the only knowable reality we have left. So there is a much closer affinity between these two methods of thought than would at first appear. Over against both of these, Christian theism affirms the absoluteness of God in the sense of an independent, perfect personal life.

2. *Some immediate inferences*

There are certain ideas that grow immediately out of the idea of the absoluteness of God. In fact, they are so closely related to it that it is doubtful if they should be spoken of as inferences; they are certain phases of this idea. Some of these we will now notice:

(1) Self-existence.

The absoluteness of God carries with it the idea that God is not dependent on anything outside himself for his own existence. He has the source and ground of his being in himself. He is not dependent on the world for life and being. This carries with it what is sometimes spoken of as life as an attribute; that is, not only that

God is living, but also that he is the source of all that lives. He is the fountain of all life. The Bible speaks of God as the living God (1 Tim. 3: 15). As the medium of God's outgoing energy, Christ is the source of life to men. In him was life, and the life was the light of men (John 1: 4). He enlightens every man that comes into the world (John 1: 9). God has given him to have life in himself (John 5: 26). He is the resurrection and the life (John 11: 25). He quickens the spiritually dead (John 5: 25). He will one day call all the dead from the tomb (John 5: 28, 29).

(2) Unity and supremacy.

The unity of God denotes that there is only one God. In the nature of the case there can be only one self-existent, absolute being. This carries with it the further thought that God in his being is undivided and indivisible. This idea of the oneness of God is usually denoted by the term monotheism. This doctrine is fundamental to both the Old and New Testaments. The conception of God as Creator of heaven and earth carries with it the monotheistic idea. Abraham was called out from his own country and kindred to worship the one true God rather than the idols worshiped in his native land. Monotheism was the foundation of the Mosaic covenant with Israel (Exodus 20: 1-6).

Christianity is as monotheistic as Judaism. The doctrine of the Trinity must not be construed in such a way as to mean tritheism. As a matter of fact, belief in the deity of Christ did not make Paul and the other early Christians any less monotheistic. The absoluteness and unity of God were held as tenaciously by them after becoming Christians as before, and held more vitally.

Monotheism emphasizes the supremacy of God. If there is only one God, he should be worshiped by all men. The universal sway of God over the world comes out clearly at places in the Old Testament, although the national exclusiveness was inconsistent with the idea.

But God was recognized as God of the whole earth (Psalm 24: 1). The prophets pronounce God's judgments on the neighboring nations, thereby recognizing his sovereignty over them (Isa., chaps. 13, 15, 17, 19, and so forth). He uses other nations to chastise Israel. In Christianity the universal element prevailed and all national exclusiveness was eliminated. This was the great issue in the case of Paul against the Judaizers.

This absolute supremacy of God is involved in Christian faith. In this faith is the element of surrender to God which contains implicitly God's universal sovereignty.

The supremacy of the one true God, then, excludes polytheism and idolatry. Jehovah is described in the Old Testament as the one true God over against all sham or false gods. Some of the most exalted language to be found in any literature is to be found in Isaiah in describing the one supreme God as over against the idols, which are vain and helpless things. (See Isa. 40: 12ff., and so forth.) Jehovah as the living God can do things. Idols cannot see, hear, nor accomplish anything. They are altogether vanity and nothing (Isa. 40: 18-29). Jehovah is God indeed. There is no measuring his power or wisdom. He fulfils the idea and ideal of God, while idols only deceive and disappoint those who trust in them.

In the New Testament, the one true God is brought to men in Jesus Christ. John says that grace and truth came through Jesus Christ (John 1: 17). This might be interpreted to mean that in experiencing the grace of God in Christ we find ultimate religious reality. We find in the next verse what that reality is when John tells us that no man has ever seen God but that the only begotten Son, who is in the bosom of the Father, has declared him. It is the grace of this God that we experience in Christ and in that experience we find ultimate religious reality in the true God.

3. *The absoluteness of God in relation to the world order*

We can understand more fully what is meant by the absoluteness or infinity of God if we apply the idea in certain definite respects to God; that is, if we consider it as applied to God in relation to the world order.

(1) His presence in the world order. What about God as related to the world order in which we live? Does the historical order mean the same to him that it does to us? How is God related to that order? Man's experience in the world order is always subject to the law of space and time. His experience takes that form. He can no more prevent his experience taking this form than he can escape himself. It is doubtful if he will ever do so. What about God? Is this true of him?

There are three terms that are usually used to denote God's relations to space and time—omnipresence, eternity, and immensity.

The omnipresence of God has reference to God's presence in the spatial and temporal order, and means that he is immanent in that order at all points of time and space. The omnipresence of God means that he is everywhere present in space and time. There is no point of space, no moment of time, where God is not present. This presence of God, however, is not to be thought of after the manner of a spatially extended object. God is not present in space after the manner of an infinitely extended substance. The spatial and temporal order is grounded rather in the mind and will of God. Since this is true, he can transcend space and time. But it is also true that because the spatial and temporal order is grounded in God, God is necessarily immanent in that order. It could not exist without him. He sustains it. His presence is the life of the universe. This is true of all orders of life and reality in the universe.

One word of caution here might be in order. The omnipresence of God does not mean that God is present everywhere in the same sense or with reference to the same end or purpose. He is not present in the rock and in the reason of Plato in the same sense. He is not present in the sinful life of Nero and the holy life of Jesus in the same sense. He is not present in hell and in heaven in the same sense or with reference to the same function or end. In one case his presence may mean torment, in another it may mean bliss. In one case he is present to sustain the natural order as natural; in another to regenerate and sanctify the believing soul.

Eternity is used to mean that God transcends all the limitations of time. This does not mean, however, that time is not real to God or that God does not know and recognize time. We must hold that time is real to God. We cannot agree with any form of idealism that makes time unreal to God and hence undermines the significance of the historical order. The historical order is real to God. He knows it as historical. The distinctions of past, present, and future belong to the very essence of the world order as historical. Hence God must know these distinctions; they must be real to him if his will is the ground of the existence of that order. But while God knows the temporal and historical order as temporal and historical, he is not limited by time as man is. He transcends these limitations. He knows the future as future, but he knows it. Man can in memory and self-consciousness, by flashes of insight into the future, transcend the limitations of time, but only very partially. What man can do partially God does completely.

The immensity of God means that he transcends the limitations imposed on man by the spatial order. God is not limited by space. What has just been said about God's relation to time will apply in a general way to space. God knows the spatial order as spatial. If this be not true, then the reality of that order is undermined, according to the theistic view of the world. But just as God transcends the limitations of time, so he transcends the limitations of space. Man can do this partially. In thought he can do so. By means of many modern inventions he can do practically in a limited way what God does fully.

(2) His knowledge of the world order.

This is denoted by the term omniscience. By the omniscience of God is meant God's perfect knowledge. God knows everything that is an object of knowledge. God does not know absurdities, such as, for instance, what would take place if an irresistible force should come in contact with an immovable object. Such a question has no meaning. It is only a question in form. It can, therefore, have no answer.

The thing that we are vitally interested in is God's knowledge of the actual world as he has made it. His knowledge of that world is perfect. This may be summed up in several statements.

a. God's knowledge is not limited by time. As stated above, God knows the temporal order. Time is real for God—not real as something outside of his control and as limiting him, but real as being known by him. The temporal and historical order is grounded in his mind and will. Therefore, he knows it completely. Since the whole temporal order of events is grounded in God's will, he knows the temporal order as a whole. It is present as a unity in his thought. There are no surprises that come to God out of the future. The fact that God is working out a purpose in the history of the world carries with it his perfect knowledge of the temporal order. This order is under his complete control. But it cannot be under his complete control unless it is under his perfect knowledge. The events of history must be foreknown of God, else the history of the world is a series of haphazard events moving toward no purpose or goal.

b. God's knowledge is not limited by space. What has been said about the temporal order applies to the spatial order. That order as grounded in his will is also known to him. God's omnipresence in both the spatial and temporal order would carry with it his perfect knowledge of that order.

c. God's knowledge is not the result of inference on his part. He does not reason from cause to effect and thus infer what will happen in the future. He knows directly. All the forces that operate in the world as causes are grounded in his will. The whole system of things in which causes operate to produce effects is so grounded. Being thus grounded in his will, all its events are directly known to him, its effects as well as its causes.

d. God foreknows also directly the free acts of men. Since man's existence as a free agent is grounded in the will of God, all the acts of man's will are known directly to God. There is an objection to this. This objection says that an act cannot be foreknown of God and be free on man's part. It is hardly necessary to say that this is not the view of the matter taken in the Bible. The biblical writers everywhere assume that an event can be foreknown and free. This is the spontaneous conviction also of man's religious consciousness. Man's consciousness as religious assumes that the future is known to God. As moral, man's consciousness assumes that man's acts are free. To destroy either idea would be to destroy an idea fundamentally necessary to religion.

But it is necessary in this connection to remember that man's acts are foreknown of God as free; not as determined. And an event may be certain in the divine mind without being necessitated on man's part. In other words, God may foreknow an event as certain and also as coming to pass as a result of man's free choice. Man does not have to do what it is certain that he will do.

e. God knows the events of the world order not simply as isolated or detached events, but in their relation to all the other events of that order. These events do not exist as unrelated; they do not come that way; they come as parts of the world order. The whole world order is grounded in God. He knows these events, therefore, as they are, namely, as a part of the world order. In other words, God knows the world order as a totality, as a unity. The whole time series is present to the mind of God in an undivided and indivisible act of knowledge. And since God knows the historical world order as a whole, he knows it in its parts, in its single events. But he knows them as events in the world order, in all their connections or relations in that order.

f. The fact that the world order is grounded in the will of God and is known by him carries with it the conclusion that every form of truth and every order of intelligence in the world order are grounded in the rational will of God. Man is an intelligent being, because he is made in the image of a God of perfect intelligence. Man's intelligence can interpret the world as a rational order, because the presence of God in the world and in man's rational nature constitutes the bond of union between the two. Man cannot rest in ignorance and darkness, because the presence of God is his constant stimulus and inspiration to search for the truth. Truth is truth, because God is what he is. Man cannot rest without knowing the truth, because God has made him as he has. Truth is not something shifting and changeable, and man's rational nature can rest only in the unchangeable truth of God.

(3) His power over the world order.

This power is described by the term omnipotence. By the omnipotence of God is meant that all the power there is in the universe, physical or spiritual, has its source in God. He, therefore, can do anything that power can do. Some things cannot be done because they are inconsistent with the order that God has ordained for the world, whether that order be conceived of as grounded in the rational nature of God or as ordained merely of God's will. As an illustration of the latter, God could not make two mountains side by side without a valley between. As an illustration of the former, he could not make two and two to be five. He could not make a lie to be the truth. Nor can God do that which is inconsistent with his own moral nature. God cannot lie. To do so would be to deny his very nature as God. To say that he cannot lie or that he can do no wrong is not to limit God's power. To do a morally wrong or rationally absurd thing is not an evidence of strength, but of weakness.

These limitations, then, if limitations they might be called, are such as are placed on God by his own moral and rational nature. God must be consistent with himself; not to do so would in no way be an evidence of power, but of the lack of power. God also respects the world order which he has established. He does not act inconsistently with that order. For instance, he respects man's freedom. He does not deal with man in such a way as to do violence to his nature as a free being. There is no limitation involved in this, however, other than a self-limitation. The only limitation is the one imposed by the nature or will of God in ordaining man's existence as free. The same may be said concerning any other limitation placed on God by the order of the world.

An objection is sometimes made to the omnipotence of God on the ground that the omnipotence of God would interfere with the freedom of man. The objection is that, if God has all power, then man has none.

But, as a matter of fact, Christian theism holds to both the absoluteness of God and to man's freedom. Both ideas are found side by side through all the Scriptures with no apparent sense of contradiction on the part of the writers. God is absolute in the sense that man's being is grounded in God and God is the ultimate source of all man's power. In this sense the almightiness of God is the ground of man's freedom rather than its antithesis.

We must keep in mind also that the sovereignty of God that grows out of his almightiness is to be thought of as moral; it is not the almightiness of sheer force. It is the rule of a righteous and loving Father, but it is nevertheless the rule of power. To think of the omnipotence of God as the sovereignty of sheer force is to think of him after the manner of Mohammedanism. The Christian conception is the thought of God as the omnipotent Person of perfect goodness and love.

III. The moral nature of God

In defining what is meant by the personality of God, we included moral consciousness as an essential element in personality. This means that God is a moral being. We must look further at what is involved in the fact that God is a moral being.

In thinking about God, the emphasis should be put on the moral nature or character of God rather than on his power or greatness. We will understand this all the more readily if we remember that the final revelation of God is given us in Jesus Christ. If any man would know the kind of God we serve, he can find out by considering Christ. He is the image of the invisible God. God is, therefore, like Christ. The dominant qualities in the life of Christ are the dominant qualities in the character of God.

Many terms are used in the Bible in reference to the moral qualities of God, such as holiness, justice, righteousness, truth, mercy, goodness, love. We can sum the matter up very well under the ideas of holiness, righteousness, and love.

1. *Holiness*

This term denoted the transcendence of God, his separation from the world and all created things. It was that quality in God which separated or distinguished him from things finite and created. This idea of transcendence or separateness from the world the term never lost. And since the term signified that in Jehovah which marked his separateness from the world, the term came to be synonymous with deity. The Holy One of Israel signified the God of Israel.[1] The term did not necessarily convey an ethical significance. This is shown by the fact that things were considered holy by virtue of their separation from secular uses and consecration to the

---

[1] See Davidson, *Old Testament Theology*, p. 145.

service of Jehovah—things such as the Temple, the sacrifices, the sabbath. Anything connected directly with the presence or service of Jehovah was considered holy. Jerusalem was the holy city because it was the place of Jehovah's dwelling and manifestation to his people. Since things and places do not possess ethical qualities within themselves, it is evident that the idea of holiness here is not primarily ethical, if that idea is present at all.

But the ethical idea comes to be prominent, especially in some of the Psalms and the Prophets. The idea of transcendence is doubtless there, but it is now his ethical transcendence. He now transcends man in ethical goodness. His ways and thoughts are not man's, but are higher than those of man (Isa. 55: 8, 9). The ethical transcendence of Jehovah comes out in Isaiah 6. The Prophet in his vision sees Jehovah on his throne, high and lifted up. The seraphim cry, "Holy, holy, holy, is Jehovah of hosts." And there was something in that vision of Jehovah in his exaltation and holiness that made the Prophet realize his own sinfulness and the sinfulness of the people in whose presence he lived. The holiness of Jehovah here is evidently ethical holiness or it would not have made the Prophet realize his own ethical unfitness. And this ethical holiness of God is evidently a goodness that transcends the human, or the vision of it would not have smitten Isaiah so powerfully with a sense of his own ethical impurity.

In the character of God as holy, as Isaiah sees it, there was evidently the element of severity. He is immediately smitten with the sense of conviction and condemnation. He confesses himself sinful and unworthy. He sees the whole moral order of things of which he is a part to be corrupt. He lives in the midst of a people of unclean lips. Yet at the same time there is the element of mercy in holiness. The coal from the altar removes his sin. There is healing power as well as condemning power in the vision of God's holiness. The holiness of God, therefore, includes the element of mercy or grace as well as the element of severity or justice.

The same thing is true in the New Testament. In what we call the Lord's Prayer, the first petition is that men may regard as sacred or holy the name or revealed character of the Father. The word used here is the verb form of the usual word for holiness in the New Testament. The Father is addressed as the Father in heaven. This suggests his transcendence. He is no democratic God in the sense that he is on the same level with the mob. Another petition addressed to the Father is that he forgive our sins. This shows again that in the character of this Holy God is the element of mercy or grace.

The holiness of God seems to be correctly defined, then, as the moral perfection of his character.[1]

It includes:

(1) His ethical transcendence. His goodness is more than that of any created being. It is goodness in the absolute, eternal, underived form. In this sense Jesus says that only God is good (Mark 10: 18).

(2) The element of severity or justice. It must condemn impurity, ethical failure, and sin in man.

(3) The mercy or grace of God. It includes all that we can conceive of as belonging to ethical goodness or perfection. Certainly from the Christian point of view God would not be perfect if he were not a God of love.

While it is true, as stated above, that the holiness of God includes the idea of his ethical transcendence, yet this does not mean that God's holiness cannot be imitated by man. The holiness of God is the reason why man should be holy and also the standard of holiness for man (Lev. 11: 44; 1 Peter 1: 16). The perfect goodness of God is the standard of goodness for man.

2. *Righteousness*

(1) Meaning of righteousness in God.

By the righteousness of God we mean the rectitude of his character. God's character is upright. In him is no sign or taint of evil. John expresses it by saying that

---
[1]See Mullins, Clarke, et al.

God is light (1 John 1: 5). Whatever else this may
mean, it signifies the absolute purity of God's character, his entire freedom from anything evil. But we
must not think of righteousness as a merely negative
quality in God. It is positive. He is not only free from
evil; he is opposed to the evil. All the energy of his
being is set against sin.

To be righteous is the very nature of his being. The
question has sometimes been debated whether righteousness is something pertaining to the nature of God or
something affirmed by the will of God. The discussion
is based on a false assumption—namely: that God's will
is exercised in an arbitrary or capricious manner. God's
will is the expression of the energy of his nature. His
will is nothing apart from his nature, and his nature is
nothing apart from his will. His being is of the nature
of a righteous, moral will. When we get to moral will,
we get to the central thing in the nature of God. The
energy of his will is always set against the wrong and in
favor of the right, because it is his nature to be righteous.
What God does is right, because his nature is righteous.

(2) God's righteousness in relation to man. In relation to man three things need emphasis:

a. God's righteousness demands righteousness in man.
This requirement expresses itself or is revealed to man
in various ways. It reveals itself in the demands of
conscience that man do the right. Man's conscience demands of him that he do the right and avoid the wrong.
This does not mean that conscience is infallible in its
decisions as to what is right and what is wrong. But
it does mean that the general demand of conscience that
one do the right so far as it is known and avoid known
wrong is a revelation of God's righteousness as mandatory
in relation to man. It means that this demand of man's
moral nature is a revelation of the righteousness of God
as demanding righteousness in man. The same demand
is revealed in the moral order of the world. The world
viewed as a moral order, as being the sphere of the

operation of moral law that condemns wrong and approves right, teaches the same lesson.

There is a still higher revelation of God's mandatory righteousness in the moral law as given in the Old and New Testament Scriptures. The Ten Commandments are a good example. These constitute the basis of moral order in the civilized world. In some respects we have, however, an advance in the standard of righteousness in the latter part of the Old Testament. In the Ten Commandments the emphasis is on the outward act. There are places in the Psalms and the Prophets where the emphasis is distinctly on the state of heart and the inner life. We have this pre-eminently when we get to the New Testament. Jesus fulfils the Old Testament law by developing its spiritual character. He shows that evil or good is a matter, first of all of the state of heart and the motive that prompts the deed. Good examples of this are his teaching in regard to murder and adultery (Matt. 5: 17ff.). He also lays emphasis on the goodness of God and calls on men to be like him (Matt. 5: 43ff.). He sums up the law and the prophets in love to God and love to men (Mark 12: 29-31). Paul says that love is the fulfilling of the law (Rom. 13: 10). He exalts faith, hope, and love and makes love supreme (1 Cor. 13).

The supreme expression of the Christian ideal of goodness we have in the character of Jesus himself. He was all that he taught that men should be. He lived up to his own teaching. In him we have the complete ideal of righteousness. He is God's perfect man. He is all that God requires of man. But what he is God requires that men shall be. Nothing short of his perfect manhood will meet the requirement of the divine righteousness.

This shows that the utilitarian conception of the moral law is wrong. The distinction between right and wrong is not grounded in experience—the right being identical with the useful or that which turns out badly. The distinction between right and wrong is grounded in God's

nature as righteous. This gives us a moral law grounded
in a transcendent and unchangeable reality. A knowledge of right and wrong on particular subjects may come
through certain social conditions; but these conditions do
not constitute the ground of the difference between the
right and the wrong.

b. God's righteousness condemns sin in man.

Man universally falls short of the standard as set for
him by a righteous God. There is none righteous, no not
one (Rom. 3: 23). As righteous, God must condemn
man's sin. The Bible all the way through represents God
as set against the sin of man. He would not be righteous if he did not condemn it. Paul does not hesitate
to speak of the wrath of God as revealed from heaven
against the unrighteousness of men (Rom. 1: 18). This
does not mean that there is anything vindictive in God.
But it does mean that God's righteousness must react
against sin and condemn it. To deny this would be to
say that God does not regard moral distinctions in dealing with men and that he treats the righteous and. the
wicked alike. This would be equivalent to saying that
he is a non-moral God. If God is a moral God, if he
recognizes the distinction between right and wrong, he
must have a different attitude toward the righteous and
the sinner. Nor does this mean that God does not love
the sinner; he both loves and condemns at the same time.
This is not to affirm an inconsistency in God; the inconsistency is in man. God loves man because of his worth
and condemns him because of his unworthiness. Man is
worth loving, but so far as he identifies himself with sin
he is not worthy of being loved. He is worth saving,
but not worthy of being saved. If he had not been worth
saving, then God's plan to save him would have been
folly. But if he had been worthy of what God did for
him, then salvation would not have been a matter of
grace. As sinful and unworthy, God condemns man, but
as a being of immeasurable worth, God loves him. If

God as righteous did not condemn man as sinful, then God's love to the sinful would not be grace.

If we would know what is the attitude of true righteousness toward sin, we can learn by looking at Jesus in his relation to sinners. He was full of compassion for sinners, but he was unsparing in his condemnation of those who persisted in wilful unbelief. To spare sin is not mercy to the sinner. The only way one can be saved from sin is, first of all, to have one's sin condemned to the fullest measure of its ill desert. To save the sinner God must, first of all, condemn the sinner in his sins. When the sinner accepts the condemnation of his sins, assumes toward his sin the same attitude of condemnation, not sparing himself in the least, then as a matter of grace he can be saved. But if one refuses to acknowl·edge the condemnation, then he must remain under the condemnation. All this we see in the life of Jesus. He condemned sin unsparingly. When the sinner humbly accepted this condemnation, turning in penitence from his sin, Jesus forgave him in mercy. But if the sinner refused to acknowledge the condemnation of his sin and hardened himself in sin, Jesus condemned him without mercy. There could be no mercy in the case. The sinner would not receive it.

c. God's righteousness moves him to redeem the sinner from sin. This is redemptive righteousness.

There is another aspect of righteousness which has sometimes been overlooked. Punitive righteousness or justice is the phase of the subject that has been given most attention in theology, but this is not the only phase of righteousness emphasized in the Scriptures. In the Psalms and some of the prophetic writings of the Old Testament, righteousness becomes a redemptive quality in God. Righteousness and redemption are shown as being almost synonymous. Especially is this true in the latter part of Isaiah. (See Psalm 51: 14; Isa. 41: 10; 42: 6; 45: 13; 46: 13; 51: 6; 61: 10.) Here God's redemptive activity grows out of and expresses his righteousness. His redemptive activity is the revelation and expression of his righteousness. In the New Testament we are told that God is faithful and righteous to forgive those who confess their sins (1 John 1: 9).

Paul tells us that in the gospel is revealed a righteousness of God from faith unto faith (Rom. 1: 17). Righteousness here is not an attribute of God, but it is a righteousness that comes to man from God. This righteousness is in contrast to the unrighteousness and evil of men who obstruct the truth by their unrighteousness (Rom. 1: 18). This righteousness is not merely forensic. Justification through faith in Jesus is a great moral and spiritual transaction that revolutionizes a man and makes him righteous. It is regenerative in its nature; and God makes men righteous because he is righteous. The righteousness which God gives to man is grounded in righteousness as an attribute of his character and reveals this attribute. Righteousness as an attribute of God is the source of righteousness in man. The righteous Lord loveth righteousness (Psalm 11: 7). He hates iniquity and sin. His hatred of iniquity and sin and love for righteousness lead him not only to condemn iniquity and sin, but also to deliver men from iniquity and sin and make them righteous. And so much does he love righteousness that in order to make men righteous he is willing to pay an infinite price for their deliverance from sin and salvation to a life of righteousness.

Righteousness in God, then, is something more than cold, abstract justice. This we can readily see if we remember that to be righteous involves all that we mean by goodness. The Christian ideal of goodness is more than justice. A good man is one who is charitable as well as just. He exercises mercy in his dealings with men. A man who was simply the embodiment of justice could never be the best man according to the Christian ideal of goodness. And this is because Christianity has revealed God as a God of goodness—one who is merciful

and gracious as well as just. The righteousness or goodness of God, then, could not be complete if it left this
element out.

3. *Love*

(1) The nature and meaning of divine love.

The love of God is difficult to define. This is not
because it is something unknown. Many of the things
we know best are most difficult to define scientifically.
The great elemental forces and facts of life are difficult
to define, not because they are unknown, but because
they are so great and far-reaching that their limits are
difficult to mark exactly. But while we cannot define
with scientific precision, we can describe some of its
qualities in such a way that we can know what we are
talking about. We can distinguish it from other things.
We will, therefore, undertake to describe some of the
qualities of love as we know it in God.

a. Love is intelligent.

Love in its true meaning is not a mere sentiment of
pleasure or good feeling toward things or persons; nor
is it a blind affection that clings to its object "through
thick and thin," irrespective of moral conditions. But
love is an intelligent principle. It is, therefore, something more than mere feeling. There is, or may be at
least, the element of feeling or sentiment in it, but it is
something more than that. The word that is usually
translated love in the New Testament, used especially
for the divine love, denotes a rational, intelligent principle. Love as intelligent has in it the element of wisdom. It sees and plans the best for its object.

b. Love is benevolent.

It is a principle of good will. It wishes good to its
objects. But true benevolence is not only wishing well,
but also doing well to others. Love acts on behalf of
others. On the natural plane God does good to all men.
His blessings are universal. He sends the rain on the

just and the unjust (Matt. 5: 45). The rain and fruitful
seasons are an expression of his good will to men. This
general benevolence of God to all men is what we might
call the divine love on its lowest plane of manifestation.
We see God's love acting in our behalf especially in the
redemptive work of Christ. Christ came as an expression and revelation of the love of God. God so loved that
he gave. He gave the best that he had—his only begotten
Son.

c. God's love is righteous.

It has respect to the eternal principles of righteousness in every expression of itself and in everything that
it does for its object. All love's giving and receiving
must be morally conditioned. The giving of self or
seeking to possess another, except in accordance with
principles of righteousness, may degenerate into ignoble
passion or base lust. Such giving and seeking is selfish
and, therefore, is not love, cannot be love in the true
sense of the word.

The meaning of the atonement is that God could not
give himself to man in such a way as to disregard moral
conditions and obligations. The integrity of God's character and of his moral government of the world must be
sustained even at infinite cost to himself. He could not
give himself to man, nor could he receive man into his
favor without regard to moral conditions. Hence before
man can be received and forgiven, he must confess and
repudiate his sins.

Because of the fact that the manifestations of God's
love are morally conditioned, there are what might be
called grades in God's love as expressed to man, dependent on man's capacity to receive and willingness to
respond to God's love. There are the manifestations of
his benevolence to all men, his general provisions for
their welfare. But the highest manifestation of love is
in his mercy and grace. God's grace is his love going out
after the unholy in character and seeking to transform
them into the image of his holy character. Those who

respond to his grace and yield to its transforming power come to know the blessedness of fellowship with the Holy One.

d. Love gives self.

All that God gives to man is meant to be an expression of himself, so that in receiving the gift man might discern the love of God and open his heart to God himself. In all that he gives he wants to give himself. He is the best of all gifts. But sometimes men are so taken up with the gift that they forget the Giver. When this is true, the gift is not a blessing, but may become a curse. Not that God sends it as a curse, but our lack of spiritual perception and appreciation turns his blessings into a curse. And, too, sometimes he may be able to awaken in us a sense of our need of him and an appreciation for him by withholding the things in which we are so absorbed as to forget him. Then the withholding is the greatest blessing he can bestow on us.

e. God's love demands man's love.

In the Old Testament God is called a "jealous" God (Exodus 20: 5). This means that he wants the undivided affection of his people. The relation between Jehovah and his people is compared to the relation between husband and wife, and an idolatrous people who do not give Jehovah their undivided loyalty and service are called an "adulterous" people. Jesus speaks of the people of his day as an evil and adulterous generation (Matt. 12: 39). He teaches also that men ought not to allow worldly sins and anxieties to interfere with their single-hearted devotion to God (Matt. 6: 19ff.).

The good of man requires that he shall render to God such devotion and service. Man finds his blessedness by giving himself wholeheartedly to God. So this requirement is truly a requirement of God's love. Love seeks the highest good of the loved one. To lead man to give himself with undivided affection to God is to promote man's highest welfare. Love is a mutual self-giving between God and man.

(2) Love the nature of God.

a. Love is not something accidental or incidental to God, but love belongs to the very nature of God.

John tells us that God is love (1 John 4: 8). Whoever, therefore, lives in love knows God, but whoever lacks love or hates his brother does not know God (1 John 4: 7ff.). Love is consequently something eternal in its nature. Because God is love and love is eternal, God's plan of salvation is eternal. In pursuance of his eternal plan of love, he now draws his people to him and imparts himself to them.

b. The fact that God is love helps us to understand that creation itself, with all else that God does, is an act of love.

There is nothing that God does that is inconsistent with love. Love is the motive in all that he does. He created because he loves. It is his delight to create moral and spiritual beings, to whom he can impart himself, and by imparting himself to them win them to himself and thereby make them holy and happy.

c. The idea that God is love essentially and eternally is closely related to the doctrine of the Trinity.

God's work of creating, preserving, guiding, and redeeming the world is an expression of his love. Love is the motive behind it all. But if God is to be a God of love in his own nature, there must be social life within the Godhead. No view of God enables us to see how this can be except the Christian doctrine of the Trinity. This doctrine enables us to see that the primary object of God's love is his eternal and only begotten Son. Eternally the Father's love has gone out to the Son in the Spirit, and in the Spirit the Son's love has answered to the love of the Father.

IV. God and the world

If there is a God of absolute power and knowledge, then there must be a relation of a peculiar kind between him and all else that exists.

1. *God created the world*

The Bible explains the origin of the world by referring it to the creative act of God. Back of the world it places God. The world, the whole material universe, it refers to God's creative power (Gen. 1: 1ff.; Col. 1: 16; Heb. 11: 3). Evidently the writer thought of the world as coming into existence because God willed it. After the material universe has been willed into existence, there is a process of development, in which higher forms of being and life appear until we get to man as the climax of the process. Each step in the process of development, as well as the first originating act, is referred to God. It is a mistake to try to find in this account a scientific description of the origin and development of the world. It is not a scientific account. Unnecessary difficulties have been caused by trying to find here a scientific or an unscientific account. It is written from the standpoint of religion. It is a religious explanation in that it has in view the religious understanding of the world and the interests of the religious life. But it must be insisted that from the religious point of view it is a valid account. The world is regarded as originating in a creative act of God. The development of the world with its different orders of life is referred to God's creative and directing power.

2. *God preserves the world*

In thinking about the relation of the world to God, we are concerned not only with reference to the origin of the world but also with reference to its continuance. Without reflecting, we might think that all God had to do was to create the world and let it alone, and it would continue to exist. Since it was in existence, it would continue unless God by a special act of his will blotted it out. But a little thought will correct this impression. The world could no more continue of its own accord than it could bring itself into existence at first. This is the view of the biblical writers. They represent the preservation of the universe as being one of the specific functions of God in relation to the world. (See Col. 1: 17; Heb. 1: 3.) Man's sense of dependence re-enforces this teaching. And just as the doctrine of creation is necessary to a religious interpretation of the world, so is the doctrine of preservation. God could not carry out a redemptive program in a world that was self-operative and thus independent of him. The Christian view of the world, therefore, as the sphere in which God is working for the establishment of his redemptive kingdom necessitates the doctrine of his preservation of the world as well as the idea that he created it.

3. *God transcends the world, yet is immanent in it*

Creation and preservation imply two things with reference to God's relation to the world: One is his distinction from the world and transcendence over it; the other is his immanence in the world. If God creates and preserves the world, then God is distinct from the world and transcends it. God transcends the world, not in the sense that he is a spatial reality bigger than the world, but in the sense that as a perfect Person he is greater than the world and is independent of it. He must not be identified with the world. He must not be swallowed up in his own creation. This is the great fault of pantheism. But if God is identical with the forces and processes of nature, then he ceases to be God. A God who is not distinct from, who does not transcend the order of, nature is no better than nature. If he does nothing more than nature can do, then he is no other than nature. And it does not help the situation to call nature God or to write Nature with a capital N. The name does not change the thing.

On the other hand, it is just as great a mistake to shut God out of his world and make him exclusively transcendent. This was the mistake of deism. The world was regarded as having been created but then left to run itself by virtue of certain inherent forces. The world was looked upon as a kind of self-operating machine. God existed above and apart from the world. If he had anything to do with the world, it was by a kind of violent interference. He had nothing to do with the ordinary processes of nature. Christian theism avoids both mistakes. It holds to the immanence of God with pantheism and to the transcendence of God with deism. God is immanent in the world. The world is dependent on God. God cannot preserve and guide the world unless he be immanent in it. He cannot act where he is not. On the other hand, creation and preservation mean nothing unless God be transcendent. He does not create and preserve the world unless he is distinct from the world.

In practical result, pantheism and deism come to the same thing on this point. If God be imprisoned in the world or shut out of the world, the practical result is that you have no God other than the world. You have a godless world.

We hold then: (1) That God created the world; (2) that God preserves the world; and (3) that God is, therefore, distinct from the world and transcends the world, but is immanent in it working out his purpose of redemption.

THE SPIRIT OF GOD

CHAPTER V

THE SPIRIT OF GOD

I. RELATION TO GOD

   1. Meaning of term spirit
   2. The Spirit of God
   3. The Spirit as personal

II. RELATION TO CHRIST

   1. Christ's earthly life under the power of the Spirit
   2. Glorified Christ imparts the Spirit

III. RELATION TO OUR SALVATION

   1. Conviction
   2. Spiritual renewal
   3. Assurance
   4. Consummation

IV. RELATION TO SERVICE

V. RELATION TO THE CHURCH

   1. Constitutes the church
   2. Inspires the work and worship of the church

CHAPTER V

THE SPIRIT OF GOD

We have not done justice to the biblical idea of God until we have considered the conception of the Spirit of God as we find it in the Bible. Much is made of the idea of the Divine Spirit in both Old and New Testaments. The work of the Divine Spirit stands for an indispensable element in biblical religion. We propose, therefore, in this chapter to treat the doctrine of the Divine Spirit as found in the Bible. We consider the Spirit in certain relations.

I. Relation to God

1. *The meaning of spirit*

Both the Hebrew and Greek terms translated "spirit" in the Bible seem originally to mean breath, or wind, and later spirit. We can readily see how the breath of man would be associated with the life principle or spirit in man, since when man's breath stops life is gone out of the body.

The term spirit is used in the Bible to denote the animating principle in man or beast. It denotes, therefore, the life of the body (Psalm 104: 29, 30; Ecc. 3: 19). It also denotes a disposition of mind or character (Psalm 51: 17; Zech. 12: 10). We use the term in that sense now, as when we speak of a charitable spirit, a spirit of forgiveness, a spirit of revenge, and so forth. It is also used to designate the disembodied soul of man after death (Ecc. 12: 7). It denotes an evil spiritual power or personality that possessed men and women and produced all sorts of physical, mental, and moral ills (Mark 5: 1ff.; 9: 14ff.).

2. *The Spirit of God*

The term Spirit of God (or some synonym) is constantly occurring in the Bible. The Spirit of God is distinguishable from God, yet is nothing apart from God. The Spirit of God is the inner reality of his being as the spirit of man is the inner reality of man's being. The Spirit constitutes the principle of understanding in God as the spirit of man is the principle of understanding in man (1 Cor. 2: 10ff.).

In general, the Spirit of God or the Spirit of Jehovah stands for the energy or power of God working toward a divinely intended end. In the Old Testament the Spirit of God worked in various ways in nature and came upon man to produce various results. The Spirit of God broods over the chaos of creation (Gen. 1: 2). The breath of God animated the dust of the ground and man became a living soul (Gen. 2: 7). The Spirit creates animal life (Psalm 104: 30). The Spirit gives physical strength (Judges 14: 6). The Spirit gives military power and skill (Judges 11: 29-33). The Spirit gives mechanical skill (Ex. 31: 3). Through the Spirit, God is omnipresent (Psalm 139: 7ff.). In the New Testament this divine presence becomes more distinctly moral in purpose and intimate in nature. Especially in Paul and John, the emphasis is put upon the divine indwelling through the Spirit (John 14: 17; Eph. 3: 16, 17). The people of God are God's temple (1 Cor. 4: 16); they are the place of the divine abode among men. The church is the house of the living God (1 Tim. 3: 15); it is the body of Christ (Rom. 12: 4ff.; 1 Cor. 12: 12ff.). It is animated and indwelt by his Spirit.

3. *The Spirit as personal*

When we deal with the Divine Spirit we ought to realize that we are not dealing with an impersonal force or power. The Spirit of God was always thought of as having personal qualities and performing personal functions. This is true even in the Old Testament. This is necessarily true since the Spirit of God is God himself present in the world or man working out his own ends or purposes.

This becomes especially clear in the New Testament as the distinctive mission and function of the Divine Spirit are brought into prominence. This phase of the matter stands especially in the writings of John and Paul. In the farewell discourse of Jesus as recorded in John, chapters 14-16, Jesus speaks of the Spirit almost as if speaking of a personal Friend. He refers to him as that One (Gk. *ekeinos*), using the masculine personal pronoun (John 16: 8, 13, 14).

Jesus speaks of the Spirit as another Paraclete. Jesus himself had been their Paraclete. As Jesus had strengthened, comforted, guided them until now; so this unseen Friend, this comforting Helper is now to be their companion and guide. This is no impersonal influence or power; it is a personal Presence.

There are three passages in Paul that are instructive on this point. One is Romans 8: 26, 27. (Cf. 1 Cor. 2: 10ff.) We do not know how to pray (or what to pray for) as we ought. The Spirit helps our infirmity. He puts into our hearts longings that cannot be expressed. But God who searches our hearts knows what is the mind (or thought) of the Spirit, because he makes intercession for us according to the will of God.

The Spirit, then, has a mind. Only a person has a mind. Only a person has thoughts.

Another passage is Ephesians 4: 30. (Cf. Isa. 63: 10.) Paul exhorts the Ephesians not to grieve the Holy Spirit in whom they are sealed unto the day of redemption. The Christian finds this grief in his own heart when he sins. It is not simply his grief; it is the grief of God's Holy Spirit living in him and striving to lead him in a holy life.

God's Holy Spirit, then, is a sensitive being—especially sensitive to moral evil. Sin grieves him. Paul here in Ephesians 4: 30 represents the Divine Spirit as capable of grief or suffering.

The third passage from Paul is 1 Corinthians 12: 11. Paul says here that in the church the Spirit distributes spiritual gifts to the members, to each one such gift as he (the Spirit) wills. A man does not choose his own gift. His function in the body is assigned him. His gift is a *gift,* and it comes not of his choice, nor of his will, but of the will of the Spirit. The Spirit *wills* as a person.

The experience of Christians indicates the personal nature of the Divine Spirit. We might notice three phases of our experience that point in this direction.

One is the fact that the Divine Spirit produces personal holiness in us. We grow in Christian character not by our own power, but by the power of the Spirit of God. The power, then, that produces moral character in us must be a personal power.

The same truth is indicated by the fact that Christian men and women find personal guidance for their lives in the Spirit of God. Those who have experienced this guidance could not be convinced that the Voice they heard was produced by a subpersonal power.

A more distinctive phase of the same thing is the sense of a divine call. He calls men to special tasks, to special fields, and guides them in fulfilling their mission. This is not the work of an impersonal power but the personal Spirit of God.

II. Relation to Christ

1. *In his earthly life and ministry he was under the power of the Spirit*

He taught and preached in the power of the Spirit (Luke 4: 18). He cast out demons by the Spirit of God (Matt. 12: 28). The Spirit had come on him at his baptism. Thus he became God's anointed, or the "Christ."

His whole being was so under the control of the Divine Spirit that his work was the work of God. His work was so completely the work of God that for men to reject him was to reject the One who sent him (Matt. 10:

40). This makes the rejection of him and his message
a dangerous thing.

This is perhaps the explanation of that awful warning
to the Pharisees about the danger of blasphemy against
the Holy Spirit (Matt. 12: 22ff.). He is not talking
here about sin against the Spirit apart from God or
apart from himself. It was his work that they were
speaking of when he warned them. They were saying
that his works were done in the power of the devil
rather than in the power of God (Matt. 12: 24). And
Jesus warns them that this is dangerous. He claims to
do his works in the power of God. His works are so
manifestly the work of God that one must be totally
blind or utterly perverse if he denied this. In either case,
truth and righteousness would mean nothing to him. He
could not or would not see them.

Jesus' work, then, was so clearly and completely the
work of God, so entirely the work of the Spirit, that for
one to deny this was a dangerous thing. His whole
personality was so possessed and controlled by the Spirit
that his work was the work of God. His work and God's
were indistinguishable.

2. *As the glorified Christ, he imparts the Divine Spirit
to his people*

John the Baptist said that the Coming One should
baptize his people in the Holy Spirit (Matt. 3: 11. Cf.
Mark 1: 8; Luke 3: 16; John 1: 33). The risen Christ
said to his disciples: "I send forth the promise of my
Father upon you" (Luke 24: 49). He breathed on the
disciples and said: "Receive ye the Holy Spirit" (John
20: 22). He bestows the Spirit on his followers. This
he had told them he would do in the Farewell Discourse
as recorded in John, chapters 14-16. (See 15: 26; 16:
7.) We have the record of the fulfilment of this on the
day of Pentecost. Peter says of Jesus: "Being therefore by (or at) the right hand of God exalted, and having
received of the Father the promise of the Holy Spirit,

he hath poured forth this, which ye see and hear" (Acts 2: 33).

The mission of the Spirit, then, is in relation to Christ. He makes Christ known as the Saviour and Lord of men. The Spirit came, not in order that men may see himself, but that they may see Christ. He is to Christ what light is to the natural world. Light exists, not so much for its own sake as that we may see other things through the medium of light. So the Spirit is the medium through which we see Christ.

The work of the Spirit is to make real in us what Christ wrought out for us. Christ wrought redemption objectively for us; the Holy Spirit works redemption experimentally within us.

The Spirit comes, then, not to displace Christ, but to make him real. The presence of the Spirit means the spiritual presence of Christ. Paul, therefore, speaks of the Spirit of God as the Spirit of Christ.

III. Relation to our salvation

1. *Conviction of sin*

Every phase of our salvation is attributable to the work of the Spirit.

Jesus says that, when the Paraclete has come, he will convict the world in regard to sin, righteousness, and judgment (John 16: 8ff.). On the day of Pentecost, when they heard the message about Jesus Christ, his death and resurrection, they were pricked in their hearts and said, "What shall we do?" (Acts 2: 37.) It is the work of the Divine Spirit thus to make men realize their sinful and lost condition and make them seek after life and righteousness. No power other than the power of God can do that for men.

2. *Spiritual renewal*

Not only can the sinner do nothing to merit his salvation; he cannot even receive salvation within and of himself. The desire for salvation and the capacity to appropriate it must be created in the sinner's heart by the Holy Spirit. The creation of the disposition and power in the sinner's heart to receive Christ is the work of the Holy Spirit. The Spirit regenerates the sinner by leading him to repentance and faith in Christ.

3. *Assurance*

The Divine Spirit also gives to us assurance of salvation. The Holy Spirit is in our hearts the Spirit of adoption, causing us to cry, "Abba, Father." "The Spirit himself beareth witness with our spirit, that we are children of God" (Rom. 8: 14-17).

4. *Consummation*

Paul clearly teaches that the indwelling Spirit is God's pledge that he will raise our bodies from the dead. The Holy Spirit is the Spirit of assurance, not only in the sense that the Spirit bears testimony to our present acceptance with God, as the Spirit of adoption causing us to cry, "Abba, Father" (Rom. 8: 14-17); but also in this same Spirit we are sealed unto the day of redemption (Eph. 4: 30). This day of redemption is the day of the redemption of the body, the resurrection day (Rom. 8: 23). The Spirit himself abiding in our hearts as the first fruits of the coming harvest of redemption makes us to groan within ourselves, looking forward to that glorious consummation. We are thus saved in hope (Rom. 8: 28).

Thus we see that man's salvation from beginning to end is attributed to the Spirit of God. It is God's power that saves man. And it is to be noticed that all that the Spirit does in saving us is in relation to Christ, as previously indicated. Men are convicted of sin in relation to Christ. They are regenerated as they are brought, through repentance and faith, into right relationship with Christ. We are brought into a consciousness of sonship to God through faith in Christ. The Holy Spirit becomes the pledge of our final redemption by forming Christ in us as the hope of glory.

This carries with it the principle that the truth of the gospel is the means used by the Spirit in our salvation.

IV. Relation to service

The Christian is just as dependent on the power of God for efficiency in service as he is for deliverance from sin. Only as one lives in fellowship with God can there be any sustained power for service to God and man.

1. *Terms used in describing the work of the Spirit*

It might help us to notice some of the terms used in the New Testament to describe the work of the Spirit.

One is the term "baptism in the Spirit." This term is used by John the Baptist in telling what Jesus would do (Matt. 3: 11, 12; John 1: 33). It is also used by Jesus (Acts 1: 5). These predictions of Jesus and of John were evidently fulfilled on the day of Pentecost, although, in describing that event, Luke does not use that term. Peter refers to the promise of Jesus as having been fulfilled in the case of Cornelius and his household (Acts 11: 16).

Another term is to be "endued" or "clothed" with divine power. This expression Jesus uses in Luke 24: 49. (Cf. Acts 1: 8.) This promise was fulfilled at Pentecost. The idea seems to be that power for service is something bestowed from without as a sovereign gift. Without it man is entirely helpless in God's service. Note this in the Old Testament (Judges 3: 10; 14: 6, 19; 15: 14; 1 Sam. 10: 10; 11: 6; 16: 13, 14).

Another expression is that of being "filled with the Spirit." This is a common expression in the New Testament (Luke 1: 41; 1: 67; 4: 1; Acts 4: 8; 6: 3; 7: 55; 9: 17; 13: 9, 52; Eph. 5: 18; et al). This expression calls attention to the inner work of the Spirit and possibly also to the more personal characteristics produced by the Spirit. It is connected with such inner and personal qualities as being filled with joy, faith, wisdom, et al. It also seems to denote the raising of the individual's powers to the "nth" degree, his being charged to the limit of his capacity with the divine presence and efficiency.

We find also the terms "poured out," "shed forth," et al, with reference to the bestowment of the Spirit (Joel 2: 28, 29; Acts 2: 17, 33; 10: 45). This suggests the freedom and fulness of the bestowal here represented. Possibly the idea expressed is about the same as being anointed with the Spirit (2 Cor. 1: 21; Acts 10: 38; 1 John 2: 20, 27). This anointing, especially in the First Epistle of John, is connected with an understanding of spiritual truth. The Spirit is our teacher in spiritual things.

Another term is the "gift of the Spirit" (Luke 11: 13; Acts 2: 38; 10: 45). This term calls attention to the freeness of the bestowment. It is not something earned or deserved, but is received as a gift.

There are other terms used in the New Testament, but these are sufficient for our purpose.

V. Relation to the church

We have been considering the Spirit mainly in relation to the individual. But the Spirit works not only in the individual, but also in the community of Christians, or the church. Much that has been said about the work of the Spirit in relation to the individual will apply also to the church. On the other hand, much said in this section will also apply to the work of the Spirit in the individual.

1. *The Holy Spirit constitutes or brings into being a church by bringing men into fellowship with one another in Jesus Christ*

We have seen that it is the work of the Divine Spirit to regenerate men by bringing men into right relation with Jesus Christ through repentance and faith. Thus they are brought into fellowship with one another. In the very nature of the case, then, the members of the church must be regenerated people.

The active agent in bringing the church into being is the Holy Spirit. A church of Jesus Christ is a product of the activity of the Spirit. As the Spirit constitutes the individual a Christian by bringing him into right relation with Christ, so the Spirit constitutes a company of individuals a church by bringing them into Christian fellowship.

2. *It is the Spirit's function to inspire and guide the worship and work of the church*

The Spirit inspires the singing, teaching, and the whole worship of each Christian and of the whole body (1 Cor. 14: 26; Rom. 8: 26, 27; Eph. 5: 18-20; Acts 4: 31). When the Spirit's presence fills the church, then it is that the fountains of praise and prayer and exhortation are opened up. There is, then, no coldness or dullness in the meeting. The church that makes out its program of worship without reference to the Holy Spirit forgets what worship is and what it is for. Oftentimes it is looked upon as a means of entertaining or pleasing the people rather than as a means of pleasing and adoring Christ as Lord and building up his body, the church. Woe to the church when the aesthetic and the entertaining take the place of the spiritual in its worship. Only so much of the aesthetic and entertaining should be allowed as will serve the ends of the spiritual.

We are not to infer from this that a church service will be spiritual by virtue of the fact that it is informal. A service may be carefully planned and intelligently directed and be spiritual. Spirituality is not synonymous with uncontrolled sentiment, nor with spontaneous combustion. God works through man's intelligence as well as his feelings. Paul says that God is a God of order, not of confusion (1 Cor. 14: 26-33). But in all the planning for a service and in the direction of it, divine guidance should be sought and spiritual aims and ends be kept uppermost.

In discussing spiritual gifts, Paul puts emphasis on the supremacy of the ethical over the miraculous and the physical. This is clearly seen in 1 Corinthians, chapters 12-14. These three chapters constitute one discussion on spiritual gifts. Whatever the gift of tongues may have been at Corinth, Paul does not consider it the supreme gift. He insists that talking does no good unless one talks so as to be understood or has some one to interpret for him. Paul does not believe in an uncontrolled emotionalism in religion. He says emphatically that the greatest thing is love. The greatest thing that God can do for any man is not to give him the power to talk with tongues or work miracles, but it is to make him a lover of his fellow man. Patient, suffering love is the greatest thing in the world.

Those people today who insist that what Christians need first of all is a restoration of the power to work miracles and speak with tongues have evidently not read Paul understandingly. Man's first need is in the moral realm. What men need first of all is to be made the right kind of men. The power to work physical miracles would not bring in the kingdom of God. But the world does need, and needs desperately, men who can love after the example of Jesus. The world's first need is Christ-like men and women. Only the Spirit of God can produce them.

THE TRINITY

CHAPTER VI

THE TRINITY

I. TRINITY IN UNITY

   1. Unity fundamental
   2. Diversity in God's manifestations
   3. Diversity becomes a trinity
   4. Two other doctrines

II. INTERPRETATIONS OF THE FACTS

   1. The Unitarian solution
   2. The modalistic solution
   3. The tritheistic method
   4. The triune nature of God
      (1) Work of Father, Son, and Spirit is each the work of God
      (2) Work of each is inclusive, not exclusive, of the work of other
      (3) Word "person" used with some reserve
      (4) The Trinity is immanent and eternal, not temporal and economic

CHAPTER VI

THE TRINITY

God is Father, Son, and Holy Spirit. Each of these is distinct from the others, and yet there is only one God.

I. Trinity in unity

1. *Unity fundamental*

In both the Old Testament and the New, God is revealed as one. In the Old Testament this is fundamental. Jehovah alone was God (Ex. 8: 10; 9: 14; Deut. 4: 35, 39; Isa. 43: 11; 45: 21). This fact was made the basis of Israel's obligation to love him with an undivided affection and devotion (Deut. 6: 4, 5). Jesus endorsed this idea of the oneness of God and also the fact that God's people owe him an undivided love (Mark 12: 29, 30). James grounds the unity of the moral law in the unity of God (James 2: 10, 11. Cf. 4: 12). The unity of God is fundamental in biblical revelation.

2. *Diversity in God's manifestations*

God is one, but there are indications even in the Old Testament that he is more than a unity. Wisdom was his companion from the beginning (Prov. 8: 22ff.). His Word went out from him to accomplish his purposes (Deut. 8: 4; 30: 14; Isa. 45: 23; Psalm 107: 20, et al). He is present in the world in his Spirit.[1] He embodies himself in his angel to help his people (Gen. 16: 7ff.; 22: 23ff.; Psalm 34: 7, et al).

3. *Diversity becomes a trinity*

In the New Testament and in Christian experience, Father, Son, and Holy Spirit are recognized as distinct. We cannot identify God absolutely and exclusively with

---

[1] See chapter on *The Spirit of God.*

either Father, Son, or Holy Spirit. It takes each of these to complete the conception of God. Even the Father does not fulfil the idea of God apart from the Son and Holy Spirit; for apart from the Son we cannot know God as Father. It is the part of God to be God within himself. It is his work also to manifest himself to man. This he does in Christ. Besides, the awakening of the response in our hearts to this revelation of himself in Christ—this also is the work of God and this is done by the Holy Spirit. The Father sends the Son, the Son reveals the Father, and the Holy Spirit enables men to apprehend the Father as revealed in the Son.

4. *Two other doctrines*

The central thing that leads to the doctrine of the Trinity is the recognition of the deity of Christ. The doctrine of the Trinity followed as a consequence of the recognition of the deity of Christ. This recognition of Christ as divine did not lead to polytheism nor to a surrender of the idea of the unity of God but to a recognition of life movement within the unity of the Godhead. Along with this recognition of the deity of Christ went belief in the personality of the Holy Spirit, so that Christians came to believe in a trinitarian life in the Godhead rather than a dual life. These three doctrines, then—the deity of Christ, the personality of the Holy Spirit, and the Trinity—are inseparably bound up together. If we accept the doctrine of the deity of Christ, the doctrine of the personality of the Holy Spirit and of the Trinity will follow.

II. Interpretations of the facts

All theories of the Trinity have been efforts to interpret these facts

1. *The Unitarian solution*

One proposed solution of the problem has been to put Christ outside the Godhead. Unitarianism has taken many forms in the course of Christian history. Sometimes it has regarded Christ as a man supernaturally endowed. Sometimes it has considered him as a supernatural being but less than God. Sometimes it has looked upon him as only a man of exceptional wisdom and goodness. But in all forms it has regarded him as less than the incarnation of God.

Of course, if Christ is only a man, there is no Trinitarian problem to solve. The question here, then, depends on the previous question of whether Christ is only a man, even though perhaps supernaturally endowed for his mission, or whether he is eternal in his being and belongs somehow within the unity of the Godhead.

2. *The Modalistic solution*

In brief, this affirmed that God was one person who manifested himself in three aspects, offices, or "modes." Hence the name modalism. Thus this method of solving the problem makes God absolutely unipersonal and makes Father, Son, and Holy Spirit to represent different manifestations of this unipersonal God. In general the Father represents God as the creator and source of all things; the Son represents God as incarnated in Jesus of Nazareth for the salvation of men; the Holy Spirit represents God as present in the hearts of men to regenerate and sanctify.

This modalistic way of representing the Trinity has some merits. It deals in earnest with the idea of the deity of Christ but it does not come to grips with the distinctions recognized in the New Testament among these phases or manifestations of the Godhead. It makes Fatherhood and Sonship to be only temporary characteristics of God rather than something essential and eternal in his nature. Nor does it have any conclusive answer to the question as to why God is manifested as a trinity rather than as an indefinite plurality. Why did God assume these three "characters" rather than four or five or a thousand?

3. *The tritheistic method*

Another method of solving this problem might be described as the tritheistic.

Much of the popular speaking and writing on the subject of the Trinity comes dangerously near to tritheism. It speaks of Father, Son, and Holy Spirit about as we speak of three human individuals. A good deal is said about "co-operation" among the three persons of the Trinity as if co-operation in this case meant that the three conferred, agreed on a plan, and all worked at it separately or conjointly. We hear about the "councils of eternity" as if three individuals met around a council table and came to an agreement.

If the word "person" as applied to the distinctions within the Godhead is to be taken in this individualistic and external sense, then we had better not use the word person in this connection. If to call these inner distinctions of the Godhead "persons" is going to be taken to mean that God is one only in this external and generic sense, then we had better speak of God as only one person rather than as three. Whatever else we are to believe about God, it is fundamental to the whole biblical revelation of God that he is One in a deeper sense than this. He is one in the sense that there is no other in the same class. Father, Son, and Holy Spirit might be spoken of as three persons, but not as three individuals. There cannot be three individuals who are infinite or absolute in their nature.

So this method of solving the problem of the Trinity by thinking of the Godhead as being three individuals of the same class who "confer" and "co-operate" does not do justice to the unity of God. Whatever our doctrine of the Trinity may be, it must not contradict the unity of God.

4. *The triune nature of God*

The true method of interpreting the Christian facts must recognize two things: the unity of God and his trinity. The unity of God is the unity of the supreme, creative Being who is the undivided source and sustainer of all things. Yet within the unity of God there is a trinity that is more than a trinity of "characters" assumed by one individual in a play. We will try to set out this interpretation as follows:

(1) The work of Father, Son, and Holy Spirit is each the work of God.

This is one of the fundamental aspects of this matter. The work of Christ is the work of God. Christ is not a "delegate" whom God sent, nor is the Holy Spirit an external agent sent by the Father and the Son. The work of Christ and of the Holy Spirit is as much the work of God as is the work of the Father.

(2) The work of each is, therefore, inclusive of the work of the other rather than exclusive.

Sometimes men talk of the "office" work of the three persons of the Trinity as if each agreed to do a certain part of the work in saving man; as if each did his work in a mutually co-operative and external way; as if the Father did his part and ceased; then the Son did his and ceased; then the Holy Spirit took up his part of the task and is working to complete the program. This is again tritheistic in its tendency. The New Testament conception is not that Father, Son, and Holy Spirit mutually and successively co-operate in carrying out a plan previously agreed upon, but rather that all work in and through each. The work of the Son is the work of the Father, and the Father works in and through the Son. The work of the Spirit is the work of Christ, and Christ works in and through the Spirit. The work of each is the work of all, and the work of all is the work of each.

Yet there is a distinction of "office" or function. The Father is the source and origin of all things; the Son is the medium of the outgoing energy and power of God; the Holy Spirit works to complete all things. But each works not so as to exclude the others, but so that the work of each is the work of all—not all separately but of the Godhead as a unity.

(3) The word "person" as applied to the distinctions within the Godhead has always been used with some reserve.

It is easy to see the reason for this—namely: the fact that it is so likely to suggest three mutually exclusive individuals. If properly qualified, this word may be used but only in a qualified sense. As already explained, it must be used, not in the sense of exclusiveness, but in the sense of inclusiveness. Perhaps after all, the most distinctive thing about personality, even in man, is not its exclusiveness, but its inclusiveness. The most personal thing about personality is not that I can say, "I am I," as over against all other I's to their exclusion, but it is rather the power of personality to include others in the circle of interest, thought, and effort. It is not the power to exclude other persons, but the power to include them. It is the power to take them into the range of one's thought and life and to put one's self into their lives. It is the power of self-giving, self-sharing. It is love.

(4) The Trinity, then, is immanent and eternal, not merely temporal and economic.

It has sometimes been held that the Trinity is only a trinity of manifestation (in line rather with modalism). To attempt to go back into the eternal being and nature of God, it has been held, is beyond man's power. Or it has been contended that to carry these personal distinctions back into the eternal nature of God would destroy his unity.

It must be granted that the main thing is the historical revelation as we have it in Christianity. The main thing is not a theory of the nature of God, but the facts of history and experience. We must in this, as in all other things, hold fast to the facts and then seek to give the best and clearest explanation possible of the facts.

But, at the same time, history and experience are the key to the interpretation of reality. The revelation must reveal God as he is. The temporal revelation must be taken as the key to eternal Being or else it is not revelation. If God is revealed as Father by Jesus Christ in time, and this is revelation, not illusion, then God must be a Father in his essential or eternal being, or revelation is not revelation. If Fatherhood is not eternal in God, if it is only an attitude or a "part" assumed in time, then Christ has not revealed God in his eternal Being. On the other hand, if one takes the revelation given us in Christ as the key to the nature of the eternal God, then Fatherhood is something eternal in the nature of God and Christ is God's Son eternally, not simply in time.[1]

---

[1]For a good discussion of this, see Fairbairn, *The Place of Christ in Modern Theology.*

THE DOCTRINE OF SIN

CHAPTER VII

THE DOCTRINE OF SIN

I. The Nature of Sin

    1. Sin has the element of wilfulness

    2. Sin as wilfulness implies knowledge

    3. Sin as unbelief

    4. Sin as guilt

        (1) Consciousness of guilt

        (2) Measure of guilt

        (3) Ground of guilt

        (4) Degrees of guilt

    5. Sin as depravity

        (1) Meaning of the term

        (2) Evidence for the doctrine

        (3) Total depravity

            a. Man's whole nature depraved

            b. Man wholly unable to deliver self from sin

            c. Without grace man becomes increasingly worse

    6. Sin brings servitude

    7. Sin is universal

    8. Sin is hereditary

    9. The salvation of infants

II. The Results of Sin

    1. Sin alienates from God

    2. Sin brings moral and spiritual degradation

    3. Sin causes social disruption

    4. Sin produces suffering

    5. Sin produces death

CHAPTER VII

THE DOCTRINE OF SIN

Any discussion that considers man in relation to God is incomplete that does not take account of the fact of sin. Much of the discussion in this realm misses the way because it either ignores or misinterprets sin. As preparatory to a consideration of the doctrine of salvation, we look at the doctrine of sin.

I. The nature of sin

Suppose we take for a tentative definition of sin the statement that sin is rebellion against the will of God. To make clear the nature of sin as rebellion against God, the following points need emphasis:

1. *The element of wilfulness in sin*

As already stated one factor in man's personality, one thing that marks him as a being created in the divine image is the power of will. To be capable of obedience or disobedience, man must have the power of choice. The obedience of physical elements or of animals to the law of their being deserves no praise because these have no choice. With them it is a matter of physical necessity or animal instinct. Their conformity to the law of their being is obedience only in a secondary sense. Man obeys because he wills to obey.

As free to obey or disobey, God addresses his commands to man. Why was man singled out at the beginning as the one being whom God had created to whom God should address a specific command, unless it be that man by virtue of his personality has the power of free obedience or disobedience? This principle as a presupposition underlies all God's dealings with man as recorded in the Bible. Man is more than mechanism; he

is a person. Even God, his Creator, respects his personality.

This comes out even more clearly in the fact that God
not only commands man, but also entreats, persuades,
exhorts him. God's respect for man's will comes out
in the fact that God uses men as his messengers to persuade their fellows to obey God. One of the most impressive things about the biblical revelation of God is
the infinite patience of God in dealing with erring and
sinful man. God was never without his witnesses and
messengers. Particularly from the time of Moses on,
after God had entered into covenant relations with Israel
as a nation, the record is one long story of the back-
sliding and unfaithfulness of Israel and of the faithful-
ness and long-suffering of Jehovah. This comes out
through the whole of Old Testament history and is the
theme of such psalms as the seventy-eighth.

This is impressively brought out in the life and teaching of Jesus. Jesus weeps over Jerusalem as he sees the
impending doom of the city. He gives as the reason for
its coming desolation that its inhabitants would not be
gathered to him (Luke 13: 34). But this comes out nowhere more clearly than in Paul's great saying in 2
Corinthians 5: 19, 20. He says God is in Christ reconciling the world unto himself. Then he adds: "We are
ambassadors therefore on behalf of Christ, as though
God were entreating by us: we beseech you on behalf
of Christ, be ye reconciled to God." It is not a surprising thing that God the Creator should command man
his creature. But it is surprising that God should entreat
man. It shows distinctly the respect that God has for
man's will. It also throws light on the element of wilfulness in man's rebellion against God.

2. *Sin as wilful implies knowledge*

If man's sin is wilful, then it must be sin against light.
When there is no knowledge of moral truth, there can
be no sin in the full sense of the term. Perhaps this is
implied in Paul's statement that where there is no law,

neither is there transgression (Rom. 4: 15). He also says that through the law is the knowledge of sin (Rom. 3: 20). In Romans 7, Paul describes a state in which he says that at one time he was alive without the law. But when the commandment came, "sin revived and I died." When he came to know a certain thing as forbidden of the law, he did not thereby refrain from doing that thing, but rather came to do it. This shows that there was an intimate connection between a knowledge of the will of God and sin as an active principle in human life. (See verses 7-11.)

But knowledge of moral and spiritual things, particularly knowledge of God and his will, presupposes revelation on God's part. As a matter of fact, we find the idea of sin in the Bible intimately related to two other ideas: revelation on God's part, and a knowledge of that revelation on man's part. In general, there are four stages in this revelation, each connected with the idea of sin in the New Testament. The first is the revelation of God in nature or the physical world. This Paul discusses in Romans 1: 18ff. The invisible things of God are clearly seen, being perceived through the things that are made, even his everlasting power and divinity. Paul says that this knowledge of God coming through nature leaves men without excuse. Although men knew God as thus revealed, they would not honor him in their lives. They rejected him, refusing to honor and serve him.

The next stage in the revelation of God as related to sin is his revelation in reason and conscience, or man's rational and moral nature. Paul says that the Gentiles, who have not the law, "are the law unto themselves; in that they show the work of the law written in their hearts, their conscience bearing witness therewith, and their thoughts one with another accusing or else excusing them" (Rom. 2: 14, 15).

A third stage in God's revelation may be denoted by the term law. This is Paul's great term when thinking of God's revelation of himself in relation to man as sinful.

By this he means primarily the Old Testament or Mosaic law. Sometimes he uses the term without the article, sometimes with it. With the article, it is clear that he means the Mosaic law. Without the article, he also means primarily the Mosaic law, but he is thinking of that law as embodying universal principles of righteousness or moral requirement. When he uses the article he is thinking of the Mosaic law more as a concrete system of particular requirements. Without the article the Mosaic law is still in mind but rather as made up of universal principles of general application.[1]

The law is the embodiment of the moral requirements of God in published ordinances. The center of the Old Testament law looked at as moral requirement is the Ten Commandments. The requirement of the law is perfect obedience to its mandates. The law as such allows for no exceptions and makes no provision for any remission of penalty.

Sin as against the moral requirement of the law, Paul calls a trespass or transgression. (See Rom. 5: 12ff., et al.)

The function of the law in relation to sin was not to justify or to save from sin, but rather to awaken one to a consciousness of sin, to one's helplessness in sin, to one's need of the Redeemer, and thus serve as the pedagogue to lead the sinner to Christ. (See Rom. 7 and Gal. 3.)

The climax of revelation in relation to sin came in the grace of God in Christ which saves from sin. We do not get the complete doctrine of sin until we see the grace of God that saves from sin. The awful blackness of sin does not make its full impression on us until we see it in contrast to the radiant grace of God. This may be illustrated in the case of Paul himself, who seems to have had a deepening consciousness of sin until in his old age he calls himself the chief of sinners (1 Tim.

---

[1] Cf. Stevens, *Pauline Theology*, p. 160.

1: 15). His own conduct in persecuting the church he thought to be right until he was given the revelation of God's grace. Then he became a guilty sinner in his own eyes. This thought is also illustrated in the teaching of Jesus. Jesus says that because of his presence and teaching in their midst, the cities of his day will receive a greater condemnation than Sodom and Gomorrah (Matt. 11: 20ff.). The servant who has the knowledge of the master's will and does it not will be beaten with many stripes, while the servant who knew not the master's will will be beaten with few stripes (Luke 12: 47, 48). Again, Jesus says that, if he had not come, those who reject him had not had sin. Now they have no excuse for their sin (John 15: 22). Men are condemned because they love darkness rather than light. The condemnation is that light is come into the world and men love darkness rather than light, because their deeds are evil (John 3: 19). The light of God's grace does two things for the sinful heart: it reveals its darkness, and it increases that darkness in case of those who reject the light of grace.

3. *What has just been said would favor the view that unbelief is the essence of sin*

This does not mean, however, unbelief in the sense of a refusal to accept a doctrine or a dogma. It is unbelief in one's rejection of moral and spiritual light, particularly as that light is embodied in Jesus Christ. It is the rejection of God's final revelation of himself as made in Christ. When this rejection becomes definite and wilful, it becomes the sin unto death (1 John 5: 13-17) It is then a wilful treading under foot of the Son of·God. counting the blood of the covenant wherewith he was sanctified an unholy thing, and doing despite to the Spirit of grace (Heb. 10: 29). It thus becomes moral suicide. It is putting out one's own spiritual eyes. It does not take place except in connection with a high degree of enlightenment. It is deliberate, wilful, malicious rejection of Christ as God's revelation, knowing that he is such a revelation. It is deliberately calling white black.

This agrees with what Jesus says about blasphemy against the Holy Spirit. The sin that men were committing which led Jesus to utter this warning was the sin of attributing his works to the power of the devil, thus denying that they were wrought by the power of God. He is thinking of the Spirit as embodied in his own life and works and thus revealing the presence of God, giving men light to see and recognize God in his own life and works. When men thus enlightened by the Spirit deliberately reject his works as the works of God and attribute them to the devil, they blaspheme the Spirit and there is never forgiveness for their sin. This is essentially unbelief in its final form as set forth by John and wilful sin as described in Hebrews.

Some have defined the essential principle of sin as selfishness—not selfishness as opposed to benevolence toward one's fellowman, but selfishness in the sense of the assertion of one's own will as opposed to submission to the will of God. To live in sin, then, is to live a life centered in self, to erect one's own will as the law of life.

4. *Viewing sin as wilful rebellion, we describe it by the term guilt*

This means that man deserves to be punished for his sin. The sense of shame and ill desert led Adam to clothe himself with fig leaves and hide himself from his Maker (Gen. 3: 8). Adam tried to shift the blame to his wife, and Eve to the serpent; but in each case there was clearly the sense of ill desert.

(1) The guilt of sin manifests itself in consciousness.

Man knows himself as blameworthy on account of his sin. This consciousness of ill desert is a general phenomenon of human life, especially of man's religious life. This is true in spite of the fact that there is a general disposition to hide one's sense of ill desert and cover up or deny one's responsibility for sin. In fact, the attempt to cover up one's guilt is itself an evidence of guilt. A clear conscience is not so quick to attempt to justify itself as a guilty one. This sense of guilt manifests itself also in the fact that men blame one another with reference to their needs.

(2) This consciousness of ill desert, however, is not to be taken as the accurate measure of the guilt of sin.

This is true with reference to one's own sin or another's. Our moral judgments are no more infallible than our judgments in other realms. In fact, it is often the case that the reverse is true—namely: that the greater one's guilt, the less is he conscious of it. This is true because of the blinding power of sin. Sin darkens the spiritual vision and warps the moral judgment. Consequently, probably the most dangerous condition that one can be in spiritually is to have no consciousness of sin and no sense of danger. For one to have no sense of ill desert is not a sign that one is without guilt; it is a sign that he is spiritually blind and in great spiritual danger. The closer one gets to God, the more conscious he is of his own unworthiness. On the other hand, if we say that we have no sin, we deceive ourselves and the truth is not in us (1 John 1: 8). Self-conscious goodness is always sham goodness. It is rotten at the core. This was one of the outstanding characteristics of the Pharisees. They thanked God that they were not like other men. They turned up their noses at "publicans and sinners." They despised Jesus for associating with such human driftwood. But these self-righteous Pharisees were the men that Jesus denounced most bitterly. Paul in his old age called himself the chief of sinners (1 Tim. 1: 15), and counted not that he had attained perfection (Phil. 3: 12, 13).

(3) The ground of guilt is the relation of man as ill deserving to God as holy.

Man's sin is ill deserving because it is against God as holy. If God were not holy, sin would not be ill deserving. The conception of any religion as to the character of sin is determined primarily by its conception of the character of God. It is against the background of God's spotless character that the blackness of sin is to be seen. This comes out clearly in the sixth chapter of Isaiah. The prophet sees Jehovah high and lifted up, the exalted and Holy One. Then he sees himself and the people among whom he lives as sinful.

(4) Men are not equally guilty before God.

In the Old Testament there were sins of ignorance and sins of presumption; sins that could be atoned for by sacrifices and sins that put one outside the covenant relation to God. Jesus recognizes this principle. The people of Sodom and Gomorrah will not have as heavy condemnation as the cities which had the benefit of his ministry and teaching (Matt. 11: 20ff.). The servant who knows not his master's will shall not have the same punishment as the one who knows but does not (Luke 12: 47, 48). Paul also recognizes the same principle. Men are held responsible for the light they have, whether that light be the light of nature, of the heart and conscience, or of the Old Testament law (Rom. 1 and 2).

It seems, then, that light and privilege are elements that enter into the determination of the degree of one's guilt. The degree of one's guilt might be said to be determined by the measure of wilfulness that enters into one's sinning (Heb. 10: 26ff.). To the extent that one sins wilfully, to that extent is one guilty and his character fixed in sin.

This principle is recognized in the social relations of life. The man with light, privilege, opportunity, ability, is held to a stricter account by his fellow men. Courts of law take into account the element of deliberateness in a man's crime in assessing his penalty.

5. *Another phase of sin is described by the term depravity*

(1) Meaning of the term depravity.

By this term is meant that state or condition of man's moral nature that makes it not only possible that he may sin on account of his power of choice, but certain that he will sin on account of his moral weakness and inherent tendency toward evil. This depravity of man's nature is inherent and universal. These two ideas— the idea that depravity is inherent and that it is universal—seem to be inseparable. Certainly, if sin is inherent, it is universal; and, on the other hand, if it is universal, there is a strong presumption that it is inherent. By saying that sin or depravity is inherent we do not mean that sin is a constituent element in human nature, or that sin and human nature are inseparable. Human nature was not created sinful or depraved. Christ did not have a depraved human nature. Besides, if sin were a constituent element in human nature, man could not be saved from sin. But in saying that depravity is inherent in human nature is meant that man as fallen is born depraved; that since Adam's time and on account of Adam's sin, all men are born with such a moral tendency toward sin that it is a moral certainty, that it is morally inevitable, that when they come to make moral choices, they will commit sin.

(2) That sin is inherent is evidenced by the direct teaching of the Scriptures.

In Psalm 51, the writer says, "In sin did my mother conceive me" (Psalm 51: 5). Jeremiah says, "The heart is deceitful . . . and desperately wicked: who can know it?" (Jer. 17: 9.) Paul says that we are by nature the children of wrath (Eph. 2: 3). Men are by nature the children of wrath in the sense that their lives of sin, which incur the wrath of God, are the natural outgrowth of their native disposition.

(3) Is man totally depraved?

That depends altogether on the definition of total depravity. If by total depravity is meant that man is as corrupt as he can be, then certainly this doctrine cannot be true. But in the sense that man is totally helpless, because of his natural inheritance, outside the provisions of God's saving grace, the doctrine is true. The matter might be summed up by saying man is totally depraved in the following sense:

a. In the sense that man's whole nature, every element and faculty of his being, has been weakened and depraved by sin. Body, soul, and spirit have passed under its power. Man's mind has been darkened, his heart depraved, his will perverted by sin.

b. It means that man is totally unable to deliver himself from the power of sin. Here is the crux of the matter. The truth for which the term total depravity stands is the total inability of man to save himself, his entire helplessness in the grasp of sin.

c. Without divine help man becomes worse and worse. Instead of total depravity meaning that man is as bad as he can be, it means that without the redeeming power of God's grace, he will forever sink deeper and deeper into sin. "This depravity does not mean that all men are as bad as some men, but it means that all the meanness in the worst man has its germ and nature in the soul of the best man."[2]

Much of the dispute over the term total depravity has been aside from the mark, because it was based on the preconception that the thing that made sin deadly was the extent to which man was affected by it. Sin was regarded as ruinous provided the sin was big enough. But it is not the extent of sin that makes it deadly; it is the nature of sin. Sin kills because it is sin, not because it is big. The very nature of sin is such that it would dethrone God and introduce moral and spiritual anarchy into God's universe. It is in direct antithesis

[2]Scarborough, L. R., *Christ's Militant Kingdom*, pp. 47, 48.

to God's nature as holy. Therefore, no sin can be tolerated in man. The very nature of sin is such that it poisons man's moral nature and ruins his spiritual life. It cuts man off from God.

6. Jesus and Paul emphasize the servitude of sin

Jesus says that the man who commits sin is the servant of sin (John 8: 34). In one place he says that the truth will free from this bondage; in another, the Son (John 8: 32, 36). Paul sets forth in Romans 6 that man is either the servant of sin or of God and righteousness. In chapter 7 he gives a vivid account of his own struggle with the power of sin, his utter inability to deliver himself and his finding deliverance in Christ. There seem to be three distinct stages in Paul's experience as set forth in this chapter. The first is a state which he speaks of as being alive without the law (verse 9a). He had no consciousness of condemnation and death, because he had not been awakened by the law to a knowledge of its demands. The second stage is one in which he becomes aware of the righteous demands of the law, but cannot live up to its demands. "The commandment came, sin revived, and I died" (verse 9b). This leads to a sense of utter helplessness and then despair. Finally comes the realization of deliverance through Christ (verse 25). This reigning principle of sin Paul recognizes as being universal, as shown in Romans 5:12-21.

7. Sin is universal

As already stated, sin is universal. That sin is universal is clearly taught in the Bible. In Genesis, following the sin of the first man, there is the intensive and extensive development of sin until the race soon became so corrupt that God sent a flood and destroyed the race, except Noah and his family. It is made clear that no man in biblical history was sinless, except Jesus himself. The very best men of both Old and New Testament times were weak and sinful. The Psalmist represents God as searching the earth, but finding none without sin (Psalm 14: 1ff.). Jesus regarded all men as sinful. He says: "If ye, then, being evil" (Luke 11: 13). This expression shows that he regards all men as evil and sinful. He teaches, as one of the fundamental things in prayer, that men should pray for forgiveness (Matt. 6: 12). They need forgiveness as universally as they need daily bread. Paul explicitly teaches that all men are sinners. All have sinned (Rom. 3: 9ff.). This presupposition underlies his argument in Romans 5: 12ff.

Experience, observation, and human history show that sin is universal. The best of men confess themselves sinners. Nor is this to be interpreted as the result of an abnormal or morbid consciousness on their part. Men who, like Paul, Luther, and John Bunyan, stand at the center of spiritual Christianity cannot be regarded as wholly misinterpreting their own relation to God. Then the consensus of opinion among men is that no man lives above moral and spiritual blame. The course of human history indicates that there is something fundamentally wrong with mankind.

8. *Sin is hereditary*

The best explanation of the universality of sin is to explain it by referring it to the corruption of human nature in the beginning of human history. The Bible gives us to understand that the first man violated God's expressed will and by doing so the stream of human history was corrupted at its source.

Whatever view one may hold as to Adam's sin and our relation to it, the fact seems to stand that when we come to the age of moral consciousness and moral activity, we find ourselves so identified with evil impulses within us and evil social forces around us that we are already practically slaves to them. These evil forces did not originate in acts of our own will. This may seem like a fact of dark and ominous aspect, but we cannot get rid of it by denying its existence. Unpleasant facts are not disposed of by denying their right to be or by calling them by euphemistic names. Men have tried long enough to heal the world's moral corruption by sprinkling rose water on it.

There are such seeds of evil tendency in the child's nature, and such social influences for evil in the world in which the child lives that it inevitably commits transgression when it comes to the age of moral responsibility. In that sense the child is a sinner. It does not have personal guilt. That is impossible where the conditions of personal responsibility are lacking. These are absent in the child's life until the powers of self-consciousness and self-determination arise. There can be no personal guilt except in the case of a personal agent.

Both the Scriptures and moral consciousness bear testimony to our responsibility for our lives in spite of our inherited natures. In fact, this evil inheritance is regarded in the Scriptures as constituting a part of our awful condition, calling for divine grace and help. The testimony of our moral consciousness on this point cannot be doubted. As evil and sinful, we acknowledge our deplorable state and renounce the sinful self. One must deny this sinful self, take up one's cross, be crucified with Christ, in order to live.

9. *The salvation of infants*

As to the question of infant salvation, it is generally agreed among evangelical theologians that those dying in infancy are saved. This is not held so much on the ground that there is specific scripture teaching to that effect as it is because of certain general principles in gospel teaching as to God's dealings with men, and because of the general view of the character of God as revealed in Christ.

There is general agreement among evangelical theologians that all disability up to the point of positive transgression and deliberate rejection of moral light is provided for in the atoning work of Christ. There is race redemption as well as race sin. No man, therefore, will be lost merely because of original or race sin. Up to the point of positive transgression or rejection of moral light, the individual is provided for in the grace of God without personal repentance and faith.

In view of these considerations, we believe that we are justified in holding that the child dying in infancy is saved. In other words, where there has been conscious and positive identification of one's self with evil, there must be also, under the grace of God, conscious and positive repudiation of evil and identification of one's self with right, before there can be deliverance from evil. Up to the point of positive identification of one's self with right or wrong, there is only the potentiality of moral life. In the case of the child, that potentiality is evil except for the positive influence of the grace of God in redeeming from this evil potentiality or the life of transgression that grows out of it. So far as the bent of the child's nature and the social influences of the world order are concerned, these are toward evil. To save the child from this evil inheritance requires the grace of God, which transcends nature and the world order.

II. The results of sin

Some of the things said here might possibly as well have been said under the head of the nature of sin. Sometimes it is difficult to tell whether a certain phase of the matter should be considered as a phase of the nature of sin or as a result of sin.

1. *Sin alienates from God*

It is of the very nature of sin to alienate man from God. This is the most serious thing about sin. All the woe of sin grows out of the fact that it cuts man off from God, "from whom all blessings flow." The curse of our age is that it has lost its consciousness of God. Worse than that, the carnal mind is hostile to God. It is not subject to the law of God. It is impossible for it to be so. This is the thing that necessitates a spiritual recreation in Christ.

2. *Sin against God also brings moral and spiritual blindness, impotence, and degradation*

God is the source of all life and light. When man by his rebellion cuts himself off from God, he is plunged into moral darkness and degradation. Paul points this out in Romans 1: 18ff. God revealed himself to men through the visible creation; but man refused to worship and serve him. As a result, God gave them up to religious and moral degradation. Low forms of religion are not always, as sometimes held, stages in man's upward progress; they are sometimes, if not always, stages in a downward process. So are moral blindness and degradation. Three times in this passage (Rom. 1: 18-32) Paul says, "God gave them up." Moral and spiritual blindness and degradation are a judicial visitation of God's wrath on man for his rebellion against God. Sin thus becomes its own punishment. Man cannot escape punishment without being delivered from sin itself.

A lesson that our age needs to learn is that immorality is the result of irreligion. Many men of this age are trying to build a moral system and leave God and religion out. Such a tower of Babel will tumble down on its builders and crush them. It cannot be done. A high moral life must be sustained by a religious dynamic.

3. *Sin also is the root cause of social disorder and disruption*

This grows out of what was said above about moral blindness and degradation.

Maladjustment with God leads to maladjustment with one's fellow man. Alienation from God causes hatreds and estrangements among men. Paul says that the gospel of Christ which brings peace for man with God also removes the alienations among men and thus brings peace between Jew and Gentile (Eph. 2: 11ff.). The only hope for social justice and righteousness among men lies in the gospel of Christ. What we are saying—that sin is the source of alienations and hatreds among men—is the other side of this truth. Social justice, therefore, can never be built on class or race hatred or exclusiveness. The only social righteousness must be a righteousness for all, not for a class.

4. *Sin produces suffering*

We know that much of human suffering is directly due to man's sin. Both the man who sins and others as well suffer because of his sins. The connection is not always easy to trace, but often it is obvious. If all the suffering of mankind due to its own perversity were taken out of the world's history, that history would make quite different reading. Here the connection is so obvious that we do not have any trouble tracing it. We cannot always trace the connection in detail, but the broad outlines are plain.

But what about the sufferings due to the disorders of nature herself, the cyclones, floods, earthquakes, volcanoes, and so forth? There is an indication in Genesis and other places that there is a connection between evil and the sin of man. In Genesis, work or labor is to be a part of man's penalty. This does not mean that work or activity as such is a part of the penalty, for man was to keep the garden even before the fall. And after redemption there is to be activity. God's servants will serve him (Rev. 22: 3). Heaven is to be no place for inactivity. But the fact that man is to earn his bread by the sweat of his brow indicates that the element of burdensome labor came in because of sin (Gen. 3: 19). Then it is said that the earth should bear thorns and thistles for man (Gen. 3: 18). This may be taken as a particular statement indicating that natural evil in general came because of man's sin and in part as penalty for his sin.

Some have concluded, because of the statement in Genesis, that there was no suffering, no animal death, no natural evil of any kind in the world before man sinned. But the Bible does not teach that all suffering, animal death, and natural evil are penal only.

Besides, if one holds that natural evil, in whole or in part, is the result of man's sin, still it is not necessary to hold that man's sin preceded in the order of time the appearance of natural evil in the world. The order in which they come in the purpose of God is not necessarily the order in which they appear in the temporal order. The disorder and natural disturbances of the world may have been intended, whether meant strictly as penalty or not, to remind man of his own sin and need of redemption. Perhaps the disorder of the physical universe is intended as a reflection of the moral universe.

To a limited extent, at least, then, natural evil or suffering may be regarded as the penalty of sin, or as a punishment for sin.

But the doctrine of providence as related to grace shows that suffering or natural evil serves another purpose in relation to sin; that is, it is used as a means under grace for the development of Christian character; it serves a redemptive end. This we know both from the teaching of the Scriptures and from Christian experience. This is involved in the saying of Jesus about the blind man in John 9. He says in substance to the disciples that they will never understand suffering and misfortune so long as they try to interpret it exclusively as the infliction of penalty for sin; they must see it as related to God's benevolent purpose toward mankind. We must remember that every phase of life is to be interpreted from the point of view of God's redemptive purpose in Christ. Law and penalty do not speak the final word. They speak a true word, but the final word is spoken by grace and truth as revealed in Jesus Christ. There is a penal aspect to suffering or natural evil; but there is also a redemptive aspect. For the man who rejects grace, suffering is primarily penal; for the redeemed man, it is primarily remedial and disciplinary. For society in general, in proportion as sin reigns, it is penal; as grace reigns, it is redemptive. We know that the race has got much of its development, mental, social, and moral, by striving to overcome natural evil.

5. Sin produces death

There are places in the Bible where the penalty of sin is summed up in the word death. God said to Adam, "In the day that thou eatest thereof thou shalt surely die" (Gen. 2: 17). Paul said, "The wages of sin is death" (Rom. 6: 23). Speaking of an unrighteous life, he says, "The end of those things is death" (Rom. 6: 21). He says again that the mind of the flesh is death (Rom. 8: 6).

The question arises as to whether this includes physical death, or is the penalty here spoken of spiritual death? There are places in the Bible where death clearly means spiritual death; for instance, when Jesus said, "He that liveth and believeth on me shall never die" (John 11: 26). He certainly does not mean that one who believes in him shall never die physically. But ordinarily death includes physical death. When the Scriptures speak of death as the penalty of sin, they do not mean either physical or spiritual death to the exclusion of the other, but they mean death as a totality, both physical and spiritual—the death of the whole man viewed from a religious or spiritual point of view. The Scripture writers never consider death from a mere biological point of view; they always regard it in its relation to God. There may be places where one aspect is emphasized, but neither phase of death is excluded.

Doubtless it would be true to say that the chief thing in the penalty of sin is spiritual death. That is the primary thing. What was said in the preceding section about natural evil as related to sin will apply largely to physical death, because physical death is the summation and consummation of natural evil. We can sum the matter up, then, by saying that for the Christian physical death is primarily redemptive and disciplinary; for the unredeemed man it becomes exclusively penal.

Looking upon the penalty of sin as being primarily spiritual and secondarily as physical death helps us also with reference to another phase of the matter. It agrees with the fact that in salvation we are first and primarily saved from spiritual death in regeneration and sanctification; but this carries with it the resurrection of the body as the consummation and completion of salvation. Just as physical death resulted from the breaking of man's fellowship with God, so the restoration of fellowship with God carries as a consequence the salvation of the body. In the order of the importance and causation, it is first the spiritual, then the physical.

The final and complete penalty of sin is eternal death, what is spoken of as the second death in the Book of Revelation (2: 11; 20: 6, 14; 21: 8). This is the banishment of soul and body from the presence of God forever. This will be discussed when we come to consider the subject of eschatology.

GOD'S PURPOSE OF SALVATION

CHAPTER VIII

GOD'S PURPOSE OF SALVATION

I. God's Purpose in its Racial Aspects

1. Indications of religious history
2. Old Testament teaching and history
3. New Testament and Christian history

II. God's Purpose as Related to the Individual

1. Meaning of the doctrine
   (1) All saving efficiency is of God
   (2) God saves in pursuance of an eternal purpose
2. Proof of the doctrine
   (1) Principle seen in the Old Testament
   (2) Teaching of the New Testament
   (3) Inference from sovereignty and omniscience of God
   (4) Seen in Christian experience
3. Objections to the doctrine
   (1) That it makes God partial
   (2) That it is unjust to the non-elect
   (3) That it is inconsistent with the freedom of man
   (4) That it discourages effort in behalf of others

GOD'S PURPOSE OF SALVATION

If what has been said about God as a God of intelligence and power who is sovereign over the world is true, then we must believe that he has a purpose with reference to the world and man that is being worked out in the course of human history. If we are correct in holding that Jesus Christ as Saviour and Lord is God's final revelation of himself to man, then this purpose of God must be a redemptive purpose. If we are right in regard to man as a sinner in his relation to God, then redemption is man's chief need.

I. God's purpose in its racial aspects

We shall first look at God's purpose of redemption in its more general aspects. We have seen how the race as a whole fell under condemnation and death. Is there any evidence that with reference to mankind as a whole God is working out a purpose? We believe there is.

1. *Indications of religious history*

The general religious history of man would indicate that God has planted in man an insatiable thirst for God so that man can never rest until he rests in God.

Man's entire religious history is a record of man's search for God. But this search for God is the result of a disposition that God has implanted in man's soul. Surely this search is not all in vain. Man's religious history is moving some whither.

2. *We get clear indications of a redemptive purpose of God in Old Testament teaching and history*

As soon as man sinned, there was a gleam of light that broke through the lowering clouds in the form of a promise to the woman—a promise that has its fulfilment only in Christ (Gen. 3: 15). There was also a bow of promise that lighted the destruction of the flood with its light of hope (Gen. 9: 9-17). The call of Abraham marks a new era in the development of God's purpose of grace (Gen. 12: 1ff.). God entered into a covenant with Abraham and his descendants by which they were made his special people for a great purpose in the world. They were not made his people, however, to the exclusion of the other nations; they were rather to be a blessing to the other nations (Gen. 12: 2, 3). Israel was to be Jehovah's missionary to the nations (Isa. 42: 1ff.). Israel, however, as a nation misinterpreted her mission. She took her call to mean the exclusion of the other nations and, therefore, she became proud and arrogant in her spirit. Yet it is the great paradox of history that Israel did not fail, because out of her came the Redeemer, the one through whom God's redemptive purpose should be accomplished and who is, therefore, the fulfilment of all that was involved in God's ideal for national Israel. Old Testament history and teaching moved to their purpose and goal in Jesus Christ.

3. *Beginning with Christ, we have further evidence of a worldwide purpose of God*

We have the evidence of this in the doctrine of the kingdom of God in the New Testament. That kingdom was initiated with the coming and work of Christ (Matt. 3: 2; Mark 1: 15). He tells that the kingdom that began in such insignificant smallness is to become a mighty affair (Matt. 13: 31-33). Many shall come from all directions (Gentiles) and shall sit down with Abraham, Isaac, and Jacob in the kingdom while the sons of the kingdom (Jews) will be cast out (Matt. 8: 11, 12). The aged Simeon greets the babe Jesus as the one who should bring a salvation which God had prepared before the face of all people. He was to be a light for revelation to the Gentiles as well as the glory of Israel (Luke 2: 31, 32). Jesus commands that his gospel be preached to all nations (Matt. 28: 19; Luke 24: 47; Acts 1: 8). The Book of Acts narrates how the gospel broke through Jewish bounds and began to lay hold on the Gentile world.

Paul carried the gospel to the very center, even to Rome. Others had even preceded him there, for there was a church in Rome before Paul went there. It is made clear in Acts that the preaching of the Word to Gentiles was done under divine guidance. Paul went to the Gentile world under a special call from God (Acts 13: 1ff. and many other passages). The Book of Revelation gives us a graphic picture, mostly in symbolic language, of the final and complete triumph of God's kingdom. The struggle is long and hard, but complete and final triumph comes at last with the coming of the New Jerusalem down to earth from God.

II. God's purpose as related to the salvation of the individual

1. *The meaning of the doctrine*

But the Scriptures teach, not only that God has a general plan that is being carried out in human history, but also that God's purpose applies to the individual. When a man is saved he is not saved as a matter of chance or accident or fate; he is saved in pursuance of an eternal purpose of God. God saves men because he intends to. He saves a particular man, at a particular time, under a given set of circumstances, because he intends to.

Election does not mean that God instituted a general plan of salvation and decreed that whosoever would should be saved and, therefore, the man who wills to be saved is elected in that he brings himself within the scope of God's plan. It is true that God has decreed that whosoever will shall be saved; but election is something more specific and personal than that. It means that God has decreed to bring certain ones, upon whom his heart has been eternally set, who are the objects of his eternal love, to faith in Jesus as Saviour. The general meaning of the doctrine of election might be summed up in two statements:

(1) All saving efficiency is of God.

The first is that, when a sinner repents of his sins and believes in Christ to the saving of his soul, he does so because God has brought him to do so. Men do not turn from sin to God on their own initiative. God must move them to do so if ever they turn. This includes all good influences, all gospel agencies, all circumstances of environment, all inner dispositions and promptings of heart and conscience that enter into one's decision. It includes the whole historical order in which one is so situated as to have gospel privileges, and this order is viewed as being providential. Especially does it include the inner promptings and leadings of the Holy Spirit.

To regard one's conversion from sin to Christ as the work of God is the spontaneous impulse of the Christian heart. When a Christian hears of some one's turning from sin, the first expression to come to his lips is, "Thank God." But if this is not the work of God, then he should not be thanked. He does not deserve credit for what he does not do. This is the view of the Scriptures as well as the spontaneous impulse of the Christian heart. In the Bible, salvation is everywhere attributed to God. To save is the work of God. But to save includes bringing about this change of mind and heart that we call conversion. It is not true that the sinner within and of himself repents and believes and then God comes into the process in forgiveness. No, God was in the process from the first. He works to produce repentance and faith. He works to bring about the conditions upon which he can forgive. He seeks the sinner. We yield to a God who draws us to himself. We seek him because he first sought us. The gospel of Christ is the gospel of a seeking God. He seeks worshipers (John 4: 23). The Son of man came to seek and to save the lost (Luke 19: 10). The seeking of the Son of man is a revelation of the heart of God. Drawing men to Christ is the work of God. Without this drawing power, men cannot come to Christ (John 6: 44).

Paul talks about God as calling men (Rom. 8: 28-30; 1 Cor. 1: 24, et al). By this calling he seems to mean more than a general gospel invitation to men to be saved by the grace of God. Paul's use of the term seems to correspond rather to what Jesus speaks of as the drawing of God in John 6: 44. It is a dealing of God with the hearts of men that results in their coming to Christ and being saved. This efficacious call does not come to all, not even to all who hear the gospel. Some are called; to them the gospel is the power of God. To others the gospel is a stumbling-block or foolishness (1 Cor. 1: 23). This call gives one a spiritual mind that enables him to get an insight into the meaning of the Cross.

This drawing power of God is necessary, because man's natural inclinations are so opposed to God and righteousness that without it man will not come to God. Paul tells us that the carnal mind is enmity against God. It is not subject to the law of God. Its nature is such that it cannot be (Rom. 8: 7). Man must be born again, because that which is born of the flesh is flesh (John 3: 6). Hence one must die to sin (Rom. 6: 2). The old man must be crucified (Rom. 6: 6). One must deny himself and take up the Cross to be a disciple of Jesus (Matt. 16: 24).

(2) God saves in pursuance of an eternal purpose.

But we must go further back yet. Not only did God work to bring us to himself; he worked in pursuance of a plan that is eternal. He did not suddenly decide to work for a certain man's salvation; he worked for the man's salvation because he purposed to do so from eternal ages (Rom. 8: 29, 30; Eph. 1: 4-11; 3: 10, 11, et al).

The doctrine of election clearly means that God takes the initiative in our salvation. It means that what he does in saving us he does because he purposed to do it. Our salvation is not a matter of chance nor accident. We are saved because God meant for us to be saved. He saves us and he does so on purpose. He works through the unceasing ages to carry out his purpose.

It hardly represents this doctrine fairly to think of it as meaning that God arbitrarily chose this man and this man to be saved and omitted that one and that one. There are depths within the divine counsel that we cannot fathom, of course. But the doctrine does stand for the fact that from all eternity God has had his heart set upon his people for good, and that through the ages he is working out his purposes of grace concerning them (2 Tim. 1: 9). But there is nothing arbitrary in his actions or purposes. Above all, there is nothing unloving or ungracious in his attitude toward any man.

Whatever of good, including salvation from sin, comes into any man's life we recognize as coming from God (James 1: 17). The doctrine of election is simply the recognition of the fact that the good that comes into our lives comes as a result of God's purpose. He purposed all the good that comes to us. He purposed our salvation. Having purposed eternally to save us, he works out in time his purpose for us. His purpose is effected in and through the social and historical order to which we belong. His purpose concerning our salvation includes all the factors and relations of this social and historical order, just as a father plans the education of his son, but plans it in view of the social and educational influences and agencies that are available or can be made available. God instituted the social and historical order with a view to our salvation. So God did not purpose our salvation as detached and unrelated units. We do not exist as such units. His plan for the salvation of any man is a part of his plan for the race. He planned my salvation as something that would be brought to me through certain social and historical influences and forces. His plan for my salvation is a part of his plan for my whole life; especially does it include all the good that I may do to others in this social and historical order to which I belong.

2. *Proof of the doctrine*

(1) One is that we see the principle of election at work in the Old Testament.

God chose Abraham and his descendants to be his people in a peculiar sense. He entered into covenant relations with them. This does not mean that other peoples and nations were shut out or were not responsible to Jehovah. They were responsible to him. He chastised the other nations for their sins and used them to chastise Israel. But there was a special relation established between him and Israel, and Jehovah took the initiative in establishing this relation.

(2) We find this doctrine clearly taught in the New Testament.

God's people are frequently spoken of as the elect (Matt. 24: 22; Luke 18: 7; 1 Peter 1: 1). In the Old Testament, Israel as a nation constituted God's elect, but in Christianity it is not national Israel that constitutes God's elect, but redeemed individuals, the spiritual Israel.

In John's Gospel, Jesus speaks of his disciples as those whom the Father had given him (John 6: 37, 39; 17: 2, 6). In some of these passages the giving is put in the past as if it might have been a pretemporal transaction in God's eternal purpose (John 17: 2, 24). It seems to precede the coming to Christ on the part of his people. It might be synonymous with the drawing that results in their coming, but it is more probable that it refers to the eternal purpose of God in pursuance of which he draws men to Christ.

Peter speaks of Christians as elect according to the foreknowledge of God (1 Peter 1: 1, 2). But perhaps the clearest statements on this question are to be found in the writings of Paul. One of Paul's clearest expressions on the subject is in Romans 8: 29, 30. Here he grounds the providence of God in his predestinating grace. We find here a chain reaching from eternity past to eternity future. This chain is made up of the links of foreknowledge, predestination, calling, justification, glorification. To foreknow in the sense here spoken of is more than to know intellectually. In the latter sense God foreknows all men. It means to set his heart on us, to know us for our good. The Lord knoweth the way of the righteous, but the way of the ungodly shall perish (Psalm 1: 6). In the day of reckoning the Lord will send away the workers of iniquity because he never knew them (Matt 7: 23). God set his heart upon the objects of his predestinating grace in eternity, and in pursuance of his eternal purpose he calls, justifies, and glorifies.

In Romans 9, Paul asserts the sovereignty of God in strong language. He quotes the Old Testament to the effect that God has mercy on whom he will, and whom he will he hardens (vs. 15). He uses the case of Jacob and Esau as an example. Unless we compare this with what Paul says in other cases, we would get the impression that God was arbitrary in his dealings with men. Certainly Paul meant to assert that he was sovereign in bestowing his grace upon sinners.

In Paul's great declaration concerning grace in Ephesians 1: 3-14, he grounds the whole thing on God's predestinating grace. God has blessed us with every spiritual blessing in Christ in pursuance of the fact that he chose us in him before the foundation of the world, having foreordained us unto adoption as sons through Jesus Christ unto himself (vv. 3, 4). Again he sets forth that we were made a heritage inasmuch as we were foreordained according to the purpose of him who works all things after the counsel of his own will (vs. 11).

(3) In the third place, the doctrine of predestination or election is an inescapable inference from the doctrine of a sovereign and omniscient God.

Known unto God are all his works from the beginning. If all the events of the universe were known to God from the beginning and God ordained the world, then God ordained all that was involved in the history of the world.

If God creates and sustains the world and is a God of intelligence; if the world in its totality and, therefore, in its details is grounded in God, then he has ordained the whole world system and each detail of that system. This is not saying that God sustains the same relation to the evil that he does to the good, nor that each event of the world order is ordained for its own sake or out of its connection; but it is saying that each event is ordained in its connections in the world system as a part of that system. Nor does this mean that God sustains the same relation to an event in nature that he does to a free act of man. Each is ordained in its connections and under its conditions. An event in nature is ordained as an event in nature, and man's free act as a free act. A deed of holiness is ordained as something that God as the Author of all good produces, and a sinful act is ordained as something which a God who respects man's freedom permits man to do, in spite of God's hatred of sin. God ordains to permit the deed rather than interfere with man's freedom.

To put the matter another way, election is saying that what God does in saving men he does because he purposed to do it. We are arguing on the assumption that as a God of wisdom he has a purpose that is being carried out in the history of the world, and that as a God of power he does all that he purposes to do. If these two propositions are accepted, election must be accepted. God does not save all men. He does save some men. Hence God did not purpose to save all, but did purpose to save some.

Moreover, if it is right that God should save some men and not save others, it is right that he should purpose to save some and not save others. One could not consistently object to God's purposing to do what one does not object to his doing.

It has been truly said, therefore, that an argument against election is an argument for universalism. Let us make that statement a little more evident. Granting the fact of sin, God could plan to do one of three things: save none and condemn all, save all and condemn none, or save some and condemn some. If God planned to do either the first or the second, there would be no election. All would be treated alike. But the third plan necessarily involves election. Any plan by which some are saved and others lost necessitates that God should choose to save some and not save others.

(4) Another argument for election is the argument from Christian experience.

As we look back upon our experience, we recognize two things as outstanding in our conversion: One is God's drawing us, and the other is our resistance to his drawing. We were saved when we ceased to resist and yielded to the God of all grace. We love him because he first loved us (1 John 4: 19). Our experience, therefore, testifies that he chose us before we chose him. He sought us before we sought him. Our seeking was in response to his seeking. Our love was in response to his love. He took the initiative in our salvation.

It is sometimes objected that this makes the sinner helpless and dependent on God. That is exactly what it does. And that is exactly what the sinner needs to recognize. Faith is assuming the attitude of entire dependence on God. Nothing else is faith. Refusing to assume this attitude is what keeps a man out of the kingdom of God. The desire to be self-sufficient and independent of God is the heart of the sin principle in our lives.

3. *Objections to the doctrine*

Most of the difficulties and objections with reference to election grow out of misinterpretations of the doctrine and hasty inference from it. The answer to the objections, therefore, will take the form mainly of clearing up the difficulties by correcting the false interpretations of the doctrine and showing that the hasty inferences are not proper conclusions from the doctrine.

(1) One objection to this doctrine is that it makes God partial.

Most likely there is lurking in the mind of the one making this objection the assumption that God is under obligation to bestow equal privileges, opportunities, and blessings on men. But as a matter of fact, God does not bestow equal blessings on men with reference to natural gifts. Men are not equal in looks, physical or mental ability, moral and spiritual endowments. He gives to one five talents, to another two, to another one. The Spirit bestows his gifts on men, to each one severally as he will (1 Cor. 12: 11). When one thanks God that he was born in a Christian land or of Christian parents, or for good health, he is recognizing the fact that God has given him blessings that he has not given to many others. The same is true if he thanks God for salvation. But the objector might say that, so far as natural blessings are concerned, these could not be equal because they come to us through natural means and in a social order that necessarily makes a difference among men. We reply that the same thing may apply in regard to religious blessings and opportunities. These also, to some extent at least, are mediated to us through natural, social, historical means, and it might be as impossible for God to reduce men to a common level of privilege and blessings here as in the case of natural gifts. To put all men on a level of religious privilege might necessitate that God take men out of the natural, historical, social connections in which they live. So the fact that God bestows more blessings on some men than on others does not mean that he is "partial" in an arbitrary way.

(2) Another objection is that it is unjust to the non-elect since it makes his salvation impossible.

If man is unable to come without the special drawing power of the Spirit and this is not given, then why is the sinner to blame? This, the objector says, would hold the sinner responsible for not doing something which he could not do.

But this objection assumes that, if God deserves the credit for the salvation of the saved, he, therefore, is responsible for the condemnation of the lost. This is not true. God desires the salvation of all. The fact that God does not save all is evidence that there are limitations on God that constitute sufficient reasons why he should not save all. We can safely say that God does all that he can consistently with his own nature, the nature of man, and the moral order of the world to save all men.

He has provided salvation for every man in Christ. He gives him the invitation. He brings influences to bear to bring him into the way of life. All this is grace. If in spite of these things the sinner will not come, he has nobody to blame but himself. As long as he is unwilling to receive the grace that God offers him, he cannot complain because God does not give him more grace.

The sinner's inability is an inability only so long as the sinner refuses to recognize his dependence on God. If he wants to come, he can come. The difficulty is on his part, not on God's. The only difficulty is in the sinner's attitude toward God. For that attitude he is responsible.

There are limitations placed on God in the matter that prevent him from carrying out his desire to see all men saved. Man's freedom and sinful perversity have something to do with it. Whatever aspects of the situation God takes account of in saving men, these he took account of in electing men to salvation. If this be not true, then God is inconsistent with himself.

It does not seem that one man is elected to salvation and another not, on the ground that the man elected is morally more deserving than the one not elected. All men are under condemnation. All are sinners. God's purpose to save any is a purpose of grace. Does God's election of one man to salvation imply that he passes over the one not elected simply because he does not desire his salvation? No; he desires the salvation of all.

But it should also be remembered that God does not save the sinner, because of the sinner's perverse and stubborn unbelief. Hence it follows that the reason God purposes not to save the sinner was because of the sinner's foreknown unbelief. To state it positively, God purposes to condemn the sinner on the ground on which he does condemn him—namely: because the sinner's attitude is such that God cannot consistently save him. God gives him over to his own doom because he would not be saved.

(3) Another objection to election is that it is inconsistent with the freedom of man.

But we must remember that God's decree of election is not to the effect that a man shall be saved irrespective of whether he repents and believes. Rather it is a decree on God's part to bring this man to repentance and faith. And God does not compel the elect to believe. He so leads and persuades them by the gracious influences of the gospel and the wooings of his Spirit that they choose to come to Christ. On the other hand, he gives the unbeliever over to his own stubborn will.

Let us remember that God's purpose of election was God's purpose to do in saving a man just what he does when he saves him. Therefore, if saving the man does not interfere with his freedom, the purpose in God's mind in pursuance of which he was saved certainly would not do so.

(4) A fourth objection to election is that it discourages effort on the part of Christians for the salvation of others.

The objector says that, if the matter is fixed one way or the other, then effort on our part is useless since we cannot change what is fixed.

But the doctrine of election does not hold that the salvation of any man is fixed as a matter of fate, or even rendered certain irrespective of conditions. God does not decree that he will save a certain man whether he ever hears the gospel or not, or whether he repents and

believes or not. Rather is it God's purpose so to direct
the providential factors of the man's life as to bring him
under gospel influences and so to incline his heart that
he will turn from sin to God.

This doctrine, on the other hand, is an encouragement
to Christian effort, if the doctrine is properly understood.
One of the values of the doctrine is that it assures us, not
only that God desires the salvation of men, but that his
heart has been eternally set upon that very thing and
that he planned the world with reference to it and so
directs it in his providence that men shall be saved. It
assures us that the purpose to redeem men from sin is
the deepest thing in the mind and purpose of God from
all eternity. What better encouragement than that could
one wish to work at the task of saving men from sin?
If this is God's eternal concern, it should be our concern
and task. We can work at it with the assurance that
we work in line with his eternal purposes and that he
works in us and through us.

THE SAVING WORK OF CHRIST

CHAPTER IX

THE SAVING WORK OF CHRIST

I. THE DEATH OF CHRIST FOR OUR SINS

    1. The fact of the atonement
        (1) Our salvation Christ's achievement
        (2) His death his redemptive act
        (3) His death and life inseparable
            a. The sinless one died for sinners
            b. His life one of self-sacrifice
        (4) His death "according to the Scriptures"
    2. The motive of the atonement
    3. The atonement and God as holy
    4. An objection considered
    5. Faith and atonement

II. THE RESURRECTION OF JESUS

    1. Through the living Christ we conquer our sins
    2. The living Christ is the assurance that death is not the end of life
    3. The living Christ is the assurance of the triumph of the Kingdom of God

III. HIS INTERCESSION FOR HIS PEOPLE

    1. Its necessity lies at the point of our sins
    2. It is the basis of our confidence in prayer
    3. It guarantees our permanent standing before God

CHAPTER IX

THE SAVING WORK OF CHRIST

We have seen something of the extent of sin in the human race and the ruin wrought by it. We have also considered God's purpose of grace, both as to the race and as to the individual. This purpose of God to save finds its revelation and means of accomplishment in Jesus Christ. Christ is Saviour. "Thou shalt call his name Jesus; for it is he that shall save his people from their sins" (Matt. 1: 21). "The Son of man came to seek and to save that which was lost" (Luke 19: 10). "Faithful is the saying, and worthy of all acceptation, that Christ Jesus came into the world to save sinners" (1 Tim. 1: 15).

I. The Death of Christ for our sins

1. *The fact of the atonement*

It will probably help us first to consider some points that stand out in the teaching of the New Testament.

(1) Our salvation Christ's achievement.

In the first place, it is made clear that Christ did something on which man's salvation depended. Our salvation was his achievement. This is shown by such statements as that of Jesus when he said that the Son of man came to give his life a ransom for many (Mark 10: 45). Whatever else this may mean, it shows that he did something that was necessary for our liberation from sin. Another statement is that of Paul when he says, "Christ redeemed us from the curse of the law, having become a curse for us" (Gal. 3: 13). The following quotations from the Book of Hebrews make this point clear: (Christ) "entered in once for all into the holy place, having obtained eternal redemption" (Heb. 9:

12). "But now once at the end of the ages hath he been manifested to put away sin by the sacrifice of himself" (9: 26). "By which will we have been sanctified through the offering of the body of Jesus Christ once for all" (10: 10). "But he (Christ), when he had offered one sacrifice for sins for ever, sat down on the right hand of God" (10: 12). "For by one offering he hath perfected for ever them that are sanctified" (10: 14). In Revelation we find this language: "Unto him that loveth us, and loosed us from our sins by his blood" (1: 5).

Other passages could be given, but these are sufficient to show that the New Testament teaches that our salvation depended on something that Christ did for us. Christ saves, and he saves by virtue of something that he accomplished. Our redemption was his achievement. He did something that makes possible for us a new relationship to God.

(2) Christ's death his redemptive act.

Another thing that comes out in the passages quoted above, and in many others, is that it was the death of Christ that constituted his redemptive act. It is significant that from the time of the great confession at Cæsarea Philippi, Jesus laid great emphasis upon his coming death. When the disciples announce their acceptance of him as Messiah, Jesus turns his attention to teaching them the kind of Messiah that he was to be—namely: a suffering Messiah. The evangelists put the emphasis on his death as the climax of a life of glorious service to God and to man. This was the goal toward which his whole life moved.

Jesus deliberately moved toward the Cross as the place where his mission of redemption should be brought to consummation. In his baptism, he was no doubt devoting himself to death for the salvation of the world.[1] The temptation to obtain his kingdom by worshiping Satan gets its point from this fact. This temptation to

---

[1]See Denny, Jas., *Death of Jesus*, and Robertson, A. T., *Epochs in the Life of Jesus*, and *The Divinity of Christ in John's Gospel*.

turn aside from the Cross was with Jesus through his life and came to its climax in the Garden of Gethsemane (John 6: 15; Matt. 26: 36ff.). With his dying breath, Jesus said, "It is finished" (John 19: 30).

There are two sayings of Jesus in the Synoptic Gospels where Jesus not only speaks of his death, but also brings out the redemptive significance of death. One of these is where he speaks of giving his life a ransom for many (Mark 10: 45). The other is at the institution of the Supper where he speaks of his blood as shed for many unto or for the remission of sins (Matt. 26: 28). These two passages condition our salvation upon his death.

In the Gospel of John, there are some definite statements on this point. One is the saying of John the Baptist concerning Jesus as the Lamb of God that takes away the sin of the world (1: 29). He is evidently thinking of Jesus as one who should be a sacrifice and thereby remove the world's sin. The saying in John 3: 14, 15, that the Son of man must be lifted up, even as Moses lifted up the serpent in the wilderness, makes our obtaining eternal life dependent on the lifting up of the Son of man. This is the idea also in the discourse on the bread of life in John 6. The bread which Jesus gives is his flesh, for the life of the world (verse 51). In John 10, Jesus sets himself forth as the good shepherd who lays down his life for the sheep (verses 14-17).

One of the constituent elements in the gospel, according to Paul, was that Christ died for our sins according to the Scriptures (1 Cor. 15: 3). Paul was determined to know nothing among the Corinthians but Jesus Christ and him crucified (1 Cor. 2: 2). While the Word of the Cross was to the Jews a stumbling-block and to the Greeks foolishness, to the called it was the power of God and the wisdom of God (1 Cor. 1: 18, 23, 24). Christ was made sin for us, that we might become the righteousness of God in him (2 Cor. 5: 21). It was by becoming a curse for us in being hanged on a tree that

Christ redeemed us from the curse of the law (Gal. 3: 13). Paul glories in nothing but the Cross. It is the power by which he is crucified to the world and the world to him (Gal. 6: 14). God sets Christ forth in his blood as a propitiation, that God might be just and the justifier of him that has faith in Jesus (Rom. 3: 21-26). We are justified in his blood (Rom. 5: 9). We are reconciled to God through the death of his Son (Rom. 5: 10). We have our redemption through his blood (Eph. 1: 7).

Peter says that we are redeemed from our vain manner of life with the precious blood of Christ (1 Peter 1: 18, 19). Christ bore our sins in his body upon the tree and by his stripes we are healed (1 Peter 2: 24, 25). In the Book of Hebrews, we are told that the new covenant of grace could not be effected except upon condition of the death of the Mediator of that covenant (9: 15ff.). Through the offering of the body of Jesus Christ once for all we are sanctified (10: 10). By this one offering he has forever perfected those who are sanctified (10: 14). This sacrifice was not something needing to be repeated, as did the sacrifices of the Levitical system. He made a complete offering once for all and thus obtained eternal redemption for us (9: 14; 10: 1ff.).

John says that Christ is the propitiation for the sins of the whole world (1 John 2: 2). In the Book of Revelation, we are told that he loosed us from our sins in his blood (1: 5). He purchased unto God with his blood men of every tribe, and tongue, and people, and nation (5: 9). God's people overcame the accuser because of the blood of the Lamb (12: 11).

Further citations from the New Testament are unnecessary. These put it beyond question that it is in the blood of Christ that our salvation is found. The Cross was his great redemptive deed. By his death he brings us eternal life.

(3) His death and life inseparable.

We are not to understand, however, that the death of Christ in its saving significance is to be separated from his life. It is true that it was the death of Christ that made atonement for our sins. But there are two things to remember about this death in relation to his life:

a. One is that it was the sinless one that died for our sins. Him who knew no sin God made to be sin for us (2 Cor. 5: 21). He died the just for the unjust (1 Peter 3: 18). If we are to regard death as the judgment of God upon sin, then his death was not a judgment upon his own sin, for he had no sin. But he was so vitally related to us that his death was God's judgment on our sin.

b. Another thing to remember is that his whole life on earth was a life of self-sacrifice. He became poor for our sakes that we through his poverty might be rich (2 Cor. 8: 9). Paul in Philippians 2: 5ff. shows that the death of the Cross was the climax of a previous life of self-emptying. His very existence on earth involved limitation and self-sacrifice. His life and his death were all of one piece, so far as moral quality is concerned.

(4) Paul tells us that the death of Christ for our sins was "according to the Scriptures" (1 Cor. 15: 3).

Jesus is regarded by all the New Testament writers as fulfilling the Old Testament sacrificial offerings. John the Baptist speaks of him as the "Lamb of God that taketh away the sin of the world" (John 1: 29). It is generally considered that John had in mind here the suffering servant of Isaiah 53. But whether he did or whether he had in mind some other Old Testament figure, the meaning is the same. He regarded Jesus as the one in whom the sacrificial lamb of the Old Testament found its significance.

The Book of Hebrews in particular emphasizes the sacrificial work of Jesus as fulfilling the Old Testament ideal of sacrifice. The writer dwells upon the superiority of Jesus as priest and also as sacrifice. The Old Testament sacrifices were intended to remove the consciousness of sin, but this they could not do effectively. Hence they had to be repeated. But Jesus offered a sacrifice once for all that completely satisfied the conscience and perfected the worshiper. Hence no repetition of the sacrifice was necessary (Heb. 9: 11-15; 10: 1ff.).

2. *The motive of the atonement*

The motive of the atonement is the love of God. God so loved the world that he gave his only begotten Son (John 3: 16). God commendeth his love toward us, in that while we were yet sinners, Christ died for us (Rom. 5: 8). Christ did not die to win for men the love of God, but as an expression of that love. It is a travesty on the New Testament view of this doctrine to represent it as meaning that God was the embodiment of justice and Christ the embodiment of love and that Christ died to win for man the love of God. The love of Christ for sinners was the love of God. The death of Christ was the love of God in action seeking to redeem men from sin; it was love going to the limit of suffering and agony to redeem the lost from the ruin of their own sin. The Cross of Christ is the pledge of God's love for a sinful and ruined race. As such, the Cross represents an act of grace. It stands for God's gracious love going out to redeem man as sinful and unworthy.

3. *The atonement and God as holy*

It will help us to understand this matter if we get clearly in mind the fact that there was a moral difficulty in God's relation to human sin which it was the purpose of the atonement to remove. Paul expresses it by saying that God's wrath was revealed against sin (Rom. 1: 18). This wrath of God against sin expresses itself in the condemnation of sin. This condemnation is the thing that necessitates justification, and the ground of justification is Christ's propitiatory work (Rom. 3: 19-26). This propitiatory work of Christ makes it possible that God should be just or righteous and the justifier of the one that believes in Jesus. Paul's thought, then, seems to be that the wrath of God condemns man, while the propitiatory work of Christ removes the wrath of

God. The implication is that without the atoning death of Christ, God could not be righteous and justify the sinner.

Christ was made to be sin for us in order that we might become the righteousness of God in him (2 Cor. 5: 21). He redeemed us from the curse of the law by being made a curse for us (Gal. 3: 13). The curse was the curse which the law pronounced. It was the curse of death. That curse came on us because of our sin. The law pronounced that curse of death upon us because of our failure to live up to its requirements (Gal. 3: 10-12). Christ redeemed us from that curse by taking the curse of death upon himself. Thus he redeemed us from the curse.

The death of Christ, then, was propitiatory. His death was propitiatory in the sense that in his death Christ endured the righteous judgment of God upon man's sin. Paul says that God set him forth as propitiatory in his blood (Rom. 3: 25). John says that he is the propitiation, not only for our sins, but for the sins of the whole world (1 John 2: 2). The Book of Hebrews says that as a faithful high priest he makes propitiation for the sins of the people (Heb. 2: 17). The Christian idea is not that God has to be propitiated before he will have mercy or love the sinner, but it is rather that God's holy character reacts against sin and that sin interposes a barrier that must be removed. God's righteous wrath against sin must be satisfied before God's mercy can go out to the sinner. God is not vindictive, but he does have regard to his own moral consistency. The propitiatory work of Christ is the revelation and expression of God's love.

The death of Christ was a vicarious work. It was substitutionary. He did something for us which we could not do for ourselves.

The matter can be simply stated as follows: On account of our sin the sentence of death came upon us. Jesus had no sin. Yet death came to him. It came on account of our sins and on behalf of us. He took upon himself the sentence of death that was due to us. By bearing that sentence he sets us free. This is what is meant when it is said that we are redeemed with the blood of Jesus (1 Peter 1: 19). The blood stands for the life which he freely gave up for us.

4. *An objection considered*

But it is objected that it would not be just, but rather the height of injustice, for one man to bear the sins of other men. It is not just, it is urged, for one man to be punished for another man's wrongdoing. If God should put the sins of the guilty on the innocent, that would show him to be a monster instead of a God of love.

In reply to this objection, let us consider the following facts: It is a law of life that men should suffer for the wrongs of others. No matter what we may say about the justice or injustice of it, it is a fact. And it is difficult to see how it could be otherwise in a social world. An arrangement by which one would suffer the exact deserts of his sins and nobody else suffer for them would hardly be a social world at all. And it is true that the innocent suffer for the guilty. Instances are too numerous to need mention. This is one of the great disciplinary laws of life. Men are often restrained from evil by the consciousness that others will suffer if they sin. Also, it is true that much of our moral development comes from suffering on behalf of others. It is a law of the Christian life that one should be willing to follow the Saviour's example in doing this.

The highest expression of love is found in this Christian law of willingness to suffer on behalf of others. This was the crowning glory of the life of Christ and is the thing that marks a man as a follower of Christ. If any man hath not the Spirit of Christ, he is none of his (Rom. 8: 9). It is love that moves one to share the sufferings of others. It was love that moved Christ to give himself for us.

Besides, this objection is based on a false assumption. The objection says that it would be unjust for God to lay the sins of one man on another man. But there are two things to be said in answer to this. One is that God did not take our sins and lay them on an unwilling victim. Christ took our sins on himself. As a matter of love, he voluntarily assumed our obligation. He laid down his life of himself (John 10: 18).

Again, the objection assumes that Christ is only one human individual among other human individuals. Perhaps the objector would be right in saying that one human individual could not bear the sins of countless other human individuals. The relation of Christ to any man or to the race as a whole is entirely different from the relation of one who is only a human individual to his fellowmen or to the race. The race exists in Christ. It was in and through him that the race was created and is preserved (John 1: 3; Col. 1: 16, 17).

The doctrine of the atonement does not mean that God laid the burden of our sins on a helpless human individual, but rather that in the Person of Christ God himself got under the burden of our sins to save us. The work of Christ is the work of God.

5. Faith and atonement

Our faith in Jesus throws light on the atonement. We trust him as Saviour from sin. We come to him confessing ourselves morally and spiritually bankrupt. We recognize that we have no standing of our own before a holy God. For such standing we must trust ourselves into his hands. We acknowledge ourselves dependent on him in the most important of all realms, the moral and spiritual; and in the most fundamental of all relations— our relation with God. We confess ourselves disqualified to deal with God as holy in our own name; our sins have disqualified us. Christ is qualified to deal with God for us. And the New Testament makes it clear that the thing that qualifies him to deal with God on our behalf is his death for us. This sets his death as the ground of our acceptance as over against our sins as the ground of our rejection. Our sins constitute our moral disqualification; his death constitutes the basis of our moral standing before God.

II. The Resurrection of Jesus

We have already given consideration to the question of the resurrection of Jesus.[2] All we need to do here is to make a summary statement as to the significance of the fact in relation to us and to our salvation.

1. *Through the living Christ we conquer our sins*

We conquer sin only in and through the Christ who rose from the dead. He conquered death because he conquered sin. He rose from the dead because he had exhausted the power of sin. He met sin in a death grapple and conquered it. Therefore, he rose victorious over death. He conquered sin for us and enables us to conquer it. The law of the Spirit of life in Christ Jesus frees us from the law of sin and death; the rule or dominion of sin and death is broken in our lives when the rule or dominion of the Spirit of life is established (Rom. 8: 2ff.). And the dominion of death is broken because the rule of sin is ended. The sting of death is sin, and when the sting of sin is extracted the power of death is destroyed (1 Cor. 15: 56, 57).

And sin can be overcome only as we are united to the living Christ. The Christ who lives forever, having conquered sin and death, the Christ who has the keys of death and Hades, is the assurance of our victory over sin (Rev. 1: 18). If he be not risen, we are yet in our sins (1 Cor. 15: 17).

2. *The Resurrection gives us the assurance that death is not the end of life*

Men have speculated as to whether we live on after death. The Resurrection of Jesus takes the question out

---

[2]Chapter IV, II, 3.

of the realm of speculative thought and puts it into the realm of fact. Moreover, the appearances and ascension of Jesus give us assurance that, for those who die in fellowship with him, death is the entrance into a more glorious life. Not only do we live beyond death, we live more abundantly. He that liveth and believeth on him shall never die (John 11: 26). As death for Jesus marked the transition into a life larger and more glorious, so will it for us. The Resurrection of Jesus is the guarantee of triumph over death for all who are united to him by faith. This is true, moreover, not only in the sense that it guarantees our entrance upon a fuller life at death, but also in the sense that it gives assurance of our resurrection, thus being the pledge of our deliverance from death on the bodily as well as on the spiritual side of our being.

3. *Again, the Resurrection gives assurance of triumph of the kingdom of God*

The living Christ who conquered death in resurrection power and who reigns in omnipotence at the right hand of God is the assurance of the final and complete triumph of the kingdom of God.

Through his Spirit and the preaching of his Word he is gradually extending his kingdom and will bring it to final triumph. He announced his program to his disciples before he went away, and in the Acts we see how he works through them to carry out that program. He does not hesitate to use persecution to thrust them out when necessary. In the Book of Revelation he stands in the midst of the candlesticks and holds the seven stars in his right hand and conducts a campaign against sin and darkness that finally results in the coming to earth of the New Jerusalem from God out of heaven and the complete sway of God therein. Moreover, one who gives himself to this living Christ and the ends of his kingdom can trust him unreservedly with life and all, knowing that he cares for his own.

III. Christ's intercession for his people

The work of Christ on behalf of his people was not ended when he ascended. Enough is said in the New Testament to assure us that he is still active on their behalf. Paul makes reference to it, as does the Book of Hebrews, and John assures us that Jesus Christ the righteous is the Advocate with the Father on behalf of the Christian who sins (Rom. 8: 34; Heb. 7: 25; 1 John 2: 1).

We have in the Gospel records at least two clear instances of Christ's intercession for his disciples while he was on earth. One is his statement to Simon: "I made supplication for thee, that thy faith fail not" (Luke 22: 32). Satan was to sift the Apostles, he was to put them through a testing that would try their faith to the limit; but Jesus made supplication for Peter individually to the end that his faith should endure the testing. The other is the intercession for those who had believed on him and those who should believe on him, as recorded in John 17. He prays that they may be kept, sanctified, and made one.

There are several references in the New Testament to the intercession of Jesus on behalf of his people after his ascension. As High Priest he offers his blood as atonement for sin and makes intercession for the people.

It appears from the Book of Hebrews that his work of intercession is based on his sacrificial work. After making atonement by the sacrifice of himself, he appears in heaven before the face of God for us (Heb. 9: 24).

1. The necessity for this intercession of Christ lies at the point of our sins

An examination of the references will show this to be true. It comes out most clearly in what John says. He is our Advocate with the Father in case we sin. Our sin, then, is the thing that necessitates his work as Advocate. It is in his character as the Righteous One that he

acts for us, implying that it is because of our unrighteousness that we need him. In the Book of Hebrews,
we are assured that he saves to the uttermost all that
come to God by him, seeing he ever liveth to make intercession for them (7: 25). This statement in its context
shows that it is with reference to complete deliverance
from sin that he wishes to assure his readers.

Here we need a word of caution. We are likely to
make the same mistake that we make with reference to
the atoning work of Christ—the mistake of thinking of
God as harsh and inaccessible, unwilling to receive us
and show mercy until he is prevailed upon by a third
party who intercedes for us. This would be a false impression. The difficulty lies not in the unwillingness of
God, but in the moral difficulty created by our relation
as sinners to God as holy. Christ is our Advocate to
take care of that difficulty. Christ as our Advocate gives
us assurance with reference to this difficulty. He pro-
vides for it. But he does so because God appointed him
as our High Priest. God took the initiative in the matter. Christ did not make himself our High Priest; he
was appointed of God (Heb. 5: 1ff.). God certainly
was interested in our case or he would not have appointed One as High Priest to act on our behalf and remove
the difficulty made by our sin. The fact that Christ is
our Priest, then, does not mean that God is harsh and
unwilling to receive us, and that God does not want us
to approach him. The intercession of Christ does not
mean that God is inaccessible while Christ is; rather it
means that God is as accessible as Christ; he has made
himself accessible in Christ.

2. *The intercession of Christ is the basis of our confidence as we approach God in prayer*

The author of the Book of Hebrews exhorts us to draw
near with boldness to the throne of grace, on the ground
that we have a High Priest who can be touched with the
feeling of our infirmities, since he has been tempted in
all points like as we are, yet without sin (Heb. 4: 14-

16). We can come with the assurance that we will receive mercy and find grace to help in time of need, because we have such a High Priest to mediate for us.

3. *The intercession of Christ guarantees our permanent standing before God and our complete deliverance from sin*

John assures us that, though we may sin, yet Jesus Christ the Righteous One is our Advocate with the Father (1 John 2: 10). The fact that he is our Advocate is our assurance that we will not lose our standing with the Father even in case we do sin. The Book of Hebrews tells us that he saves to the uttermost all who come unto God through him, seeing he ever liveth to make intercession for them (Heb. 7: 25). Here is the guarantee of our final and complete deliverance from sin and its curse. Because he lives, we shall live also (John 14: 19). Being reconciled to God through the death of his Son, much more shall we be saved by his life (Rom. 5: 10).

If any one should object to the discussion in this chapter on the ground that it does not locate the saving work of Christ in any one thing that he does, we grant the fact, but do not admit it as a thing objectionable. The New Testament does not unify our view of salvation by making it depend on any one event, even any one thing that Christ did for us. Our view is to find its center and unity, not in an event, but in Christ himself. It is his Person that gives significance to what he did. In him we find salvation, not in some event detached from him. He conquered sin in his own life, he died for our sins, he rose from the dead, and ascended to the right hand of God. He ever lives to make intercession for us. All this he did for us. In the complete Christ who did this we find salvation from sin. The guarantee of our right to come to God and of our standing with him is not in the atonement as an event apart from Christ's person, but it is in the Person who suffered for us and who is now active on our behalf.

BECOMING A CHRISTIAN,
OR, THE BEGINNING OF SALVATION

CHAPTER X

BECOMING A CHRISTIAN,
OR, THE BEGINNING OF SALVATION

I. THE CONDITIONS OF SALVATION

    1. Repentance
        (1) Other terms used
        (2) What is repentance?
           a. Conviction of sin
           b. Contrition for sin
           c. Renunciation of sin
        (3) Repentance and reformation
        (4) Christian life a life of repentance
        (5) Repentance and conversion
    2. Faith
        (1) Meaning of faith
           a. Christ the object of faith
           b. Two aspects of faith
               (a) Receiving Christ as Saviour
               (b) Submission to Christ as Lord
        (2) An objection to Christian faith
        (3) Why salvation is by faith
        (4) Relation of faith to a life of righteousness

II. GOD'S SAVING ACT

    1. In Christ we have forgiveness of sins
        (1) Scriptures setting forth forgiveness
        (2) Meaning of forgiveness
    2. In Christ we are justified
        (1) Doctrine defined
        (2) A one-sided statement of the doctrine
    3. In Christ we are reconciled to God
    4. In Christ we are adopted
    5. In Christ we have new life
        (1) New Testament terms used

     (2) Nature of the change
        a. Moral and spiritual renewal
        b. Wrought by the Spirit of God
   6. In Christ we are sanctified
     (1) Meaning of the term
     (2) All Christians sanctified

III. UNION WITH CHRIST
   1. It is taught by the New Testament
   2. It is by faith
   3. It is with the living Christ
   4. It is union with God
   5. It does not mean pantheism
   6. It sums up all salvation

IV. THE CONSCIOUSNESS OF SALVATION
   1. The normal Christian experience
     (1) Consciousness of sin
     (2) Conscious communion with God
   2. The lack of assurance
   3. What is necessary to assurance

CHAPTER X

BECOMING A CHRISTIAN,
OR, THE BEGINNING OF SALVATION

In this chapter we will discuss the experience of salvation. We do not mean by this, however, that becoming a Christian is all of salvation. Salvation in its completeness includes everything from the new birth to the final resurrection. In this chapter we will consider the initiation of the Christian life.

I. The conditions of salvation

We will consider first what are usually called the conditions of salvation. By this we mean the spiritual attitude one must assume in receiving the grace of God that saves from sin. In other words, what must one do to become a Christian?

There are many terms used in the New Testament to describe the experience of becoming a Christian. Perhaps the essential elements can all be summed up in the two terms, repentance and faith. It is no accident that the experience of becoming a Christian has two fundamental aspects, for in this experience man is concerned with two fundamental relations of life. One is his relation to sin; the other, his relation to God as a God of grace, revealed in Christ as Saviour. The inward turning from sin is repentance; turning to Christ as Saviour is faith. Each implies the other. Neither is possible without the other. At the same time and in the same act that one turns from sin he turns to Christ. Sin and Christ are the opposite poles of the moral universe, and one cannot turn from one without turning to the other. Repentance and faith are not two acts or moral attitudes; they are two aspects of one act or attitude.

1. *Repentance*

(1) Other terms used to describe repentance.

Repentance is not the only term, by any means, used in the New Testament to describe the act or attitude denoted by that word. Jesus says: "If any man will come after me, let him deny himself, and take up his cross, and follow me" (Matt. 16: 24). To deny one's self means to renounce self as sinful and selfish; to renounce the old self as unworthy. To take up the Cross is to die; to die to the old self and give oneself to a new Master, Jesus Christ. Jesus says also: "Whosoever would save his life shall lose it" (Matt. 16: 25). To lose one's life here is to give it away to another, to give it to Christ and one's fellows in service. He puts this over against saving one's life in such a way as to lose it. To save it (so as to lose it) means to keep it for oneself, to live the self-centered life. To lose it (so as to save it) is to renounce the self-centered life. Paul speaks about Christians as those who are crucified with Christ (Gal. 2: 20), and about those who have crucified the flesh with the affections and the lusts thereof (Gal. 5: 24). He glories in the Cross through which the world has been crucified to him and he to the world (Gal. 6: 14). All these are different ways of expressing the idea of repentance.

(2) What is repentance?

The term that is translated repentance in the New Testament means a change of mind. This involves at least three things.

a. Either as an element in repentance or as a precedent condition, it involves the understanding of one's condition as a sinner. One must come to realize something of the guilt and condemnation of his sin. This is ordinarily spoken of as conviction of sin. Some theologians speak of it as the intellectual element in repentance. It comes as a result of hearing gospel truth and the enlightening work of the Holy Spirit. One cannot repent until he comes to see something of the nature of his sin. This does not mean that the consciousness of sin must be present in the same form and to the same extent in every case. In some cases the consciousness of sin may take the form of a sense of guilt and condemnation. In others it may be the sense of moral failure. But in every case the hearing of the gospel intensifies this consciousness of sin. In some cases at first it is nothing more than a vague uneasiness, a consciousness that somehow things are not right with us. The hearing of the gospel intensifies and clarifies this, so that it becomes a definite consciousness of sin. Sin comes to be seen as sin. This means that it comes to be seen as against God. As seen in relation to a God of holy love, it comes to be seen in its true character.

b. A second thing involved in repentance is that the love of sin shall die in one's heart. This is usually spoken of as the emotional element in repentance. One may see himself ever so clearly as a sinner and even understand the ruin involved in sin, but unless the love of sin dies in his heart, it will make no difference in his life. He has not repented.

This is not to be identified with fear of punishment. One may have fear of punishment without gospel repentance. This fear of punishment may produce what has been termed "hell-scared religion." But unless there is something more in one's religion than the fear of punishment, he will not escape punishment. This fear of punishment may be intensified into remorse of conscience, so that one has no rest day or night. But remorse of conscience is not repentance. That is to say, repentance is a gospel grace, not simply a state of mind produced by a knowledge of the law, which brings a message of condemnation for sin, but no message of salvation from sin.

One may often have great emotion because of sin and yet not repent. He may freely weep, but when the emotion passes he goes back to his old sins.

The emotional element in true repentance may be described as godly sorrow that worketh repentance (2 Cor. 7: 10). It is a sorrow that grows out of a true understanding of our sin as it is related to a God of grace. It is contrition. "A broken and a contrite heart, O God, thou wilt not despise" (Psalm 51: 17). When one has this contrition on account of sin, it will lead on to the third and final element in repentance.

c. The third element is the renunciation of sin. It is the repudiation of sin by an act of will. Because the love of sin dies in one's heart, there is a revulsion of one's whole moral nature against it. Sin is repudiated, not so much because one sees that he will be punished for sin, as because one sees sin in its true nature and comes to hate it. This leads to a changed life in regard to sin. "How shall we, that are dead to sin, live any longer therein" (Rom. 6: 2)? Such a thing is a moral impossibility. Repentance is never complete until the will thus repudiates sin. This repudiation of sin and a contrite heart on account of sin always go together; they are two aspects of one state of mind.

This shows that the change of mind here spoken of is not simply an intellectual change. The mind includes the whole moral nature of man. To make up one's mind is not simply an act of the intellect. To repent is to think back over one's course, to see the wrongness of it, and make up one's mind to change. It is no superficial matter; it goes down to the depths of the moral life. This change is an inner change. It is such a change as revolutionizes one's life in relation to sin.

(3) Repentance and reformation.

There may be a marked change in the outer life following repentance, or there may not be. Sometimes evil habits have so fastened themselves on to the life that such an inner revolution is the only thing that will change them. Sometimes there may be a marked change in the habits of life without inner repentance. Sometimes the outward life may have been so correct, judged by the

standards of social morality, that no special outward
reformation was needed. So you may have reformation
following repentance, or you may have repentance without reformation where it is not needed.

We are not to conclude, however, that because reformation is not needed in some cases repentance is not
needed. Reformation as ordinarily spoken of means a
change in which vicious moral habits are left off. A man
may have no vicious moral habits, but yet need to repent
of sin toward God. Not all men are grossly immoral,
but all men are sinners. Sin is against God. Repentance
is the repudiation of sin as against God. Repentance,
therefore, is a religious act or attitude of mind. It is
not simply the repudiation of the act of sin; it is the
repudiation of self as evil and sinful. It is to deny one's
self and take up the Cross (Matt. 16: 24). It means
death to the sinful self.

(4) The Christian life a life of repentance.

We should not think of repentance as being an act
performed at the beginning of the Christian life, not
needing to be repeated. It is an attitude that belongs
to the Christian life as a whole. The initial act of repentance is the beginning of a life of repentance. Jesus
says we should take up the Cross daily (Luke 9: 23).
Paul says that Christians have died to sin (Rom. 6: 2),
but he also exhorts them to reckon themselves to be dead
to sin (Rom. 6: 11). The sinful self has to be crucified
daily. The old man, as Paul calls him (Col. 3: 9), has
more lives than the proverbial cat. He will not stay
dead when killed. Oftentimes the deepest repentance
does not come at the beginning of the Christian life.
When one first emerges from the darkness of sin, his
eyes are not yet accustomed enough to the new light of
the gospel to see sin in all its heinousness. The more
one lives in fellowship with a holy God, the more one
sees himself as sinful and corrupt. It is not a sign of
special piety to hear one boasting of his own goodness.

The term good is one that Jesus says men should use with a good deal of caution (Mark 10: 18).

(5) Repentance and conversion.

It is sometimes said that conversion is the outer change corresponding to repentance, or repentance and faith, as an inner change.[1]

Sometimes it is said that conversion is made up of repentance and faith—repentance and faith being the elements in conversion.[2] Neither of these statements is objectionable. Conversion means a turning. It is that change in which one turns from sin to God. It is such a change as is evident, or becomes evident, to men. In that sense, it is an outward change. Yet when Jesus speaks of conversion, he lays emphasis on the inner qualities of mind and heart. He says that one must turn and become as a little child in order to get into the kingdom of God (Matt. 18: 3).

2. *Faith*

(1) The meaning of faith.

Faith is the aspect of conversion in which the soul turns to Christ for salvation. As shown above, it is inseparably connected with repentance. Since repentance is a believing response to the truth of the gospel concerning us as sinners, it might be included in faith. In some places in the New Testament we find faith alone stated as the condition of salvation; in others we find repentance alone; in still others we find both; while in others yet we find other terms carrying the same meaning as these terms.

Faith is a term of such rich content and deep significance that it is difficult to define it in a simple statement. Christian faith, however, might be defined as trust in Jesus Christ as Saviour and surrender to him as Lord.

a. Christ the object of faith. This implies that faith is something more than belief of a doctrine or the ac-

---

[1] See Mullins, *The Christian Religion in Its Doctrinal Expression.*
[2] See Strong, *Systematic Theology.*

ceptance of a dogma. No doctrine, however important, can be the object of faith in the full sense of the term. One can believe a doctrine with his intellect. He can trust a person with his heart or will. Nor is the church the object of faith. The Roman Catholic Church makes faith implicit surrender to the church, so that one is pledged to believe in the realm of doctrine what the church prescribes to be believed and practice in the realm of morals what the church prescribes to be practiced. One believes in Christ only on the authority of the church. But this falls far short of Christian faith. It is indeed a fatal perversion of faith. It puts the church in important respects where Christ belongs and calls for submission to the church such as a Christian can yield only to Christ. It enslaves the mind and conscience to the church and its hierarchy.

The place of doctrine in relation to faith is to present Christ to us as the object of faith and then to help explain the meaning of Christ as we know him in experience. Doctrine, then, has an important place in the life of faith, but no doctrine as such can be the object of faith.

Christ is the object of faith by virtue of the fact that he is the incarnation of God and is, therefore, the revelation of God's saving grace. He is the object of saving faith because he is the one who atones for sin and is thereby the one who achieves redemption for us.

Faith in Christ and faith in God are indistinguishable. We can say that we trust in Christ for salvation or that we trust in God through Christ. In the New Testament and in Christian experience, faith in Christ is faith in God.

b. Perhaps the meaning of faith can be made a little clearer if we remind ourselves of two aspects of the act of saving faith.

(a) One is that in saving faith we receive Christ as Saviour. There are many ways of expressing this in the New Testament. It is called coming to Christ. "Him that cometh to me I will in no wise cast out" (John 6: 37). "Come unto me, all ye that labor and are heavy laden" (Matt. 11: 28). It is called receiving him. "But as many as received him, to them gave he the right (authority or power) to become children of God" (John 1: 12). It is called eating his flesh and drinking his blood. Christ says that unless we eat his flesh and drink his blood, we have no life in us; but if we eat his flesh and drink his blood, he abides in us and we in him (John 6: 52, 59). This statement of Jesus has no reference to partaking of the Lord's Supper, but it does refer to that which our partaking of the Supper symbolizes. In the Old Testament this act of faith is called a looking. "Look unto me, and be ye saved, all the ends of the earth" (Isa. 45: 22). It is called a hearing. "Incline your ear, and come unto me; hear, and your soul shall live" (Isa. 55: 3). Men are said to call upon the Lord. "It shall come to pass, that whosoever shall call upon the name of the Lord shall be saved" (Acts 2: 21; Rom. 10: 13). But the most common term is the one translated as a verb "believe," and as a noun "faith." The passages are too numerous to quote or even refer to. The meaning of the word carries with it the idea of trust, confidence, repose in one. (See John 3: 14-16, 18, 36; Acts 10: 43; 13: 38, 39; 16: 31; Rom. 1: 16; Gal. 3: 26; Eph. 2: 8, et al.)

(b) The other aspect of faith that needs emphasizing is that in faith one submits to Christ as Lord. In the same act in which we receive him as Saviour, we give ourselves to him as Lord. We become his servants by virtue of the fact that he saves us from sin. Jesus emphasizes this in relation to his disciples. The very term disciple implies that we become learners in his school. We must have the teachable spirit, the spirit of humility and submission. This is why Jesus says we must become as little children and have the spirit of humility (Matt. 18: 1-4). Jesus emphasized this childlike humility in contrast to the spirit of pride and selfishness that desired the greatest place for self in the kingdom. The same thought is brought out clearly in Matthew 11: 25-30. Here Jesus thanks the Father that the truth has been concealed from the wise and prudent, the proud and self-sufficient in spirit, but that he has revealed it unto babes, those who are humble and teachable. Jesus says that no one can know the Father except those to whom the Son wills to reveal him. Therefore, if a man would know God, he must enter the school of Christ, take his yoke, submit to his authority, have the spirit of meekness after the supreme example of Jesus himself. The demand for supreme authority in our lives comes out in those passages where he says that he must come ahead of father, mother, brother, sister, wife, houses, or lands, even of life itself (Matt. 10: 34ff.; Luke 14: 26); also in the passage where he says that one cannot be his disciple unless he forsakes all (Luke 14: 33); where he demands of the rich young ruler that he sell all and follow him (Mark 10: 21); where he refuses to allow one to go back to bury the dead or bid farewell to his loved ones (Luke 9: 57-62); where he makes the acknowledgment of one before the Father to depend on the confession of him by that one before men (Matt. 10: 32, 33); where he teaches that obedience to his teaching is the only solid foundation for character and destiny (Matt. 7: 24-27); where he claims that he as judge will be the arbiter of the final destinies of men (Matt. 25: 31ff.). So we see that even in the Synoptic Gospels Jesus presents himself as absolute Lord of conscience and of life, calling for self-surrender on our part.

In John's Gospel, we find the same truth. Jesus is one with the Father (10: 30); the way, the truth, and the life (14: 6); the bread of life (6: 35); the light of the world (8: 12; 9: 5); the true vine of which his disciples are branches (15: 1ff.); the good shepherd who gives his life for the sheep (10: 11); the mediator of creation (1: 3); the life of the world (1: 4); the eternal Son of God (1: 18). In short, all the finalities of the soul are found in him. To believe on him is not to be condemned (3: 18), but to have eternal life (3: 36); not to believe on him is to be condemned, to have God's wrath abide on us.

Paul speaks of the obedience of faith (Rom. 1: 5). This may mean the obedience that grows out of faith, or it may mean the obedience that is identical with faith. Whichever construction is put upon it, it is sure that Christian faith has at its heart submission to Christ as Lord. Paul delighted to call himself the slave of Jesus Christ. In Romans 6, he shows that a Christian is one who has become the servant of righteousness (verse 18). Paul and Peter speak of obeying the gospel (2 Thess. 1: 8; 1 Peter 4: 17). This is not submission to baptism but submission to the Christ who is presented in the gospel as Saviour and Lord.

(2) An objection to Christian faith.

Here is the point where the modern objection to Christianity becomes sharpest. This objection, however, does not usually assume the guise of an objection; it usually appears in the form of an explanation that devitalizes the gospel by removing the objectionable feature. It claims the name of Christ and lauds him as the great religious leader and hero, but objects to making him Lord of the conscience and of life. In the name of freedom and the autonomy of personal life, objection is made to what the objector considers an abject surrender of one's conscience and will to another. Such a surrender, it is claimed, would destroy our freedom and degrade our personality.

But, as a matter of fact, those who assume this attitude of surrender toward Christ do not find their personalities degraded, their wills weakened, nor their freedom lost. They find, on the other hand, that their wills are set free and that they are given a power over themselves and their environment, and especially over moral evil that they never knew before and in many cases that they never dreamed possible. It is this freedom in the gospel that Paul urges the Galatians that they should not surrender but contend for (Gal. 5: 1). The point to remember here, however, is that this freedom comes only by a faith that makes one the willing slave of Jesus Christ. This is one of the paradoxes of the gospel for which logic furnishes no explanation; it is understood only when experienced. As a matter of experience, however, it is as clear and definite as the experience of vision or hearing.

(3) Why salvation is conditioned upon faith.

Paul says that justification is by faith that it might be according to grace (Rom. 4: 16). Faith and grace are correlative ideas; each implies the other. If salvation is to be of grace on God's part, it must be by faith on man's part. Salvation by grace means salvation as a free gift on God's part. But God cannot give except as man receives. Receiving salvation as an unmerited gift on God's part is faith. God gives salvation, man receives it.

Opposed to Paul's idea of salvation by grace through faith was the doctrine of salvation by works; that is, that man by his obedience to the law was to deserve salvation. Paul strenuously opposed this on the ground that it would utterly pervert the gospel. When the Judaizers insisted that Gentiles who accepted the gospel should also be circumcized and keep the law, Paul objected, holding that faith in Christ was sufficient to save. He said that this would make salvation a matter of debt on God's part rather than a matter of grace (Rom. 4: 4).

There are, then, no conditions of salvation that have been prescribed in any arbitrary way. The only conditions are the conditions that are necessarily involved in the relations of a God of mercy who would, as a matter of grace, save an undeserving sinner and the sinner that he would save. The moral relations in the case make it impossible for God to save the sinner who does not recognize and acknowledge his sinful condition and cast himself in his helplessness upon a God of grace. That is to say, God cannot save a sinner without making the sinner willing to be saved. In this sense, repentance and faith are not conditions of salvation; they rather constitute salvation; that is, saving a sinner means to bring him to that state of mind in which he renounces sin and trusts himself to a God of grace. As the necessary moral relations involved in the case, repentance and faith are the universal and invariable conditions of salvation. Or using faith as including repentance, we may say that faith, and faith alone, is the condition of salvation. God himself could not save the sinner without faith on the sinner's part. To say that he could would be to say that God saved a man without saving him.

It follows, then, that the conditions of salvation have never changed. To say that some men were saved in one age of the world on one set of conditions, and other men in another age of the world on other conditions is to make God an arbitrary God. It is nonsense to say that men were saved in Old Testament times by the law and in New Testament times by the gospel. Not one man was ever saved by the law, because no man could keep its requirements. (See Acts 13: 39; Rom. 7: 10ff.; Gal. 2: 16.) To say that men were saved by the law would make void the gospel of the grace of God. Men were saved in Old Testament times by faith in God and his promises of grace. (See Rom. 4.)

Moreover, faith as a condition of salvation is not an act by which the man merits or earns anything; it is the act by which the bankrupt sinner receives the grace of God. It is an act in which the sinner puts all his trust for salvation in another and in what that other has done for him. It is not an act in which the sinner makes any claims for himself; it is rather an act in which he acknowledges that he cannot help himself and in which he signs away his life to another. It is an act of utter self-abandon to another. So there is involved in the act of faith the very opposite of any claim to doing anything by which one wins the favor of God; it is an act in which one acknowledges the utter impossibility of doing this and by which one casts himself on Christ and what he has done for his acceptance with God.

(4) The relation of faith to a life of righteousness.

The objection is sometimes made to the doctrine of salvation by grace through faith that it would encourage one to live a life of spiritual ease and sin rather than one of good works and righteousness. This has been a standing objection since the days of Paul. Doubtless he had come across it many times in his contest with the Judaizers. Paul shows (Rom. 6: 1ff.) that a Christian is one who has died to sin and been made alive to righteousness by faith in Christ. This constitutes a moral guarantee (the only kind of guarantee that will apply in the case) that the Christian will live a life of righteousness. It is morally impossible for him to do anything else.

It is sometimes thought that James and Paul do not agree on this question. Paul says that one is justified by faith apart from works of law (Rom. 3: 28). James says that a man is justified by works and not by faith only (James 2: 24). But we must remember two differences in point of view between Paul and James. One is that they are using the term works in somewhat different senses. Paul is talking about legalistic works, works as a basis for meriting the favor of God. And Paul's view was that as a basis for a sinner's acceptance with God, works of law were utterly useless. James is talking about works as the outgrowth and expression of a living faith. Again, Paul's question was: Upon what condition is a sinner justified before God? His answer is: Upon condition of faith, not on condition of works as a meritorious basis. James' question was: What kind of faith is it that justifies? Is it faith that produces good works, or faith that only repeats a formal creed? His answer is that faith that produces no works is a dead faith, and he contends that that kind of faith will not save (James 2: 14). No doubt Paul would have endorsed James' contention, and James would have agreed with Paul. There is no contradiction unless one insists on taking the author's words apart from their connection and without reference to the author's intention. In that case language has no meaning whatever.

It is not true that salvation by faith encourages one to a life of sin and discourages a life of righteousness. On the other hand, faith in Christ as Saviour from sin is the only thing that will lift one out of a self-centered life and produce a life of righteousness. True righteousness is not possible as long as one lives a self-centered life. But in the act of faith one looks beyond self; he trusts in another. He gives himself up to another. Moreover, faith unites to Christ and his Spirit becomes the controlling power of the Christian's life. As Christ gave himself for us, so those who follow him will give themselves to him and to the service of their fellows. Gratitude to God for a salvation received as the gift of his grace will not let one live for self while the world is dying for what he can give.

II. God's Saving Act

It has been customary to regard God's saving work from two points of view: the juristic or forensic, and the experimental or biological. In one of these, it is said, we come into a new standing with God; in the other we are given newness of life. In one we are changed in our relation with God; in the other we are changed in our moral nature. In one we are justified; in the other regenerated. One is objective; the other subjective. One takes place outside of us; the other within us.

This may be a valid distinction, but we must remember that it can be pressed too far. A good deal of discussion has been had as to which of these aspects of salvation preceded the other; which was fundamental and which secondary. But we must remember that these are not two separated acts on God's part. God does not justify in one act and regenerate in another. These are two ways of regarding the one saving act of God. Neither aspect precedes the other. Neither is complete without the other.

And it is doubtful if more is not lost than gained in trying to class the terms used in the New Testament for God's saving activity under one of these two heads. It would probably be better to understand that the one saving act of God may be looked at from a number of points of view and that this is what we have in the different terms used in the New Testament with reference to God's saving activity. We will consider some of the terms used in the Bible to set forth what God does for us in Christ in saving us.

1. *In Christ we have forgiveness of sins*

(1) Scriptures setting forth this idea.

This is one of the fundamental blessings in salvation. Salvation is deliverance from sin. In Old Testament times emphasis was laid on other forms of deliverance, such as deliverance from enemies (Psalm 27: 1ff.; Jer. 23: 5ff.), deliverance from disease (Psalm 103: 3), and deliverance from death (Psalm 49: 14, 15). But even in the Old Testament, salvation from sin was the chief blessing. We might look at several passages in which forgiveness of sins is set forth. In Psalm 32, David speaks of the blessedness of the man "whose transgression is forgiven, whose sin is covered." The Lord does not impute to him iniquity, and in his spirit there is no guile. As long as he kept silence and refused to confess his sin, God's hand was heavy upon him; he was scorched with the drought of summer. But when he confessed his sin, the Lord forgave the iniquity of his sin. We have a close parallel to this in Psalm 51. This Psalm is a classic, and will be to the end of time, in which a soul convicted of sin pours out its confession to a God of mercy and pleads for forgiveness and cleansing. The penitent in each of these cases has come to recognize that sin has broken his communion with God and that there is no possibility of peace and joy for him until his sin is forgiven and he is cleansed from its defilement. In Psalm 103, along with the blessing of being healed of disease, praise is ascribed to Jehovah because he forgives iniquities (verse 3). He does not deal with us after our sins, nor reward us according to our iniquities (verse 10). Because of his transcendent lovingkindness (verse 11) and fatherly pity (verse 13), he removes our transgressions as far from us as the east is from the west (verse 12).

In Jeremiah 31: 31-34, the Prophet tells about a new covenant that Jehovah will make with his people. This covenant will not be like the old covenant; it will be based on a greater deliverance than the deliverance from Egypt; it will be based on a deliverance from sin. He will forgive their iniquity, and their sin will he remember no more. This will give such an inner knowledge of God that they will keep this covenant. By this forgiveness the knowledge of God will be put in their hearts.

In the New Testament the forgiveness of sins is one of the fundamental blessings that men were to receive in the Messianic salvation. John the Baptist was to "go before the face of the Lord to make ready his ways; to give knowledge of salvation unto his people in the remission of their sins" (Luke 1: 76, 77). Forgiveness of sins was one of the elemental blessings that Jesus taught his disciples to pray for (Matt. 6: 12; Luke 11: 4). After the Resurrection, Jesus commissioned his disciples to preach, in his name, remission of sins, upon condition of repentance, to all the nations (Luke 24: 47). Peter announced to the people at Pentecost that after repentance they should be baptized unto the remission of sins (Acts 2: 38). He preached to Cornelius and the company assembled at his house that the prophets all bear witness that through the name of Jesus every one who believes on him shall receive remission of sins (Acts 10: 43).

In Ephesians 1: 7 Paul says: "In whom (Christ) we have our redemption through his blood, the forgiveness

of our trespasses." (Cf. Col. 1: 14.) This seems to identify redemption and forgiveness of sins; at least, it makes
forgiveness the chief element in redemption. Without
forgiveness there is no redemption.

This list of passages is by no means exhaustive, but
it is representative of the teaching of the Bible on the
subject. It shows that forgiveness of sins was the
fundamental blessing of the gospel of Christ. That idea
was not unknown to Old Testament saints, but the idea
comes out in its clearness and fulness in the new dispen-
sation. The Book of Hebrews shows that the forgiveness of sins was an essential element in the new covenant.
It was in the forgiveness of sins that men should know
God (8: 11, 12). This was in accordance with the prophecy of Jeremiah (Jer. 31: 31-34).

(2) The meaning of forgiveness.

We might inquire a little more particularly as to what
is meant by the forgiveness of sins. The term translated to forgive in the New Testament means to send
away. It is exactly our term to remit, send back or
away. To remit sins is to put them away. But still
the question remains: To put them away in what sense?
What does it mean to put away sins? It does not mean
to put away in any mechanical or spatial sense. Sins
cannot be put away thus. To remit sins is evidently a
figure of speech. Sometimes the matter was thought of
as analogous to the releasing of a debtor. Jesus thought
of it thus when he taught the disciples to pray: "Forgive us our debts, as we also have forgiven our debtors"
(Matt. 6: 12). We have the impressive statements in the
Old Testament that God puts our sins behind his back
(Isa. 38: 34) and remembers them no more (Jer. 31:
34). He casts them in the depths of the sea (Micah 7:
19). He washes us, and makes us whiter than snow
(Psalm 51: 7).

It is not exactly true to say that to forgive sin is
to make us as if we had not sinned. This is not true
in the consciousness of a forgiven sinner. The con-

sciousness of a sinner is not the same as the consciousness of one who has not sinned. "Once a sinner always
a sinner—in this sense at least, that he who has but
once sinned can never be as if he had never sinned. His
very blessedness to all eternity is a different thing from
the blessedness of the sinless. The man whose iniquity
is not imputed is a very different being from the man
whose iniquity was never committed."[3]

But forgiveness does mean that sin is removed as a
barrier to our fellowship with God. Sin breaks man's
fellowship with God. It is a personal offense against
God. "Against thee, thee only, have I sinned, and done
that which is evil in thy sight" (Psalm 51: 4). "Your
iniquities have separated between you and your God, and
your sins have hid his face from you, so that he will not
hear" (Isa. 59: 2). As the Holy One of Israel, Jehovah
will not accept the offerings of a sinful and rebellious
people, nor hear their prayers. They must repent of their
sins and do the right (Isa. 1). But when sin is forgiven,
the block to fellowship is removed. The cloud that shut
out the face of God is blotted out. In this sense sin is
remitted, sent away. It is like the revival of human
fellowship after friends or loved ones have been separated
by a wrong done by one to another. Forgiveness sought
and obtained renews the former intimacy of confidence
and love. It is this that gives to one the uplifting sense
of freedom, peace, and joy upon realizing that his sins
are forgiven. He is released from the enslaving sense
of guilt. A great burden is gone from the soul. A new
light comes in. Often the whole face of nature seems
to be transformed. A joy unspeakable and full of glory
comes into the soul. We realize that we are loosed from
our sins (Rev. 1: 5), which have bound and enslaved us.

Forgiveness is a personal act that law, physical, social,
or moral, cannot explain. Law knows nothing of forgiveness. There are those today who insist that law
reigns in the world, and that there can be no variation

---

[3]Forsythe, P. T., *Christian Perfection*, pp. 5, 6.

from the reign of law; law is supreme and invariable. It does not make any difference what form the law may take; it may be physical law or it may be moral; but if law speaks the last word, forgiveness is excluded. There can be forgiveness only where personality and personal relations are the ultimate reality. God is a person and God is more than law, physical or moral. If a man does not believe in a personal God, he cannot believe in for-giveness of sins. On the other hand, the experience of the forgiveness of sins gives one such an assurance of relationship with a personal God that one cannot lose the consciousness of God without also losing the sense of forgiven sin. This transcendent act of God is an act that not only carries with it the idea of God's personality; it is also an act of grace on his part. As such it tran-scends law. Grace does not nullify law, but transcends it. Law cannot forgive, but God can. Law cannot for-give, because law knows nothing about grace. Grace is a personal quality. It is the highest conceivable quality of moral character. Forgiveness, therefore, is an act that transcends law. The God of grace rises above, but does not violate or nullify law.

The grace of God that forgives sins and thus restores the sinner to the fellowship of a holy God will finally deliver the forgiven sinner from all the evil consequences of his sin. This is true both with reference to the indi-vidual and to the redeemed race. Sin broke man's fel-lowship with God and brought spiritual death, followed by a whole horde of evils consequent upon sin and spir-itual death. When sin is forgiven, man's fellowship with God is restored and as a consequence all the ills that followed upon sin will be removed. But this cannot be done at a bound. To do so would probably mean violent-ly to dislocate man from his historical, social, and moral connections as a member of the race and as a part of the order of nature.

For instance, a body that is maimed by disease, caused by sin, is not, usually at least, restored to perfect soundness upon the forgiveness of sin. If one wastes the strength of youth in prodigal living, God will gladly forgive the penitent prodigal when he returns home, but the substance of his physical and sometimes his mental manhood is not given back to him in this life. Again, the social results of our sins are forgiven. God forgave David his awful sins in connection with Bathsheba and Uriah, but the sword never departed from David's house until his death. Many a bitter tear he shed over the consequences of his sin, although he knew the sweetness of God's forgiving grace.

But while we are not at once delivered from all the consequences of our sins, when we are forgiven, we are put in such a relation with God that all the ills of life may become redemptive forces in our lives working for the one supreme purpose of transforming us into the image of Christ. (See Rom. 8: 28ff.)

The experience of the forgiveness of sins as a gracious act on God's part not only removes sin as a barrier to fellowship with God, it gives one an insight into the character of God that otherwise would be impossible. In other words, the forgiven sinner understands God, and consequently has a fellowship with God that would be impossible for a man who had never sinned. How could a man who had never sinned understand that element in God's character that we express by the term grace? The grace of God is the most glorious element in his character according to the Christian view. This grace we know only in its redeeming work in our lives. A sinless being can never know a God of grace. The conception would have no meaning to him. Redemption in Christ, then, does not put man back in the place of an unfallen Adam. It puts him on a new basis, gives him an insight into God's character and fellowship with God that such an unfallen man could not have. For instance, the redeemed sinner will, as a result of an experience of God's grace in saving him, have reproduced in his life the quality of grace in relation to his fellows. This is seen in that the redeemed man has in him the spirit of grace as manifested in his evangelistic and missionary spirit. Such a spirit is not something incidental or accidental in the Christian life; it is of the essence of Christianity. An unfallen Adam might be a man of legalistic justice; he could hardly be a man of grace.

We might say, then, that the forgiveness of sins is the fundamental blessing in salvation, and that the forgiveness of sins through the grace of God changes the whole of life into a redemptive order. The ills of life that before were of a fundamentally retributive aspect now become primarily remedial and redemptive in that they can, by God's grace, be made to contribute to the development of Christian character.

2. *In Christ we are justified*

(1) The doctrine defined.

Justification is the act of God in which the sinner, hitherto condemned on account of his sin, upon condition of faith in Christ, is forgiven and received into the divine favor. Justification is mainly, if not exclusively, a Pauline doctrine in the New Testament. Paul uses this term mainly rather than the term forgiveness of sins. In Paul's writings is the only place the doctrine is stated with anything like thoroughness or completeness. He sets the doctrine forth in the Letters to the Galatians and the Romans. There is so much in common between the ideas of forgiveness of sins and justification that it will not be necessary to give a full treatment of justification here. Practically all that has been said about forgiveness will apply to justification. As previously stated, they do not denote two acts of God or experiences on the part of the sinner, but they denote the same transaction looked at from somewhat different points of view. Justification, however, is a somewhat different idea from the forgiveness of sins.

Note two differences: One is that justification is a forensic or law term. The word means to declare just.

It is the legal term for acquitting one accused of crime. It is the term that Paul uses for the act of pardoning or acquitting the sinner condemned on account of sin. But it does not denote, as some say, the act of pardoning without being received into God's favor. God is not neutral toward man. So when the sinner is pardoned, he is restored to the divine favor. The thing that necessitates justification is the removal of this condemnation. Forgiveness is more of a personal idea; it removes sin as that which breaks our personal fellowship with God. Justification deals with sin as that which brings on us the condemnation of the law.

Another difference is that justification is something that takes place once for all. It is never repeated. It does not need repeating. It brings one into a new relation with God which is never reversible. Forgiveness needs repeating in the life of the Christian as often as sin weakens or breaks his fellowship with God. But the justified sinner never comes again under the condemnation of the law. Therefore, he never needs to be justified again. This is the advantage of Paul's use of this idea. It denotes that the penitent sinner is brought into a relation with God which he will never lose. He comes not again into condemnation.

(2) A one-sided statement of the doctrine.

This doctrine has sometimes suffered from a one-sided interpretation and a wrong emphasis. The emphasis with some theologians has been on the fact that it is a declarative rather than an efficient act on God's part; that is, we are told, it is an act in which the sinner is regarded and treated as righteous rather than an act in which he is made righteous. The emphasis is placed on the fact that it is a legal or forensic term. For one to be declared "not guilty" in court, it is said, does not mean that one has not committed the crime of which he is accused; it means that he is released so far as the law is concerned. So, we are told, justification is an act in which God declared the sinner just in his relation with the law; but it does not mean that one is actually righteous; nor does it mean that God makes him righteous.

But the emphasis on justification as a declarative or forensic act as distinguished from an efficient act is hardly just. Justification is an efficient act; it does make one righteous. It makes one righteous in his relation with God, and there is nothing more fundamental in one's life than his relation with God. The distinction has sometimes been made that justification gives one a new standing before God, while regeneration gives one a new life; justification gives one a new relation to God, regeneration gives one a new nature. But this is a distinction and a contrast that is wholly foreign to Paul's mind. To Paul, condemnation and death were one and inseparable, and so were justification and life. The thing that brought life to the man dead in trespasses and sins was the justifying act of God which brought him into right relation with God. Paul speaks of it as the justification of life (Rom. 5: 18). Jesus says that the one who believes has eternal life and comes not into condemnation (John 5: 24).

Instead of its being true that Paul's doctrine of justification by faith is legalistic, on the other hand, Paul set forth his doctrine in opposition to the legalistic system of the Judaizers. These Judaizers insisted that Paul's Gentile converts to Christianity must not only have faith in Christ to be saved but must also be circumcised and keep the Jewish law. Paul stoutly insisted that this would mean the perversion of the whole gospel order; that faith and faith alone saved from sin; that the Christian was free from all bonds of legalism for salvation. We are justified by faith apart from works of law (Rom. 3: 28).

3. *In Christ we are reconciled to God*

This is another term used by Paul to denote God's act of saving the sinner. This term means practically the same as justification. It views sin as causing an alienation or estrangement between God and man. When this alienation is removed, the sinner is said to be reconciled to God.

That reconciliation is synonymous with justification is seen in Romans 5: 9, 10. In verse 9, Paul speaks of being justified in the blood of Jesus; in verse 10, he speaks of being reconciled to God through the death of his Son. It is clear that these two expressions refer to the same experience. Paul's statement in 2 Corinthians 5: 19 shows the same thing, for he defines reconciliation as being the non-imputation of trespasses.

A question that arises in regard to reconciliation is whether man's reconciliation to God consists in the removal of man's enmity toward God, or whether it is the removal of God's displeasure toward man, or whether it is both. It is evidently both. The two passages above referred to as showing that reconciliation and justification are synonymous would show that it is both. If reconciliation is synonymous with justification or the non-imputation of sin, then it involves a change in God's attitude toward man. So for the sinner to be reconciled to God means that the sinner shall receive the pardoning grace of God. Doubtless it is meant to describe a mutual transaction, but the emphasis seems to be on the removal of God's displeasure in the non-imputation of sin.

4. *In Christ we are adopted into the family of God*

The term adoption seems to be used in three senses or rather with reference to three different applications. In Romans 9: 4, Paul uses it with reference to Israel as a nation in her peculiar relation to Jehovah. In Romans 8: 23, he uses it with reference to the redemption of the body in the resurrection for which the Christian anxiously waits. But the usual application of the term is with reference to our being made God's children spiritually when we become Christians. The term is a forensic term, as justification is, and denotes the act by which one not naturally a child is made legally the child and heir of the one who adopts him. The term, however,

is not to be taken as describing a merely legalistic transaction. Paul, in Romans 8: 15 and Galatians 4: 5, emphasizes the conscious possession of the Spirit in connection with our adoption or as a consequence of it, and
shows that by this conscious possession of the Spirit we
are delivered from the bondage of fear and of legalism.
He also points out the fact that as a consequence of our
adoption, we not only are made sons of God but also
heirs and, therefore, inherit with Christ all the spiritual
riches of God.

It is evident that this term is, on one side, synonymous
with justification, and, on the other, with regeneration.
It is a legal term like justification used to describe what
God does for us in saving us. Justification emphasizes
our new standing as sons in relation to God. Like regeneration, it puts our salvation in terms of sonship—
adoption being the legal term, regeneration the experimental or biological term. The two ideas are so closely
related that we will not dwell on adoption here but will
pass on to discuss regeneration.

5. *In Christ we have new life*

(1) Some New Testament terms used for this idea.

One of the most common terms used in theology and
in preaching to describe God's saving act is the term
regeneration. The term means to beget or generate
again. Our term new birth means practically the same.
The term regeneration has passed into religious term-
inology mainly from the influence of the expression of
Jesus in John 3: 3, 7, where he speaks of being begotten
or born again or more properly from above. Peter uses
the same verb (compounded with a preposition) in 1
Peter 1: 3, 23. John uses the expression repeatedly in
his First Epistle. There are other terms in the New
Testament used to describe this experience of being renewed in the grace of God. One is Paul's figure of a
new creation. In 2 Corinthians 5: 17, he says, "If any
man is in Christ, he is a new creature" (literally, "there

is a new creation"). Here the Apostle describes this saving act on God's part as being a creative act in which he so renews one that "the old things are passed away; behold, they are become new." He says in Gal. 6: 15, "For neither is circumcision anything, nor uncircumcision, but a new creature" (literally creation). In Ephesians 2: 10, 15; 4: 24, and Colossians 3: 10, he uses the same figure. In Romans 2: 29, Paul says that true circumcision is that of the heart, in the spirit, not in the letter. This evidently refers to regeneration as that which makes one a member of the true spiritual Israel. Another figure found in Paul's writings and in some other places is that of death and resurrection. In Romans 6: 1ff., Paul sets forth the idea that the Christian is one who has died to sin and risen to walk in newness of life. This death to sin was set forth further back as meaning repentance. That is true. To die to sin is to repent if we look at it as a human act; if we look at it from the point of view of the divine efficiency, it is equivalent to regeneration. In Galatians 2: 20, Paul says: "I have been crucified with Christ; and it is no longer I that live, but Christ liveth in me." In Galatians 6: 14, he glories in the Cross through which the world has been crucified to him and he to the world. (See also Gal. 5: 24 and Col. 2: 20.) This reminds us of the saying of Jesus that, if any man would come after him, he must deny himself and take up his cross. One shall lose his life by saving it and save it by losing it (Matt. 16: 24, 25). "Except a grain of wheat fall into the earth and die, it abideth alone; but if it die, it beareth much fruit" (John 12: 24). "The hour cometh, and now is, when the dead shall hear the voice of the Son of God; and they that hear shall live" (John 5: 25).

(2) The nature of the change.

What kind of a change is regeneration? Just what is it that takes place when a man is born again?

a. This change is primarily of the nature of a moral and spiritual renewal. It is a change the main significance of which is to be found in the realm of character. In this change the fundamental moral disposition is changed. The affections and activities of life no longer center in self, but in God. Love for God and for one's fellows becomes the controlling factor in life. One dies to sin and rises to walk in newness of life (Rom. 6: 1ff.). Regeneration is a transaction in which the moral nature is so changed that one can never again rest in a life of sin. Righteousness becomes the passion of the soul. This does not mean that all evil or sinful propensities are at a stroke eliminated from one's being; but it does mean that such a revolutionary transaction has taken place in the soul that it can never rest until it is free from sin. The dominant passion of the soul becomes love for righteousness and hatred for sin. In principle the soul is made sinless. This is why the man that is begotten of God cannot sin. He cannot live in sin as his natural and native element as formerly he did; he cannot habitually sin, cannot continually sin; he cannot live a life of sin (1 John 3: 6-9).

b. This change is one that is wrought in the moral nature of man by the Spirit of God. Nothing but divine power could produce the change. Both experience and the Scriptures bear testimony to this. It is a new creation in which old things pass away and all things are made new (2 Cor. 5: 17). It is a birth from above in which one is cleansed (born of water) and given a spiritual disposition (born of the Spirit) (John 3: 3ff.). It is a change that is not of blood (natural descent), nor of the will of man (human nature on its higher, spiritual side), nor of the will of the flesh (human nature on its lower side), but of God (John 1: 12). God's power works this change. The gospel is the power of God unto salvation (Rom. 1: 16). God draws men to Christ (John 6: 44).

Christian experience bears witness to the same truth. The man who experiences regeneration knows as well as he knows daylight from darkness that he himself did not work the change. He submitted to God, and God changed him. He knows the power that deals with him as something new in his experience. He knows it as some power different and higher in nature than the social forces that influence his life. It is the spontaneous impulse of the Christian heart to thank God for one's own salvation or for the salvation of another.

6. *In Christ we are sanctified*

(1) Meaning of the term.

It is customary at this point in treatises on theology to discuss the doctrine of "sanctification." It means, first of all, consecration or dedication to God. This use is frequent in the Old Testament and is not unknown in the New. Used in this sense it included things as well as persons and did not possess moral significance. But the words holy and holiness did come to have ethical significance in the Old Testament. So do the terms sanctify and sanctification in the New Testament. Things are sanctified as they are consecrated to God, as they are regarded and treated as sacred or dedicated to the divine service. But since the character of God was regarded as ethically righteous, it was recognized that men who are acceptable for his service must be also righteous in character. And when applied to persons in the New Testament, the idea is fundamentally ethical. The term is used in the New Testament both for the initiation of the Christian life and for its development. The New Testament speaks of all Christians as "saints" or "sanctified ones" (Acts 9: 13; Rom. 1: 7; 1 Cor. 1: 2; 2 Cor. 1: 1; Eph. 1: 1; Phil. 1: 1; Col. 1: 2). In this sense the term is synonymous with justification or regeneration. This is sometimes called positional sanctification, as distinguished from progressive sanctification. Then it is used with reference to the progressive cleansing or purification of the soul (1 Thess. 5: 23; Heb. 12: 14). It is in this sense that the term is usually used in discussion in systems of theology. But there are very few places in the New Testament where the term is unquestionably used in the sense of a progressive work. The preponderating use of the term is in its application to a definite act at the beginning of the Christian life.

(2) All Christians sanctified.

Every Christian, then, however imperfect he may be, is sanctified in the sense that he is dedicated or consecrated to God by the power of the Spirit and by his own act of faith. We have seen that one element in faith is surrender to Christ as Lord. Faith is thus an act of dedication. One dedicates himself to God and separates himself from all that opp'oses his consecration to God. There should be, normally there will be, a deepening consecration to God and his service, and a more complete separation of oneself from all the forces and factors of life that hinder this consecration; but this is only the carrying out of what was involved in that first act of consecration.

Every Christian is sanctified also in the sense of an inner purification or transformation of character. In this sense sanctification means about the same as regeneration. One who is dedicated to a God of love and righteousness will necessarily become like him in character. The thing that renews one in heart and character is the fact that he is dedicated by an act of self-surrender to a righteous God. Fellowship with a holy God produces holiness in man. Here again there should be progressive sanctification; but the prevailing use of the term in the New Testament is in the sense of the initial dedication or cleansing from sin.

III. Union with Christ

We have seen that salvation is by faith. Faith saves because it is the bond that unites the soul to God in Christ. Our salvation is in Christ Jesus. In him we find God and salvation from sin. "Jehovah is my light and my salvation" (Psalm 27: 1). His power and his alone can redeem from sin. In finding him we find salvation.

1. *The New Testament clearly teaches this union*

This union of the believer with Christ is represented in many ways in the New Testament. But it is Paul and John that present to us most clearly and fully this union. Paul and John, in the good sense of the word, are mystics. They emphasize this immediate contact of the soul with the living Christ. In John's Gospel Christ is the bread of life (6: 35); by eating his flesh and drinking his blood we dwell in him and he in us (6: 56); he is the good shepherd in whose hands we find safety (10: 27, 28); he is the vine, we are the branches (15: 1ff.); he is in us, we are in him (14: 20). Paul also uses a number of expressions that set forth this union with Christ. Christ is the head, we are members of his body (Rom. 12: 4ff.; 1 Cor. 12: 12ff.); he is the husband, the church the wife (Eph. 5: 22ff.); he is to us what the foundation is to a building (1 Cor. 3: 10ff.; Eph. 2: 20). We are crucified with Christ (Gal. 2: 20); we are risen with him (Col. 3: 1); we are buried with him in baptism (Rom. 6: 4); we suffer with him and shall be glorified with him (Rom. 8: 17). In union with him, Paul says he can do all things (Phil. 4: 13). He is so vitally related to Christ that he can say, "For to me to live is Christ" (Phil. 1: 21).

2. *This union with Christ is by faith*

In John 6: 56, Jesus says that if we eat his flesh and drink his blood we abide in him and he in us. This means faith. In Galatians 2: 20, Paul says that the life which he now lives, which is Christ living in him, is by faith in the Son of God. In Ephesians 3: 17, Paul prays for the Ephesians that Christ may dwell in their hearts through faith.

3. *This union is with the living Christ*

This conception of union with Christ by faith has no meaning apart from the New Testament teaching that Jesus is now the risen, reigning Lord. The faith that saves is not simply faith that looks back to the historic

Jesus; it looks up to the living Christ. Christ is a living person with whom we must be vitally united by faith if he saves us from our sins. The cry "back to Christ," meaning back to the historic Jesus of the Synoptic Gospels and away from the transcendent Christ of Paul and John, is a motto that means to devitalize Christianity, for merely a historic Christ cannot save; he must be superhistoric. As a matter of fact, the Christ of the Synoptic Gospels is just as transcendent as the Christ of John and Paul. But some of the critics think they get in the Synoptic Gospels a Christ with no element in him that cannot be measured in terms of human life and history. The Christ who is presented in the New Testament as the object of saving faith is the Jesus who, having been slain by wicked hands, was raised from the dead by God (Acts 2: 23, 24; 5: 30, 31). He is the Christ who in the Spirit can be called Lord (1 Cor. 12: 3). We do not merely reach back by a stretch of imagination over nineteen centuries to the Christ who lives and reigns at the right hand of God.

4. *This union with the living Christ is union with God*

The significance of this union with Christ is that in him we come to know God with all that that implies. To talk about union with Christ signifies nothing if he is nothing more than a historic character whom we know through the New Testament records. These records are essential, for the Christ we know in Christian experience is not another than the historic Christ, yet he is more than historic. He not only lived a life in time and space, but in his Resurrection and ascension he transcended the historical order. And when we know him as the transcendent Christ we are conscious that in knowing him we know God. In our consciousness, union with Christ is union with God. No man knows the Father except the one to whom the Son wills to reveal him (Matt. 11: 27). For a knowledge of God we are absolutely dependent on Jesus Christ, his only begotten Son. But in and through the Son we do know the Father. It is not a question between knowing God in Christ and knowing God outside of Christ; it is a choice between knowing God in Christ and not knowing him at all. The claims of Jesus in this respect are absolutely true to experience and have been vindicated in experience. Outside an experimental knowledge of Jesus Christ as Saviour and Lord, men may speculate about God and come to hold certain opinions about him that are correct; but they never come to know God himself. But by faith in Jesus as Saviour and Lord, men are vitally united to God in an experience that constitutes such a knowledge of God as means nothing less than salvation from sin.

5. *This union with Christ is not to be interpreted after the pantheistic fashion*

Our union with Christ does not mean the losing of the finite self in the infinite All. The surrender of our wills to the will of God in Christ does not mean the losing of our wills; it does not mean to annul personality; it does not mean the throwing off of moral responsibility by merging oneself in the impersonal Absolute. It means rather the finding of oneself. The prodigal son went home to his father when he came to himself (Luke 15: 17). One never comes to himself until he comes to Christ. When one comes to Christ he finds his will invigorated, his mind quickened, his moral nature renewed —he finds himself.

6. *Doctor Strong was true to New Testament teaching* when he summed up our salvation in the idea of union with Christ and made that the controlling idea in his discussion of salvation.[4] Every blessing that we enjoy as Christians grows out of our union with Christ. A full discussion, therefore, of union with Christ would involve all that follows in regard to salvation.

---

[4] See *Systematic Theology*, Vol. III.

IV. The consciousness of salvation

One of the outstanding things about salvation in the Christian sense of the term is that it is a conscious transaction. This was presupposed in all that has been said about salvation, but it is well now to give special consideration to it.

1. *The normal Christian experience*

The normal Christian experience is one in which the Christian has conscious acceptance with God. The whole religious atmosphere seems to change with the coming of Jesus. Old Testament saints had conscious communion with God, but they did not have that full note of joy and confidence in their relation with God that we find in the New Testament. Especially is it true from Pentecost on that men had this full assurance of acceptance with God. Forgiveness of sins was no merely external transaction that the forgiven sinner might happen to hear about or not.

(1) In the first place, there was the consciousness of sin.

This was produced by the preaching of the gospel. The man who had no consciousness of sin and in whom it could not be produced by the Word of God was hopeless. The more the sinner is conscious of sin, the more is he likely to rejoice in salvation and love the God who forgives in mercy (Luke 7: 41ff.).

(2) Salvation from sin was a transaction in which one was brought into conscious communion with God.

In this transaction one finds God. He comes to know God (John 17: 3). God comes to possess man and man to possess God. He shall be their God and they shall be his people (Heb. 8: 10). In a real sense a man has no God until he comes to possess him in this great revolutionary crisis of life. In this crisis a covenant is sealed by which the soul becomes consciously given over to him. When sin was removed and the soul came into fellowship with God, the soul was often flooded with joy (Acts 8:

8; 13: 52, et al). The justified man had a heritage of peace to which he was entitled by virtue of his new relation with God (Rom. 5: 1). Another element that came as a result of this fellowship with God in Christ was hope (Rom. 8: 24). New Testament Christians were forward looking.

This does not mean that all Christian experiences were alike then any more than they are now. Some were more emotional and cataclysmic than others. Lydia did not seem to have the agitation of soul that the jailer had (Acts 16). There are varieties of Christian experience, just as there are differences among men in every other respect. But every normal Christian experience is an experience of conscious acceptance with God in the forgiveness of sins, an experience that brings love, joy, peace, and hope to the soul.

2. *The lack of assurance*

Yet it must be recognized that there are cases of those who have been regenerated who do not have clear and definite consciousness of acceptance with God. This is recognized in the New Testament and is verified in Christian experience. John says that he wrote his Gospel that men might have life by believing in Jesus as the Christ (John 20: 31). He says he wrote the First Epistle in order that those who believe may know that they have eternal life (1 John 5: 13). This clearly implies two things: One is that it is the privilege of a saved man to know that he is saved; the other is that a man may be saved and not have this assurance. If salvation and assurance were inseparable, then John's writing to bring to Christians assurance was superfluous labor.

Sometimes assurance is lacking in the beginning of the Christian life; sometimes one may have it and lose it. Sometimes the lack of assurance is caused by sin and disobedience in the life; sometimes it is due to a lack of understanding of some of the fundamental and elemental things in the Christian life, such as the ground of our forgiveness in the atoning work of Christ, or faith as the essential and all-inclusive condition of salvation. In some cases, the lack of assurance is caused by the fact that one did not get just the kind of experience he was looking for. Some people want the kind of religious experience Paul had, and, therefore, are constantly dissatisfied with the one God has given them. In still other cases, lack of assurance is due to intellectual perplexities. One may be disturbed because he cannot work out to his own satisfaction all the problems concerning God and his dealings with man.

3. What is necessary to assurance

A word might be said now as to how assurance is produced or what is necessary to assurance.

In the first place, one needs a clear understanding and a firm grasp of the elemental things in salvation. This is not to say that he needs to be an expert theologian. He does not. Nor is it to say with the Catholic creeds that, if he does not believe certain dogmas, he shall be anathema. But he does need a firm grasp on the fact that Christ has made full provision for our sins and that we are saved by faith in him. There can be no definite assurance of salvation where one does not definitely grasp this fact. Sometimes one may know that he has been changed without having a clear consciousness of salvation, but this clear consciousness of salvation will come when one firmly grasps the fact that it is faith in the crucified and risen Redeemer that saves. Along with this there must be definite surrender to Christ as Lord. The will must be surrendered to him. There must be no conscious and wilful disobedience to Christ.

Putting together what has been said, it will be seen that the sum of it is that one must have clear and definite faith to have assurance of acceptance with God. Faith brings its own assurance. And nothing but faith is necessary.

Doctor Strong says: "The ground of faith (meaning saving faith) is the external word of promise. The ground of assurance, on the other hand, is the inward witness of the Spirit that we fulfil the conditions of the promise."[5] This statement is somewhat misleading. It makes the impression that the ground of saving faith is one thing, and that the ground of the faith that brings assurance is another thing. But this is a mistake. The faith that saves is the faith that assures. Saving faith carries its own assurance, and, if it does not, it is because the faith is not clear and definite. So, if one needs assurance, he will not get it by having developed in him a new kind of faith or faith in a different object. Assurance will come when faith is clarified, strengthened, and aware of what it is about. Christ is always the object of faith, and the Holy Spirit always is the power that produces faith in Christ. This is true both in salvation and assurance. In other words, Christ and the Holy Spirit both bear the same relation to saving faith that they do to assuring faith, for these are one faith, not two.

There are pointed out in the New Testament certain ethical and spiritual qualities that mark the regenerated man. Some of these are the possession of the Spirit (Rom. 8: 9, 14; 1 John 3: 24), obedience to Christ or God (John 14: 15, 21; 1 John 2: 34), a life of righteousness and of victory over sin (1 John 3: 6-9), love of the brotherhood (1 John 3: 10ff.), the power to discern the truth (1 John 2: 27). These are all the result of our faith in Christ. When we are asked to look at these as evidences of regeneration, we are simply asked to let our faith become clear and self-conscious and know what it is about. We are not asked to take something outside of or beyond saving faith as evidence of our salvation.

---

[5]*Systematic Theology*, Vol. III, p. 844.

THE NATURE OF THE CHRISTIAN LIFE

CHAPTER XI

THE NATURE OF THE CHRISTIAN LIFE

I. THE CHRISTIAN'S MISSION AND WORK

    1. To work out and exemplify the life implanted in regeneration

    2. To bring others into saving relations with Christ and to develop the new life in them

    3. To do all the good he can in every realm of life

II. PROVIDENCE

    1. Providence and redemption

    2. Providence and faith

III. PRAYER

    1. Elements in prayer

    2. Purpose and scope of prayer

    3. Conditions of answer to prayer

IV. THE PERSISTENCE OF THE CHRISTIAN LIFE

    1. Meaning of "final perseverance of the saints"

    2. Evidence that the regenerated will persevere

        (1) Eternal life

        (2) Union with Christ

        (3) Intercession of Christ

        (4) "Sealing" of the Spirit

        (5) Definite statements in the New Testament

    3. Objections to the doctrine

        (1) That it is inconsistent with freedom of man

        (2) That it encourages one to a life of sin

        (3) That the Bible teaches "falling from grace"

            a. Some passages teach that perseverance is necessary to final salvation

            b. Some teach that perseverance is an evidence of regeneration

c. Some teach that those not persevering are "false professors"
d. Some emphasize lack of development and loss of reward
e. Some emphasize danger of rejecting gospel truth

V. The Growth of the Christian Life

1. Need of growth
2. Foes of growth
3. Means of growth
4. Conditions of growth
5. Perfection theory of growth
6. Goal of growth

CHAPTER XI

THE NATURE OF THE CHRISTIAN LIFE

Having seen something of how the Christian life begins in an act of faith on man's part and an act of forgiveness and regeneration on God's part, in which the sinner is brought into conscious fellowship with God and renewed in the moral image of Jesus Christ, let us turn our attention now to the life that the Christian lives in pursuance of this act of faith and in fulfilment and completion of God's saving act. It is our purpose in this chapter to consider only some of the outstanding and more important phases of this life.

I. The Christian's mission and work

To discuss in full the Christian's mission and work would necessitate the treatment of several of the phases of practical theology. This would manifestly be out of order here. What we are concerned with is simply to consider briefly some of the fundamental principles of that life, especially when it is viewed as a life of redemption.

1. *Work out and exemplify life implanted in regeneration*

The first thing that we mention is that the Christian's mission is to work out and exemplify in his daily activities the life implanted in his heart when he becomes a Christian.

This life seeks embodiment and expression. This is expressed in many ways in the New Testament. The Christian is said to follow Christ (Mark 1: 16ff.; 2: 14). He is a disciple; that is, a learner in the school of Christ (Matt. 28: 19). The Spirit of Christ is in him and he is led by the Spirit (Rom. 8: 9ff., 14). Christ lives in him

(Gal. 2: 20), and he strives to bring every thought into subjection to Christ (2 Cor. 10: 5). He is to work out his salvation, because it is God that works in him both to will and to do (Phil. 2: 12, 13). We are not meaning to say here that the Christian life is simply the embodiment of some principle of divine life implanted at the time of regeneration which lives on independently of further re-enforcement from the divine presence. God continues to work in us, as the above references show. He continues to energize in us and through us, and our mission is to work down and out to the limit what God works in us in the way of willing and doing.

2. *The Christian's mission, in another phase of it, is to bring others into saving relations with Christ and to develop the Christ-life in them*

Every Christian should be an evangelist, a herald of good news. In this sense every Christian should be a preacher. This is the spontaneous impulse of the new life in us—to bring somebody else to know Christ and enjoy the great blessing that he brings. Our mission is to bear witness to him from Jerusalem to the uttermost part of the earth. Any form of Christianity that does not have throbbing through it a mighty missionary and evangelistic impulse is a degenerated form. And the Christian's mission is to do all he can to develop the Christ-life in others after they are brought into saving relation with him.

3. *The Christian's mission is to do all the good he can in every realm of life, in every possible way*

He is to seek to make regnant the will of God in the whole extent of human life and society. There are those today who set over against each other evangelistic effort and social service. They would disparage one in favor of the other. Those who emphasize evangelism and decry social service seem to think that anything except direct religious work is irreligious. Every good work is religious, if done with a motive to glorify God.

There is no conflict between serving God and helping men. Surely the Christ who healed the bodies of men and performed a miracle to feed the hungry multitude does not represent a God who is displeased with anything that makes this world a better place in which to live. The type of piety that thinks that the only function of religion is to cause a man to withdraw into some monastery and save his own soul and let the world go to the devil—that type of piety belongs to the middle ages, if it belongs anywhere. Nor is it the only function of Christianity to save the souls of men from hell in the next life; they need to be made righteous in every relation of life. The regeneration of the individual and the regeneration of society should never be put over against each other as antithetical things; it is not a question of one to the exclusion of the other. They are rather two things that are mutually dependent. The only way to regenerate society is through the regeneration of the individual units of society. And the only power that can regenerate the individual is the gospel of Christ. Nor has the gospel done its full work in the life of the individual unless he is made right in every relation of life. The gospel makes a man live right in the world, not withdraw from the world. Jesus taught his disciples to pray that God's kingdom might come and God's will be done on earth as it is in heaven (Matt. 6: 10).

II. Providence

What has been said about God and his relation to the world would involve the thought that he exercises a providential care over the world.[1] More particularly would this be true with reference to mankind. If God created man in his own image,[2] then surely he has a purpose for man that he is working out with reference to man.

---

[1] See Chapter V.
[2] See Chapter II.

1. *Providence and redemption*

But it is when we come to the idea of redemption that the providential purpose of God comes most distinctly into view.[3] Only a consciousness of redemption can give one a definite assurance of God's loving providential guidance in his life. To understand the doctrine of providence, then, we must see it from the point of view of redemption. This comes out clearly in Paul's statement in Romans 8: 28, 29. The emphasis is usually laid on Paul's statement that all things work together for good to those that love God. But we must see this in the light of the following statement that God has predestinated those whom he foreknew to be conformed to the image of his Son. The Apostle here shows that what God had in mind for his people was that they should be made like Jesus Christ. That was the thing he purposed for them from all eternity. It was with reference to that that he made the world and directs it. His moral government of the world is directed to that end. This world was made for the purpose of developing Christian character in it. The whole historical order is a redemptive order.

When Paul says that all things work together for good, in order to understand him we must see what the good is that he had in mind. He is not saying that all things work together for our comfort or ease, for our physical health, or for the gathering of material wealth. There might be a better world than this one for these things, but God is not concerned primarily about these. He is concerned, first of all, that we should become like Christ. To that end he makes all things to work.

In thinking of the idea of providence, we should consider it in relation to the development of the kingdom of God in the world as well as in relation to the redemption of the individual. The coming of the kingdom and the redemption of the individual are vitally interlinked. The salvation of each individual is a factor in

[3] See Chapter IX.

the coming of the kingdom. The kingdom comes through the saving of individuals. In studying God's purpose of redemption, we saw that it was not to be interpreted to mean that God purposed to save the individual as an isolated unit, without reference to his connections in the social and historical order to which he belongs. So we are not to take the idea of providence to mean that God works for the good of the individual without reference to his place in society or in the kingdom of God. The good of the individual is a phase of the common good. The whole of biblical history shows that God is working toward an end that includes more than the good of individuals selected out of the mass; he is working toward a universal kingdom of good as the goal of history.

Providence, then, is both general and particular. The idea of a general providence that did not include the minutest affairs and cares of life does not agree with Jesus' view of God. He says that not a sparrow falls to the ground without his notice. He clothes and feeds his people (Matt. 6: 26ff.; 10: 29ff.) We can cast all our anxiety upon him, realizing that he cares for us (1 Peter 5: 7). By keeping in constant communion with the Lord, we can live above anxiety and have the peace of God to guard our hearts and our thoughts (Phil. 4: 6, 7).

2. *Providence and faith*

What has been said will show that God's providence is not something that works in a mechanical or necessary manner. Since the good that God is working out for us is the good of redemption, our obtaining that good is conditioned upon our faith. Redemption is not something that comes to man automatically or mechanically. Redemption is a moral and spiritual matter and is morally and spiritually conditioned. The idea of providence has been too often presented as if it meant that everything that came into our lives was within itself a good independently of our attitude toward God and his providential dealings with us. This is not true. Whether or not the things that come into our lives are a blessing to us depends on how they are received. If received in the spirit of submission and trust in God, all things work together for good. Otherwise what was intended for our good may even prove to be a curse. It is to those that love God that all things work for good; and they work for good to the extent that we love God or are led to love him by the things that come to us.

The matter might be put thus: The reason that all things work together for good to the Christian is that the Christian is one in whom the dominant motive and passion of life is love to God. Since this is the dominant force in life, everything in life causes it to grow. When one is properly related to God, everything in life draws one closer to him and makes one more like him in character. Love to God is the alchemy that has the power of transmuting all the baser metals of life into the pure gold of Christian character.

This shows that the New Testament does not consider all things as good within themselves. Nor does Paul say that all these things within and of themselves work for good. His statement implies that it is because of God that all things work for good. It might be translated that God works all things for good; but whether it should be translated that way or not, that was clearly Paul's thought. The New Testament doctrine was that every detail of life, even the smallest, was under his control and he directs it all for our good.

It is God who makes all things work together for our good; and their being good to us is conditioned upon our faith and love toward him. In other words, all else becomes good to us. To the extent that one comes unto fellowship with God does he overcome evil and transmute it into a means for good.

III. Prayer

One of the most important things in the Christian life is prayer. Prayer is elemental and fundamental. The only thing we can do here is to consider in a brief way some of the more important aspects of this subject in its vital relation to the Christian life.

1. *Elements in prayer*

There are a number of elements or factors that enter into prayer—one might call them varieties of prayer. In the broadest sense of the term, prayer is communion of the soul with God; that is, it is the conscious outgoing of the soul in spiritual fellowship with God. The soul reaches out in thought and aspiration after God and usually in spoken word expresses itself to him. There is also in this communion the side of waiting in an attentive and receptive attitude on God for spiritual light, strength, and guidance. It is the recognition of the unseen Companion. It is taking definite and conscious recognition of God.

One of the specific elements in prayer as communion with God is adoration. It is the recognition of the worth and worthiness of his character and giving expression to this recognition. It is the proper response of the soul in worshipful recognition of the character of God as holy love.

There enters into prayer also the element of thanksgiving. Thanksgiving is the expression of our recognition of God as the source of our blessings and an acknowledgment of the fact that God's gifts to us put us under obligations to the Giver. In adoration we are recognizing the worth of God's character; in thanksgiving we are recognizing our indebtedness to him for his blessings to us which are an expression of his goodness of character.

As we hold fellowship with God, we become more and more conscious of our unworthiness in his sight. So confession of sin becomes a necessary element in prayer to God. Jesus laid emphasis on this factor in prayer. He taught that God blessed the publican who confessed his unworthiness rather than the self-righteous Pharisee who told the Lord about his goodness (Luke 18: 9ff.).

Petition is a prominent element in prayer. It is to be feared that with many people it is about the only factor. For some people it seems to be about all there is in prayer. It certainly should not be the only thing in prayer, but it is very naturally a prominent one. Intercession is a special form of petition. It is asking God for a blessing on someone else rather than on self. This is an outstanding feature of prayer as we have it presented in the Bible, both by precept and example. Abraham pleading for Sodom (Gen. 18: 22ff.), Moses for Israel (Ex. 32: 31ff.; Deut. 9: 25ff.), Paul for the Jews (Rom. 9: 1ff.; 10: 1), are outstanding examples.

2. *The purpose and scope of prayer*

It has been stated that prayer is communion with God. We might ask, What is the purpose of prayer? We might say in accordance with this idea that the main purpose of prayer is the right adjustment of man's relations with God. Prayer is a matter of personal relations and adjustments. It is man as a person dealing directly with God as a Person. In dealing with God, man is dealing with an unseen and spiritual reality. Prayer is a recognition of the fact that this reality is a Person, not simply an impersonal force or an abstract principle. Mrs. Eddy says that God is principle.[4] God is more than principle. He is a Person. And prayer is direct dealing on man's part with this supreme spiritual power.

Where there is no recognition of the personality of God, there can be no prayer in the true sense of the word. There may be meditation, reflection, but these are not prayer. There can be no adoration, thanksgiving, petition, no personal communion of any kind. The supreme thing that man needs is God himself rather than something that God can give. God is himself the supreme blessing; he is man's chief need. When God gives himself he gives all else; without God nothing else meets his need.

---

[4] *Science and Health*, pp. 107, 111, 112, 113, 115, *et al.*, edition of 1913.

About what should man pray? What constitutes a proper subject of prayer? The answer is, Anything that concerns man is a proper subject of prayer. This means that anything that is of concern to man is also of concern to God. The God and Father of our Lord Jesus Christ is interested in anything and everything that touches the lives of his human children. This does not mean that we can ask God for anything we want and get it—far from it. But it does mean that in any situation, perplexed by any problem, we may bring ourselves with our problem to God, and when we find the right personal adjustment with God, he will solve or help us to solve our problem.

Prayer is not an effort on the part of man to persuade an unwilling God to bestow some good on man; rather is it such an adjustment of man's personal relations with God as makes it possible for God to bestow a blessing he desires to bestow. It is not bringing a reluctant God into harmony with man's will; it is rather bringing man into harmony with God's will, so that God can do his highest will concerning man. This is shown in the fact that the Holy Spirit makes intercession for us. The reason for this is that we do not know how to pray as we ought (Rom. 8: 26, 27). The Spirit makes intercession for us with groanings that cannot be uttered. This intercession is not intercession apart from ours, but it is intercession in and through us. The groanings unutterable are the groanings of the human spirit possessed and moved by the Divine Spirit. The Spirit moves us to pray in accordance with the divine will, and, therefore, God answers our petitions. Man cannot pray in accordance with the divine will except as he prays under the tuition and guidance of the Divine Spirit. When man desires any good, seeks any good, accomplishes any good, he finds that God desired, sought, and accomplished that good with him, in him, and through him. God takes the initiative in all good, and prayer is no exception to the rule. In every desire of good, in every heart yearn-

ing and longing, "unuttered or expressed," God is seeking
to bring to pass his will for good to men. In prayer,
then, man is not striving against God, but striving with
God to bring to pass that which God wills should be
brought to pass.

We might sum up, then, by saying that the purpose of
prayer is that man may keep himself in fellowship with
God and thus God can work in and through man to carry
out his purpose of grace in the world. Its scope is universal in that anything that concerns us is a proper subject for prayer.

3. Conditions of answer to prayer

In one sense, there is no such thing as unanswered
prayer. Taking prayer in the sense of communion with
God, one does not commune with God and fail to get a
response from God. The very idea of communion carries with it a mutual activity on the part of God and
man; so that, if God should not respond to man's approach, there would not be communion; there would only
be an unsuccessful effort on man's part to establish communion. What man seeks, or should seek, in prayer is
not, first of all, something that God may give, but he
should seek God himself. So that, if there is prayer in
the sense of communion with God, this carries with it
the idea of a response on God's part, and this response
is God's answer to man's· approach. In this sense there
is no prayer that is not answered.

Usually, however, when men speak of unanswered
prayer, they have reference to petitionary prayer. That
is, they mean that man asks for something and does not
get what he asks for. In this sense there may be unanswered prayers. Men ask God for things they do not
get. This may be due to the fact that they ask God for
things that God in his wisdom sees best that they should
not have. He gives good things (Matt. 7: 7-11), and
we must always in asking submit to his wisdom as to
whether it is best that we should have what we ask for.

There are certain spiritual conditions, however, that

are necessary to our obtaining and maintaining communion with God. Without these there can be no conscious fellowship with God. They are conditions of obtaining our petitions of God, because they are conditions of communion with God. A number of these conditions are named in the New Testament. One of them is faith (Matt. 21: 22; James 1: 6). If one prays in faith, God grants his petition. This does not mean that one can ask for just anything and believe, and then get what he asks for. One cannot have faith except as one is drawn into spiritual unity with God. This guarantees two things: One is that one will not ask contrary to God's will; man's will will be submitted to God's. The other is that one will be under the guidance of the Spirit—and the Spirit does not lead us to trust God for something that it is not his will for us to have. Faith is a condition of successful prayer and, therefore, carries with it two other conditions—praying in accordance with the will of God (1 John 5: 14), and praying under the guidance of the Spirit (Rom. 8: 26, 27). It is stated in another way in John 14: 13. We are to pray in the name of Jesus; that is, as those who live for him, those who seek to do his work in the world, those who represent him. We can pray in his name only as we live in spiritual unity with him. In John 15: 7, this thought is presented in another way: We are to abide in Christ and have his Word abiding in us. In other places men are urged to be persistent in prayer (Luke 11: 5ff.; 18: 1ff.). But persistence is simply one evidence of faith. It is faith holding on in spite of delay and discouragement.

Whatever term is used, then, in naming the condition of successful prayer, it is always in essence the same—namely: spiritual harmony or unity with God, surrender to his will. There must be no conscious holding back of ourselves from God. If we expect him to give himself to us, there must be the completest giving of ourselves to him.

IV. The persistence of the Christian life

There is a wide difference of opinion on the question as to whether the Christian life will with certainty persist in the face of all opposition. Is it possible for the new life begotten in regeneration to perish? Can a Christian fall away and be lost?

1. *The "final perseverance of the saints"*

Let us first make clear what is involved in the doctrine usually known as the final perseverance of the saints.

This does not involve the antinomian position that, since one is in justification delivered from sin, he is, therefore, made eternally safe, no matter what he may become in character and life. This is a perversion of the truth that becomes about as great a heresy as the one which it denies. The New Testament teaching is not that a justified man is saved irrespective of what he may be in character; it is rather that the justifying and regenerating grace of God so revolutionizes his character that he can never be again what he was before. It is not that the Christian is saved whether he persists in faith or not; it is that he will persist in faith and will, therefore, attain to final salvation. The New Testament teaches that in one sense the Christian is saved when he believes (John 3: 36; Eph. 2: 8). In another sense, he is to be saved at the last day (1 Thess. 5: 8; Tit. 3: 7; 1 Peter 1: 5). This latter is usually called salvation in the eschatological sense; it is completed in the resurrection. Salvation includes everything between regeneration and resurrection. Perseverance is a condition of salvation in the eschatological sense. He that endureth to the end shall be saved (Mark 13: 13). In the Book of Revelation the emphasis is on the fact that it is the one who overcomes, who is faithful unto death, that gets the victor's crown (2: 7, 17, 26; 3: 5, 12, 21). It is sometimes said that we do not have to hold on to Christ, because he holds on to us. He does hold on to us, but we must also hold on to him. He holds us by causing us to hold to him. That is, the perseverance of the saints is based on the preservation of the saints. We persevere because he keeps. But it is not true to say that, because he keeps us, we do not need to persevere.

One mistake that is sometimes made in regard to this matter is that, when one speaks of perseverance as a condition of salvation, people immediately think of perseverance in works. That is, they think perseverance as a condition of salvation means that one is brought into saving relationship with God through faith and then put on a basis of works and from there on must earn or deserve his salvation. But it does not mean this; it means that one must persevere as he began—namely: in faith. Salvation is by grace on God's part and by faith on man's part. It is altogether of grace on God's part and altogether by faith on man's part. It begins in faith, continues in faith, and is consummated in faith. We are kept by the power of God, through faith, unto a salvation ready to be revealed in the last day (1 Peter 1: 5). God keeps us, but he keeps us through faith, not independently of faith. Man is not saved by trusting for a moment. The Christian life is a life of trust. Perseverance is not something beyond faith as a condition of salvation; it is of the nature of faith to persevere; if it does not persevere, it is not faith. To say that one must persevere to be saved is simply saying that the faith that saves is a faith that persists. If it does not persist, it does not have vitality enough to save.

2. Evidence that the regenerated will persevere

What is some of the evidence for the view that the truly regenerated man will persevere in faith to the end? Or, to put it the other way, what evidence do we have that God will keep his children to the end, that he will cause us to persevere?

(1) The life brought to us in Christ is described in many places in the New Testament as eternal life.

This at least suggests that it is enduring in its quality. Four times in John 6 Jesus sweeps everything up to the "last day" and says that in that day he will raise those that believe in him.

Remember that the doctrine as we maintain it is that God preserves the Christian by causing him to persevere in faith. In regeneration his moral nature is so revolutionized that he persists in faith in God and, therefore, in a life of righteousness. This is John's view in 1 John 3: 6-9. He says that the one who is begotten (or born) of God does not commit sin; that is, he does not live a life of sin. John says it is a moral impossibility; he cannot sin. Not that there is any external constraint laid on him; his freedom is not interfered with. But he is given a new life by faith in Christ that cannot compromise with sin and that sin can never overcome. In regeneration there is something put within a man that will never let him rest in sin; he must fight sin until it is vanquished. This is not enslavement; it is freedom. Nor does this mean that one never commits an act of sin after he becomes a Christian; it means rather that the general course of life is changed. John uses the present tense that denotes a habit of life, a constant attitude. It is this new life within, which is imperishable in its nature, that guarantees persistence in the fight on sin until sin is conquered.

(2) The fact that we are by faith brought into vital union with Christ is a guarantee that the new life will persist.

He becomes our life, our all. Because he lives, we shall live also (John 14: 19). Christ dwells in us and we in him. And he that is in us is greater than he that is in the world (1 John 4: 4). The living Christ, to whom we are united by faith, having justified us in his blood, will deliver us in the end from the wrath of God (Rom. 5: 9, 10).

(3) This doctrine is also supported by the fact of Christ's intercession for the Christian.

Just before Peter's denial of Jesus, the Master said to him: "Simon, Simon, behold, Satan asked to have you (the apostles), that he might sift you as wheat; but I made supplication for thee (the one individual), that thy faith fail not" (Luke 22: 31, 32). Here we see that Jesus made intercession for Simon individually, and his request for him was that his faith should not fail. Jesus says that, while he was in the world, he kept those that the Father gave him. He so guarded them that not one of them was lost, save the son of perdition (Judas Iscariot, who was never saved). Now, since he is going away, he prays the Father to keep them (John 17: 11-15). These two examples of prayer for his disciples may give us some idea of the kind of intercession Christ is making now on behalf of his people. The ground of our safety is the fact that Jesus is now living and active on our behalf. This is specifically expressed in the Book of Hebrews: "Wherefore also he is able to save to the uttermost them that draw near unto God through him, seeing he ever liveth to make intercession for them" (7: 25). The thought here is that he saves completely, to the end, because of his living to make intercession for those who come to God through him. His intercessory work guarantees the completeness of their salvation.

(4) Paul expresses the thought of the believer's security in a somewhat different way under the idea of the sealing of the Spirit.

Upon hearing and believing the gospel, we were sealed with the Holy Spirit of promise (Eph. 1: 13). The Holy Spirit dwelling within us is God's promise or pledge that our redemption will be completed in the resurrection of the body. In the Holy Spirit we are sealed unto the day of redemption (Eph. 4: 30). This is the meaning of Paul's expression that God has given us the earnest of the Spirit (2 Cor. 1: 22; 5: 5; Eph. 1: 14). The word translated earnest here means pledge money that one put up as a forfeit to guarantee that he would not go back on a contract or trade entered into but would carry out his part of the contract. The Holy Spirit is the Spirit dwelling within us as God's guarantee that we shall enter into the full possession of our inheritance in the redemption of our bodies. God pledges himself to complete our redemption. The Spirit not only bears witness to our present acceptance with God, but also bears witness to the fact that we are heirs of God and joint heirs with Christ (Rom. 8: 17). As heirs of God, we look forward to the time when we shall enter into possession of our full inheritance. We have the first fruits of the Spirit; that is, the Spirit as dwelling within us is a beginning, a sample, of the fuller possession that we are to have later on. This gives us that groaning within ourselves, that eternal dissatisfaction with ourselves as we are, and that eager longing for the adoption, to wit, the redemption of our bodies that will consummate our salvation. This makes our salvation a hope salvation. We hope for fuller blessings than we now enjoy, and the Spirit within is God's guarantee that we shall enter upon that fuller possession. (See Rom. 8: 23-25.)

(5) We have certain definite statements in the New Testament that cannot be explained on any other hypothesis.

We can consider only a few of the outstanding ones. Jesus says that he gives to his sheep eternal life and they shall never perish, and no one shall snatch them out of his Father's hand (John 10: 28, 29). Here the unequivocal declaration of Jesus that those to whom he gives eternal life shall never perish would be difficult to harmonize with any view that allowed a Christian to fall away and perish. Jesus says again that the one who hears his Word and believes on the One who sent him has eternal life and comes not into condemnation (John 5: 24). In Romans 8: 35-39, after Paul enumerates the things that might be thought able to separate one from the love of God, he concludes by saying that none of these shall be able to separate us from the love of God which is in Christ Jesus our Lord. Peter says that we are kept by the power of God through faith unto a salvation ready to be revealed in the last day (1 Peter 1: 5).

These passages seem clearly to affirm that God keeps those that believe in Christ and that there is no possibility of their perishing.

3. *Objections to the doctrine*

(1) One objection is that it would be inconsistent with our freedom.

But this is due to a misunderstanding. The doctrine does not say that a man is saved whether he chooses to be saved or not, but rather that his character is so revolutionized that he will certainly choose to hold on to Christ and thus be saved. To begin a life of righteousness through faith in Christ does not interfere with one's freedom: then why should we hold that the continuance of such a life interferes with freedom? If one can have faith at the time of regeneration and at the same time be free, why can he not have faith through the rest of his life and be free? If faith does not destroy one's freedom at the beginning of the Christian life, why should it be thought to do so later on? This doctrine does not hold that one must continue to be a Christian whether he desires to do so or not, but rather that his likes and dislikes will be so changed that he will choose to continue in the Christian faith.

(2) Another objection is that this doctrine encourages one to a life of sin. It is said that, if one has the assurance of final salvation, then he is at liberty to live as he pleases.

But it must be remembered that this doctrine is predicated on the presupposition that one is regenerated, and that regeneration means that one's moral nature is so renewed in the image of Christ that he can never again rest in sin. If the deepest longing of one's heart is for a life of sin, then, of course, he will live a life of sin. That is inevitable. But the fact that he longs for a life of sin is evidence that he has not been regenerated. There can be no external constraint nor fear of punishment that will keep an unrenewed man from living in sin. On the other hand, the regenerated man will conquer sin because the deepest passion of his soul is love for God and hatred of sin.

It is a misrepresentation of this doctrine to say that it means that, if one ever becomes a Christian, he is saved, no matter how he may live. One might as well say that, if one is born a white man, he will be a white man all his life, even though he should change to a Negro. If one is born a white man, he will be a white man all his life just because his changing to anything else is an impossibility. Likewise, if one is made a Christian by the power of God's regenerating grace, he remains a Christian forever, because it is a moral and spiritual impossibility ever to become anything else. It is not true, then, that God saves a regenerated man anyhow. God saves him a very particular how; and that how is that God puts within him, by virtue of his union with Christ by faith, an imperishable life. That imperishable life becomes a moral guarantee that the Christian will persevere in faith and finally conquer sin. This doctrine does not mean that we will conquer sin whether we fight it or not; rather does it mean that we have the promise of such help as to assure victory. Therefore, we fight sin with courage and hope.

(3) Another objection is that the Bible teaches the opposite doctrine popularly called "falling from grace"; that is, that one may be saved and then fall away and be lost.

Sometimes the opposing doctrine is stated as being that one must "hold out faithful" or he will be lost. But theologians of all schools grant that one must "hold out faithful"; that is, if one should cease to have faith, he would be lost. The point at issue is whether or not a truly regenerated man will cease to have faith. It is not a question as to whether persistence in faith is necessary or not; it is rather the question as to whether there is anything in God's relation to the Christian and in the nature of the new life begotten in regeneration that guarantees the persistence of the believer in faith. To cite passages in the New Testament that teach the necessity of perseverance in faith or that such perseverance is necessary to final salvation, is altogether a different thing from showing that the New Testament teaches that one may be a Christian and then fall away and be lost. With this in mind, we maintain that the passages claimed to teach apostacy would come rather under one of the following heads:

a. Passages that teach that persevering faith is necessary to final deliverance from sin. Under this head we would put such passages as Matthew 24: 13; Mark 13: 13; 1 Corinthians 15: 2; Revelation 2: 7, 11, 17, 26; 3: 5, 12, 21. Other passages of like import could be found. These show that it takes a faith of persevering, conquering power to save.

Here we must remember that a thing may be certain from the standpoint of God's purpose and yet humanly conditioned and from that point of view contingent. A good illustration of this is found in Paul's experience in the storm on his way to Rome as a prisoner (Acts 27: 14ff.). In the midst of the storm Paul told the company on the ship that God had assured him that they would all, without the loss of a man, be saved (vv. 22-25). Yet later on when the sailors were about to escape in the boat, Paul told the soldiers that, if the sailors got out in the boat, they (the soldiers) could not be saved (vv. 30-32).

The salvation of a man elected to salvation is from all eternity certain in the mind and purpose of God, yet it is conditioned upon faith; and it is conditioned upon a faith that perseveres and conquers. A man may be elected to salvation and yet his salvation conditioned upon the fact that somebody shall preach to him the gospel. One might ask: "Suppose God should elect a man to salvation and then the proper conditions not arise?" One might as well suppose any other absurdity. That assumption assumes that a set of conditions might arise that God did not know about and had not provided for. Such is the assumption that a regenerated man should not persevere in faith.

b. There are other passages where the thought probably is that perseverance in faith is evidence of regeneration and godly character. Perhaps this is the significance of John 8: 31; Heb. 3: 6, 14; 4: 14; 2 John 9. Possibly this is one of the thoughts underlying John 15: 1ff. (especially verses 6, 7).

c. This thought stated in another way means that those who have faith only in name and profession fall away and thereby manifest the superficial character of their faith. (See Matt. 13: 20, 21; Mark 4: 16, 17; 2 Peter 2: 20-22; 1 John 2: 19.)

d. There are other passages where the writer is emphasizing the lack of development in Christian character or the loss of reward for faithful service. (See 1 Cor. 3: 14, 15; Heb. 5: 12-6: 8; 2 Peter 1: 8-11.)

e. Still other passages seem to be emphasizing the danger of rejecting gospel truth on the part of the unregenerate when one knows it, especially where there has been spiritual enlightenment to understand the truth. (See Matt. 12: 43-45; Luke 11: 24-26; Heb. 10: 26-31; 2 Peter 2: 20-22; 1 John 5: 16.)

V. The growth of the Christian life

It is customary to discuss the development of the Christian life under the term sanctification. But, as already stated, the prevailing use of this term in the New Testament is to denote the initiation of the Christian life, not its development. Besides, the term sanctify (or sanctification) is only one of a number of terms used to denote the development of the Christian life. For these reasons, we prefer to use the expression growth or development of the Christian life.

1. *The need of growth*

That the new life begun in regeneration needs development would hardly seem to need proof. That this life is susceptible of growth and needs to grow is everywhere assumed in the New Testament. This is shown by some of the terms used for Christians. One of the earliest and most common designations for them was disciples. A disciple is a learner, a pupil in the school of Christ. Becoming a Christian is enrolling in the school. One must start in the elementary things and advance grade by grade. Then the Christian is sometimes called a soldier. When one enlists in the army, he must go through a course of drilling and discipline before he can become an effective soldier. Undeveloped Christians are called babes. Christian teachers sometimes rebuked these babes and manifested sorrow and disappointment because they had not made development in the Christian life (1 Cor. 3: 1ff.; Heb. 5: 12ff.). Peter exhorts Christians to grow in grace (2 Peter 3: 18).

While not many have theoretically denied the need of growth in the Christian life, yet as a practical matter it has been greatly neglected in church life, especially in those denominations that have laid emphasis on the need of conversion as a definite, conscious experience and that have, therefore, placed great stress upon public evangelism and revivals. Some other religious bodies have emphasized teaching and training to the neglect of preaching and evangelism. To get the best results, the two phases of work must go together. Those who have emphasized evangelism have seemed at times to forget that conversion was only the beginning of the Christian life. They have forgotten that the new convert who is today rejoicing in his new experience and walking on the delectable mountains may tomorrow be a prisoner in the castle of doubt or even floundering in the Slough of Despond. They have forgotten that old habits of sin must often be conquered and that the whole emotional, intellectual, and volitional life of the convert, with all his social relations and activities, needs to be brought into captivity to Christ.

2. *Foes to growth*

There are certain things that stand in the way of growth. Let us look at the opposing forces, the forces that must be overcome if any progress is to be made in the Christian life. Sometimes one is deceived by the thought that, when he becomes a Christian, all his struggles are over; but it would be nearer the truth to say that his struggles are just begun. The difference between his present and his past condition is not that he is now put beyond the need of struggle and effort; the difference is rather that now he is given a disposition that will not let him rest in sin and that makes it possible for him to overcome it. But his enemies are not dead and he must fight.

The forces to be overcome can be summed up in the three familiar words, the world, the flesh, and the devil.

By the flesh is meant human nature in its sinful disposition, out from under the dominion of the Spirit. It is unsanctified human nature. The Christian man finds that he is now two instead of one. There is the "old man" and the "new," the "flesh" and the "spirit," and between these there is ceaseless warfare. The flesh has been crucified, but it must be put to death daily. This must be done until the life on earth is over. The flesh cannot be put to death once for all so that it does not need to be done again. And unless the flesh is kept in subjection, there can be no progress in the Christian life. Progress in the Christian life depends upon the overcoming of those impulses and tendencies in one's life that oppose the will of God.

But opposition to progress in the Christian life comes not only from within but also from without. The world sums up all those forces operative in human society around us that stand opposed to the will of God. The general currents of life around us are set against the development of true spirituality. Jesus did not find a very congenial atmosphere when he was on earth, and he did not encourage his disciples to expect that they would.

On the other hand, he warned them that they would be treated as he had been (Matt. 10: 24ff.). Not everybody would receive them and their message (Luke 10: 16). Woe unto them when all men should speak well of them (Luke 6: 26). Paul says that the man who lives a godly life shall suffer persecution (2 Tim. 3: 12). Peter exhorts his hearers to save themselves from a crooked generation (Acts 2: 40). John regards the world as evil and perishing (1 John 2: 15-17). But the Christian has within him a power that enables him to overcome the world (1 John 4: 4; 5: 4, 5).

The devil is the prince of this world (John 12: 31; 14: 30). He is the one who inspires and directs all these evil forces within and without and uses them to tear down Christian character. He delights to test God's people. He puts them in his sieve and shakes them up when he can (Luke 22: 31ff.). But his power is limited. He can only test God's people as he is given permission and to the extent that he is permitted (Job 1: 12; Luke 22: 31). Only the chaff is destroyed by his sifting, the wheat is preserved. The Christian should resist the devil and he will flee (James 4: 7). We can overcome him in the blood of Jesus and the word of our testimony (Rev. 12: 11).

While these are the foes of the spiritual life and will hinder the development of that life unless we overcome them, yet if we conquer these foes, they can by being overcome be made to contribute to our spiritual life by struggling against these enemies and by the grace of God overcoming them.

3. *The means of growth*

By the means of growth we intend those agencies and forces that contribute directly to our advancement in the Christian life. These are sometimes spoken of as means of grace. They include all those means or agencies by which we become familiar with the principles of the gospel of Christ and more fully appropriate that gospel. They are the same as the means by which we are brought into saving contact with the gospel, such as the church, the ministry, the ordinances, the Bible, prayer, personal influence, and testimony.

This does not signify that any of these things within themselves have the power to augment the spiritual life. They no more have the power to do that than they have the power at first to regenerate or make alive. It is the power of God alone that can regenerate or develop the regenerate life. This idea is suggested by the expression, "means of grace." These things are means by which we are enabled to appropriate the grace of God. Our development in the spiritual life is just as much a matter of grace as our justification or regeneration. We can no more make ourselves grow than we can make ourselves alive at first. They are equally the work of God and equally a work of grace. Paul, speaking of his efficiency in the Christian life, says, "By the grace of God I am what I am" (1 Cor. 15: 10).

4. *The condition of growth*

The condition of growth is the same as the condition of entrance upon the Christian life—namely: repentance and faith; or, using faith as inclusive of repentance, we might say it is faith alone. There must be continued and increasing repudiation of sin and opposition to it in our lives and continued and increasing dependence on Christ. Since our development in the Christian life is a work of grace on God's part, it must be a matter of faith on our part by which we appropriate his grace. To put it another way, our growth in the Christian life is the growth of our faith. The increase of faith is the growth of the divine life within us. This is due to the fact that faith is the means or condition of our union with Christ. This does not mean that faith is the only Christian grace, but it means that faith is the means of our fellowship with Christ by which these other graces are developed. Faith is the root principle of the Christian life. It is the germinal grace. Out of it grow all the other graces.

There must be struggle on our part against evil. Faith must not only trust and rest in the Lord; it must also agonize in its contention against sin and evil. There is the rest of faith, but there is also the struggle of faith. The statement is sometimes made to the effect that one cannot any more make himself grow spiritually than he can cause himself to grow physically; that all one can do is to conform to the laws of growth and he will naturally grow without effort on his part. It is true that all Christian development is the work of God and that we grow by conforming to the laws of growth. But there is a difference between physical and spiritual development and the laws governing each. And one of the laws of spiritual development is that there must be struggle against evil in oneself and in the world around him. There must be consecrated service to God and man and striving after holiness. "Blessed are they that hunger and thirst after righteousness: for they shall be filled" (Matt. 5: 6). But the hungering and thirsting after righteousness must be more than a passing desire; it must be the deepest passion of the soul; it must be such a passion of the soul as to control and direct the energies and activities of life. God will give to one all the righteousness he wants; but he must want it; must want it so that he would fight for it, even die for it. Righteousness of character is no easily won achievement. The most difficult thing in the world is to be righteous. One must be willing to wade through the fires of hell to attain it.

But some one asks, "Is not righteousness the gift of God's grace?" Yes, it is. But God can give only as we receive, only as we attain. The experience of regeneration is no easy-going transaction in which the soul is passively quickened into life; it is the supreme crisis of the soul in which the soul agonizes after God and righteousness and renounces forever sin and Satan. And the progressive sanctification of the life or growth in grace is of the same nature. God makes the soul righteous by creating this passion for righteousness in the soul. He gives, but he gives through our effort. Our achievement is his bestowal. God feeds the birds, but he feeds them through their efforts. God gives the farmer his harvest, but he does so through the farmer's planting and cultivation of the soil and his toil in gathering the harvest. He gives a man an education, but he gives it through years of toil and self-denying study. He gives the musician his skill in winning music from his instrument, but he does so through study and practice. We thank him daily for bread which he gives by the labor of brain and hand. So he gives righteousness of character, but he gives it through struggle and effort. Faith receives what God gives, and God gives what faith achieves.

5. *The perfection theory of growth*

In different forms there has arisen in Christian history the theory that man may attain perfection in this life. Sometimes it is held that this is attained in a great crisis. This crisis has sometimes been spoken of as a second work of grace. This work is spoken of as sanctification over against the first work of grace in regeneration or justification. People are exhorted to seek this experience as definitely as they sought the experience of regeneration. According to this theory, "carnal" Christians or "babes" in Christ are in a moment made into "spiritual" Christians.

There are a number of serious objections to this view. One is that it tends to produce in those holding it a self-satisfied spirit and a pharisaical attitude toward others. They look upon other Christians as "babes" and as "carnal." It is never a good indication for one to claim to be free from sin. The closer one gets to God, the less likely is he to claim to be sinless.

Again, those who hold this view usually lower the standard of righteousness. By being free from sin they often mean free from deliberate and conscious acts of transgression. Or they may mean by Christian perfection a heart of love toward God and a sincere purpose to serve him and do his will. They rarely go so far as to claim that all promptings and tendencies toward evil are taken out of one's nature. So when one comes to discuss perfection, it would be necessary for him, first, to define what he means by perfection. Most anyone could reach a standard of perfection if we would let him bring the standard of perfection down low enough. Any man could reach the stars if he could bring the stars near enough to the earth. Those who hold this view use such words as "holiness" and "sanctify" with a good deal of glibness and freedom.

This theory is also wrong with reference to its view of Christian growth. Christians do not attain to maturity at one bound. Sin is not completely eradicated from the nature of man at a stroke. One cannot help but feel that those who hold this view do not see as they ought the radical nature of sin and do not realize its stubborn hold upon man.

This theory does not agree with the teaching of the Bible. There are places where men are spoken of as perfect, such as Noah and Job (Gen. 6: 9; Job 1: 1). Men were commanded to be perfect (Gen. 17: 1; Deut. 18: 13). The word translated "perfect" here probably means blameless, free from fault, whole-hearted, sincere—using all these terms in a relative, not an absolute sense. A perfect man was a full-grown, well-developed, sincere servant of God. (See in N. T. 1 Cor. 2: 6; Eph. 4: 13; Phil. 3: 15; Heb. 5: 14; 6: 1. In some of these passages the Greek word is translated "perfect," in others, "full-grown.") The pure in heart shall see God (Matt. 5: 8), and without sanctification no man shall see him (Heb. 12: 14); but we are not to conclude that perfect purity of heart or perfect holiness is to be attained at one leap. John describes the regenerated man as one who does not commit sin, but practices righteousness (1 John 2: 29; 3: 6-9). This evidently does not mean that the regenerated man never commits an act of sin; much less does it mean that the nature or disposition to sin is entirely removed in regeneration. John uses here the present tense of the verb, as elsewhere, to denote a continuous or habitual course of conduct, a fixed or settled tendency of life. Besides, whatever he means by "sinneth not" and "doeth no sin" he affirms as true of every regenerated man, not of Christians who have been "sanctified" in a second work of grace. If he means by these expressions absolute sinlessness, then he affirms that all Christians are sinless. That would be affirming too much, even for the modern "sanctificationist" or the most enthusiastic "holy-roller."

Besides, the same author says: "If we say that we have no sin, we deceive ourselves, and the truth is not in us" (1 John 1: 8). Here he is evidently speaking of Christians and from a Christian point of view. It is hardly probable that he would affirm here that no man can claim to be free from sin, and then in the third chapter affirm that all Christians are sinless.

Paul's statement in Philippians 3 is instructive on this point. He does not count that he has obtained or been made perfect (verse 12). He does not count that he has laid hold (verse 13). But he stretches forward with all his might, striving to lay hold of that for which Christ has laid hold of him (verses 12-14). He implies that the "perfect" or full-grown Christian is the one who recognizes his imperfection. The one who claims to be sinless, therefore, claims more than Paul could claim. But he does not thereby show himself a man of wisdom, but rather advertises himself as one who is lacking in spiritual discernment.

6. *The goal of development*

The goal or standard toward which we are to strive is nothing less than that of a perfect Christian character. According to the meaning of the law in its spiritual content, this would demand that one love God with all the powers of his being and his neighbor as himself (Mark 12: 29-31). Christ himself was the embodiment and revelation of what God would have man to be. To be like Christ is, therefore, the goal of the Christian's ambition. Or, as Jesus puts it in Matthew 5: 48, we are to strive to be as perfect in character as the Heavenly Father himself is perfect. Here is an ideal that remains as a constant challenge to higher endeavor and attainment in the Christian life. No matter what heights of attainment in character one may climb, he finds other heights still towering above him and challenging him to yet greater achievements. To attain these we must do more than sing, "Lord, plant my feet on higher ground"; we must also climb.

Protestant theology has usually held that the complete purification of the soul from sin was accomplished at death when the soul passed into the presence of the Lord and beheld him in beatific vision. While it might be difficult to find scriptural statements that clearly and explicitly teach this, yet it seems to be thoroughly in harmony with scriptural principles and a fair inference from what is taught about the soul's passing into his presence at death. So far as the complete transformation of soul and body is concerned, that seems to be put at the final appearing of Christ when we shall see him as he is (1 John 3: 2). There is nothing, however, in this to forbid the idea that we shall go on growing in knowledge and character even throughout the endless ages.

THE CHURCH

CHAPTER XII

THE CHURCH

I. MEMBERSHIP OF THE CHURCH

    1. A first essential

    2. Baptism a qualification

    3. A voluntary matter

II. OFFICERS OF THE CHURCH

    1. Apostles, prophets, evangelists, and teachers

    2. Pastors

    3. Deacons

    4. Other officers

III. GOVERNMENT OF THE CHURCH

    1. Forms of church government

    2. Reasons for a democratic organization

    3. Importance of the doctrine

IV. THE MISSION OF THE CHURCH

    1. Fellowship and upbuilding of members

    2. Spread of gospel at home and abroad

    3. Promotion of righteousness among men

    4. Co-operative efforts

CHAPTER XII

THE CHURCH

In speaking of a Christian church, we do not mean simply a religious organization, as, for instance, when people speak of "the Jewish church." Nor do we mean an organization covering a large scope of territory, such as a nation or a state in the United States. We use the term rather in an institutional sense, as we speak of the home or the state as institutions. Nor are we concerned here with the more general use of the term church such as we find in Ephesians 5: 22-33 and in a few other places in the New Testament. The only ecclesiastical organization found in the New Testament was that of a local church.

The church is not a pre-Christian or extra-Christian institution. It grew out of the redemptive mission and work of Jesus Christ. The Christian church, therefore, should not be identified with the Old Testament order of things.

The first church in the New Testament seems to have been a growth. Perhaps we could not designate any particular time as the day of its organization or "setting up." Jesus gathered around him a group, including the apostles and others, with a more or less definite organization. After his ascension, one hundred and twenty of these met together in Jerusalem (Acts 1: 15) until the coming of the Spirit, when a great multitude was added to them. Officers were added later on, and perhaps other features of organization.

I. Membership of the church

One of the most important questions concerning the church is the question as to who should belong to it. Who should be members of the church?

1. *A first essential*

Only those should be received into church membership who give credible evidence that they have received Christ as Saviour and Lord. Becoming a Christian is a voluntary matter, and only Christians should be members of the church. This grows out of the fact that the church is a Christian institution. Doctor Hodge identifies the Christian church with the commonwealth of Israel.[1] If this idea were carried out to its logical conclusions, it would destroy the distinctiveness of Christianity as a spiritual religion and make it a state religion like the Judaism of the Old Testament.

That the church should be composed of the regenerate only, the New Testament makes clear. Concerning that original one hundred and twenty names that constituted the members of the church at Jerusalem, doubtless most of them had been the personal disciples of Jesus. They were all evidently followers of his or they would not have adhered to the company of his followers in such circumstances. As for those who were added to them, as revealed in the Acts, in practically every case they are described in such a way as to make it clear that they voluntarily received the Word of the gospel, repented of their sins, and believed in Christ as Saviour (Acts 2: 41, 42, 47; 4: 4; 13: 48, 52; 16: 32-34, et al). And there is no evidence whatever to indicate that the contrary was true of any of them. Paul in writing to the churches always addresses them as saints, faithful in Christ, and in such other terms as to leave no doubt that they were all professing Christians (Rom. 1: 7; 6: 1ff.; 1 Cor. 1: 1, 2; 2 Cor. 1: 1).

Moreover, the nature and mission of the church carries with it the view that only regenerate people should belong to the church. The church is a spiritual organization; it is the body of Christ (Rom. 12: 4, 5; 1 Cor. 12: 12ff.). Only those, therefore, who are animated by his life should be members of the body.

---

[1] *Systematic Theology*, Vol. III, pp. 548, 549.

The work of the church is spiritual. It has a spiritual function. To do this work it must be a spiritual body. An unregenerated church cannot be the means of conveying the renewing grace of God to an unregenerate society around it.

Moreover, if regeneration is an absolute necessity to Christian character and regeneration depends on the voluntary acceptance of the gospel, then for a child to be reared in the church, or an adult to be received into the church without regeneration is a perilous thing. The inevitable tendency of such a procedure is to encourage the unregenerate church member to think that somehow his church membership makes him a Christian and turns him in his mind away from the necessity of definitely repenting of sin and trusting in Christ for salvation.

Doctor Hodge objects to the doctrine of a regenerated church membership on the ground that man cannot tell with certainty who is regenerated and who is not.[2] We do not maintain that the ideal in the matter can be perfectly attained. Of course, there have been some unregenerated people in the churches and always will be, no doubt, but this does not prove the doctrine wrong. It only proves the necessity of guarding the more carefully the membership of the churches. This argument is of the same nature as the one by the anti-prohibitionists against the prohibition of the liquor traffic to the effect that prohibition could not be enforced. The law cannot be perfectly enforced, but neither can any other. If a regenerated church membership is the ideal, then we should maintain it as nearly as possible. And we maintain that the authority of New Testament teaching and the very nature of the church as a Christian institution commits us to the view that only the regenerate should be members of the church.

2. Baptism a qualification

Baptism is a necessary qualification for church membership. This is shown in Paul's argument in Romans

---

[2] See previous reference to *Systematic Theology*.

6: 1ff. in which he argues on the assumption that all Christians have been baptized. This statement would be accepted with practical unanimity among all Christian denominations. Perhaps the Quakers and some other minor exceptions might be found. Of course, there would be serious division when it came to the questions of who should be baptized and what constituted baptism. These questions will be discussed in the next chapter. The question as to who should be baptized will have an important bearing on the question of a regenerate church membership, as discussed in the preceding section.

3. *A voluntary matter*

What has been said, and what will be said later on in regard to the qualifications for baptism, make it evident that church membership is always a voluntary matter. There can be no such thing as becoming a member of Christ's church by being born into a certain family or nation. One became a member of the Jewish nation by natural birth, and one becomes today a member of a certain family or nation that way. But one cannot become a member of the church of Christ that way. Nor can one come into the church by any ceremony performed by proxy or through vows taken on one's behalf by someone else. Every man must hear, repent, believe, be baptized, and join the church for himself. Becoming a Christian is a matter of personal choice, and so is every Christian duty; and where personal choice is absent, no act can have moral or religious value.

II. Officers of the church

Practically every organization must have officers. Evidently the churches of the New Testament had them. The question of the officers of the church, however, is not a matter so vitally related to its existence as the question discussed in the preceding division concerning the qualifications of its members nor as the ones yet to be discussed concerning the form of its government and the mission of the church. A church might exist and perform its functions without officers, but it could not exist as a church if its members were unregenerate. It would then cease to possess the Spirit of Christ and would necessarily cease to function as his body. Yet a church cannot do its best work without officers.

1. *Apostles, prophets, evangelists, and teachers*[3] (1 Cor. 12: 28, 29; Eph. 4: 11).

These officials are mentioned in the New Testament, but do not seem to have been officers of local churches. The Apostles evidently possessed a high degree of authority among the early churches, because of their relation to Christ and their apostolic call and mission (Mark 3: 13ff; Acts 1: 21ff.). They might be called the authentic founders and guides of the early churches. Their peculiar relation to Christ made it impossible for them to have any successors.

The prophets were probably functionaries rather than officials; that is, prophecy was speaking forth a message under the direct inspiration of the Spirit. It was a gift, more or less temporary in its nature, that might be given either to an official or to others in the church. It is likely, therefore, that there was no official prophetic class, but a prophetic gift conferred at special times upon certain Christians.

Some have thought that the evangelists spoken of in the New Testament were more like our modern missionaries. As to teaching, it was probably a function performed by pastors and others. A pastor was to be "apt to teach" as a qualification (1 Tim. 3: 2). Pastors and teachers are mentioned together by Paul in such a way as to make the impression that they were not separate officers but two functions of one office (Eph. 4: 11). No doubt teaching was a very important function in the New Testament churches, and doubtless was one of the duties of the pastors. But there may have been also

---

[3]On this section, Cf. Dargan's *Ecclesiology*.

persons who had this as their special function in the churches.

2. *Pastors*

The most significant officer in the New Testament as connected with a local church was that of pastor. There are three terms used in the New Testament for that office—pastor, elder, and bishop. In Acts 20, in the account of Paul's meeting with the elders of the church at Ephesus, in verse 17, they are called "elders," while in verse 28 Paul calls them "bishops" (AS). The verb translated "feed" in verse 28 means to tend as a shepherd, act as shepherd. This is the verb corresponding to the noun that is translated "pastor." So here in one passage, the same men are called "elders" and "bishops" and they are exhorted to "pastor" the flock. Again, in Titus 1: 5, 7, Paul uses the terms "elders" and "bishops" to apply to the same office. In 1 Peter 5: 1, 2, Peter addresses the "elders," and exhorts them to "pastor" or "shepherd" the flock.[4]

The duties of the pastors are not defined in detail in the New Testament. Evidently they were intended to exercise general oversight in spiritual matters, teach their people, and guide in all the activities of the church. Their character and spiritual attainments must be such as to qualify them for such leadership (1 Tim. 3: 1ff.; Titus 1: 5ff.; 1 Peter 5: 1ff.).

3. *Deacons*

Deacons were another class of officers in the churches of the New Testament. The choosing of the seven in Acts 6 is usually considered the origin of the office of deacon. They are not called deacons, however, in that chapter, and there is no positive proof that this was the origin of that office.

The qualifications of deacons were to be much the same as those of pastors or bishops (1 Tim. 3: 8ff.). Not much is said to throw light on their duties or functions,

[4]See Dargan, pp. 87, 88.

but it is usually considered that they should have charge of the financial or business affairs of the church. It is evident from their qualifications, however, that they were to perform their duties for spiritual purposes or ends. It follows, therefore, that no man should be made a deacon merely because he is a good business man. Doubtless he should have business ability, but he should also have the highest moral and spiritual qualities as well.

4. *Other officers*

While pastors and deacons are the only officers of a local church clearly referred to in the New Testament, we cannot be sure that the churches had no others. Certain it is that churches since then, even those claiming to follow most closely the New Testament, have had various other officers; such as clerk, treasurer, trustee, Sunday school superintendent, and so forth. On what ground can this be justified? On the ground of necessity. The appointment or election of such officers comes within the range of method, as Doctor Gambrell would say, where we are to use common sense and judgment in carrying out the task committed to us by our Saviour and Lord. The commission given to us justifies us in using any means or adopting any methods that are consistent with the principles of the gospel and the fundamentals of ecclesiology, such as a regenerate church membership and a democratic organization of the church. This principle would not justify us in the appointment of "bishops" in the modern acceptation of the term, for this would interfere with a democratic organization of the church (soon to be discussed) and the spiritual freedom of the children of God, and would, therefore, be anti-Christian in principle.

III. Government of the church

Under what form of government should the affairs of the church be managed?

1. *Different forms of church government*

In general, there are about four different forms of church government: the monarchical, in which the ultimate authority is in the hands of one man, as the Roman Catholic Church with the pope of Rome as its head; the episcopal, in which the church is governed by a college or a body of bishops; the presbyterial, in which the local church is governed by elders, with higher courts of appeal; and the democratic, in which the local congregation is self-governing, and in which there is no body outside to which the local congregation is responsible with reference to its own internal affairs. Of course, there are many modifications and combinations of these four general types of organization.

Baptists are democratic in their church government. Each local church is self-governing and independent in the management of its affairs. They apply the term "church" to no organization including more than the local congregation, and regard all boards, associations, and conventions simply as bodies organized for convenience in co-operative work and advice with reference to matters of interest common to the churches.

2. *Why the church should be democratic in organization*

Several reasons might be given why the church should be organized in a democratic manner.

First, the New Testament churches were organized on this plan. There is no evidence that there were any "ruling elders," or "bishops," or any other official class in the New Testament that managed the affairs of the churches. In the case of a difficulty between brethren, as recorded in Matthew 18, Jesus makes the church the court of last appeal.

In the sixth chapter of Acts, the apostles asked the multitude to "look out" seven men whom they should appoint over the distribution of the church's help to the widows; and the saying pleased the "whole multitude," and they (the multitude) chose the seven. In Acts 15, when the dispute arose about whether Gentile converts should be required to keep the law, the "whole church" (verse 22) decided the matter under the leadership and advice of the apostles.

In 1 Corinthians 5, Paul gives advice to the church at Corinth about how to deal with the incestuous man. He does not give the church any order after the manner of a modern bishop. In fact, Paul always advised, exhorted, instructed the churches that he dealt with. He claimed apostolic authority against the assaults of his adversaries; but he did not seem to think that even apostolic authority authorized him to exercise coercion in dealing with a church. And if Paul did not have the right to give orders to churches, we believe no man since has had such a right.

Moreover, we ground this doctrine of a democratic church on some fundamental principles in the Christian religion, as well as on New Testament practice and precept.

One of these is the absolute Lordship of Christ. He claimed to be the Lord of all men. To recognize his lordship in the spiritual realm is inconsistent with recognizing the authority of priest or bishop or pope in the realm of religion. The Christian cannot recognize any master in the spiritual realm, in the realm of conscience, without to that extent denying the Lordship of Jesus. This necessarily makes the church a democratic organization.

Again, the doctrine of salvation by grace through faith carries with it a democratic organization of the church. When men recognize themselves as hopeless, helpless, sinners saved by grace, all artificial distinctions among them will melt away. There will be then no Jew and Gentile, bond nor free, priest, bishop nor pope, no clergy and laity. Historically, the departure from a democratic organization of the church came hand in hand with a change that substituted a priestly mediation of salvation through "sacraments" for salvation by grace through faith. Salvation mediated by priests goes with and necessitates the rule of the priestly class, but salvation by grace implies a democratic church.

Another thing that would indicate that the church should be a democratic body is the fact that the Holy Spirit dwells in every Christian to make known the will of Christ, not simply in the official class of the church. There is no class in the church that has a monopoly on the indwelling Spirit of God. The purpose of the Spirit's indwelling is to make Christ's will effective in the church and through the church in the world. But since the Spirit dwells in all believers, every believer should have the privilege of making known the will of Christ as the Spirit has revealed it to him. An episcopal government or government by any official class is based on the assumption that the Spirit resides in a special way in the bishops or the clergy or the elders. A democratic government of the church is based on the assumption that the Spirit dwells in all believers, and that a man's understanding of the will of God is limited by his spiritual perception, not by his official position. In a democratic organization of the church, bishops do not constitute the church, but the bishop simply performs certain functions for the congregation by appointment of the congregation. All these functions—preaching, administering the ordinances, and so on—are the functions of the whole congregation of believers, not of official clergymen.

3. *Importance of the doctrine*

We believe that what has been said will justify the position that the question of democratic organization of the church is not a question of small moment. We believe that it is essential to a true church. No other form of organization is consistent with a spiritual religion, and any other form of organization tends towards a formal and sacramental religion. To the extent that the church departs from a democratic organization and government, to that extent does it cease to be Christian in its principles and life.

IV. The mission of the church

The mission of the church corresponds to that of the individual Christian as set out in the last chapter. We may sum up the mission of the church as follows:

1. *Fellowship and mutual upbuilding of the members*

Paul laid great stress on the idea of fellowship among Christians and on the obligation of Christians so to conduct themselves as to build up interest in the Christian life. Especially did he recognize the duty of the stronger to help the weaker brethren in their trials and temptations. Mutual love and helpfulness should be the controlling power in the church. He also recognized that sometimes it was necessary for unruly and disorderly members to be expelled from the body (1 Cor. 5: 1ff. See also Matt. 18: 15ff.).

2. *The spread of the gospel at home and abroad*

One of the primary functions of the church is to give the gospel to the world. The church of Christ is to find its marching orders in his commission to preach the gospel to the whole world. Any organization claiming to be a church is false to Christ that is not missionary in spirit and in practice.

3. *The promotion of righteousness among men*

The church of Christ should promote social righteousness and human welfare in all spheres of life. Christ was devoted to human welfare—physical, moral, and spiritual. Individual churches, groups of individual Christians or groups of churches should foster movements and institutions for the promotion of human welfare. Orphans' homes, hospitals, Christian schools, and other benevolent institutions may and should be promoted to help men. These are often an effective embodiment and manifestation of the Spirit of Christ. The people of Christ cannot afford to be indifferent toward any movement for social betterment. Economic, political, and social questions are never settled until settled on Christian principles.

There are some movements and organizations, however, which are benevolent in their aim, with which Christians as individuals may identify themselves, with which churches as such should not. Christ's churches must remember that their function is primarily spiritual and that they cannot afford to identify themselves with movements that tend to be partisan in their character.

4. *Co-operative efforts*

Churches may sometimes best carry out their mission by combination of efforts. Such combinations have been made in the past for purposes of encouragement and fellowship and also for practical ends in doing missionary and benevolent work. Mission boards, associations, and conventions of all kinds represent such co-operative effort on the part of individual Christians and churches.

In all such movements it should be remembered that the voluntary principle should be maintained for both the individual and the church, and the independence of the local churches should be strictly safeguarded.

THE ORDINANCES

CHAPTER XIII

THE ORDINANCES

I. BAPTISM

  1. Purpose of baptism
    (1) Not for salvation
    (2) Symbol of salvation
    (3) Salvation conditioned on faith in Christ
    (4) Prophecy of resurrection
  2. Act of baptism
    (1) New Testament descriptions suggest immersion
    (2) Greek words used mean immersion
    (3) Meaning of the ordinance conforms to immersion
  3. Candidate for baptism
  4. The administrator of baptism

II. THE LORD'S SUPPER

  1. Meaning of the Supper
  2. "Close communion"

III. THE PERPETUITY OF THE ORDINANCES

CHAPTER XIII

THE ORDINANCES

Christ instituted two ceremonial ordinances and committed them to his people for perpetual observance—baptism and the Lord's Supper. These two ceremonies are pictorial representations of the fundamental facts of the gospel and of our salvation through the gospel. Over against this view is the view of the Roman Catholic Church that these two ordinances, with five others, are "sacraments" that convey grace to the participant. Underlying the multiplication of "sacraments" is the assumption that nothing is "holy" or good except as it is consecrated and made so by the "Holy Church." Even the ground in which the body is buried is unholy until consecrated by the Church (the Roman Church, of course).

One reason, perhaps the fundamental reason, that Christians have recognized only baptism and the Lord's Supper as gospel ordinances is because other ceremonies that have been proposed do not have essential relation to the gospel. These two do. They were instituted by Christ, for a very obvious reason. That reason is that they are adapted to set forth the facts of the gospel and our experience of salvation through grace.

I. Baptism

Jesus submitted to baptism at the hands of John (Mark 1: 9-11), administered the ordinance (through his disciples), and commanded his people to do so as part of their work to the end of the age (Matt. 28: 19). It is, therefore, worthy of our careful consideration.

1. *The purpose of baptism*

One of the most important considerations concerning this ordinance is its meaning or significance. We will consider this first. What is the purpose of the administration of this ordinance?

(1) Baptism does not save, nor does it help to save. It is not a condition of salvation, nor of the remission of sins. It does not convey grace; in the historical significance of the term, therefore, it is not a "sacrament."

The Roman Catholic Church (with some others) holds that in the act of baptism the soul is regenerated, that one's sins, actual and original, are remitted. We are actually and literally baptized into Christ and our sins are actually washed away. There is, therefore, no salvation without baptism.

The Disciples hold a somewhat similar position. They do not hold that baptism within itself regenerates or saves, but that it is the culmination or climax of the regenerating process; that baptism is one of the conditions of the remission of sins; that it is for the remission of sins in the sense that one submits to baptism for the purpose of obtaining the remission of sins.

Although these two positions are not exactly the same, they are enough alike that we can discuss them together, each one holding in general that baptism is essential to salvation.

There are a number of passages in the New Testament that are used to prove that baptism is necessary to salvation. One is Mark 16: 16, where Jesus tells his disciples: "He that believeth and is baptized shall be saved; he that disbelieveth shall be condemned." Another is John 3: 5, where Jesus tells Nicodemus that one cannot enter into the kingdom of God unless he be born of water and the Spirit, and the similar statement of Paul in Titus 3: 5, where he speaks of the washing of regeneration and renewing of the Holy Spirit. Then there is Peter's statement recorded in Acts 2: 38, exhorting the people to "repent, and be baptized every one of you in the name

of Jesus Christ for (Gk. *eis*, into) the remission of sins."
Also we have the statement of Ananaias in Acts 22: 16
saying to Saul, "Arise, and be baptized, and wash away
thy sins." Paul also in Romans 6: 1-4, speaks of our
being baptized into Christ and into his death.

As to Mark 16: 16, it may be said that the textual evidence is against its genuineness, and it would not, therefore, be safe to quote it as a genuine part of Mark's Gospel. Furthermore, it is to be noted that when the matter
is put negatively it is said that he that believeth not shall
be condemned, as if faith were the deciding factor, rather
than baptism.

John 3: 5 and Titus 3: 5 probably do not refer to baptism at all, but rather to the cleansing power of God's
Spirit in regeneration, which is symbolized in baptism.
But if they be taken as referring to baptism, the remark
that follows about the other passages would apply equally to them.

As to the other passages, the following may be said:
They may be interpreted in one of two ways—either literally or symbolically. For instance, Acts 2: 38 means
literally that one is baptized into the remission of sins,
or symbolically he is so baptized. Paul, in Romans 6: 3,
means that either literally or symbolically one is baptized into Christ and into his death. Acts 22: 16 means
that either literally or symbolically, in a picture, one's
sins are washed away. And the same thing is true of
every other passage in the New Testament that is
claimed to teach the idea that baptism saves or is a condition of salvation. Between these two methods of interpreting these passages there is no logical standing
ground. There can be no half-way position. That is the
weakness of the position of the Disciples. It tries to
make baptism a condition of salvation without holding
with the Catholics that baptism actually and literally
washes away sins.

As a matter of fact, when one thinks about it, he
recognizes that the word into (*eis* in Greek) implies mo-

tion spatially when meant literally; but to talk about being literally baptized into Christ, into his death, or into the remission of sins is to talk nonsense. But one must either hold that or grant that being baptized into the remission of sins, into Christ, or into his death, is figurative language. One might baptize another literally into the Jordan as John baptized Jesus (Mark 1: 9, AS, margin); but one cannot baptize another literally into Christ, or his death, or the remission of sins, because these are spiritual and not physical or spatial realities for us. To try to mix the two and hold that one by being spatially (i. e., literally) baptized into water can be thereby baptized spiritually into Christ is to try to identify two things that are so fundamentally different that they cannot be identified. The spatial may picture, or represent, or symbolize the spiritual, but the two cannot be identified. To identify the spatial and the spiritual is to nullify or destroy the spiritual. That is exactly what Romanism has done by trying to identify spiritual realities with the spatial and historical forms of religion.

Moreover, to interpret these passages literally, i. e., in such a way as to make baptism a condition of salvation, is to make the New Testament fundamentally a self-contradictory book. This would introduce an inconsistency into the very heart of its doctrine of salvation. This is evident if we look at the numerous passages in the New Testament where it is plainly taught that the only conditions of salvation are spiritual. It is abundantly set forth in the New Testament that repentance and faith are the only conditions of salvation—conditions that are primarily and only spiritual. Salvation is a spiritual transaction and depends on spiritual conditions alone. And to make salvation depend on any outward ceremony or act is to destroy the nature of Christianity as a spiritual religion. It is to make God a "grand master of red tape." It is to make him an arbitrary God. God is not arbitrary. He has not arbitrarily "prescribed" any conditions of salvation. The only conditions of salvation are the ones necessarily involved in the relations of a God of grace to a sinner whom he would save from sin.

From what has been said, it follows that the conditions of salvation are universal and unchangeable. God did not save people one way in Old Testament times and another way in New Testament times. Salvation has always been by grace on God's part and by faith on man's part. God saved Abraham by faith before the law was given. Grace antedates law, therefore, in God's dealings with man (i. e., the Old Testament or Mosaic law) (Romans 4: 9ff. Gal. 3: 15ff.). No man was ever saved by keeping the law.

Nor is it true that the "law of pardon" was established on the day of Pentecost, including baptism as a condition. On that assumption, Jesus never told men himself how to get into the kingdom of God, nor how to be saved. Such passages as John 1: 12; 3: 14, 15, 16, 18, 36; 5: 24, and many others promising salvation on the sole condition of faith in Christ could not be claimed by us as valid today. On such a method of interpretation, the fact that Jesus saved the paralytic man (Mark 2: 5), the sinful woman (Luke 7: 47, 48), and the thief on the Cross (Luke 23: 42, 43) would offer to sinners today no encouragement to believe that they, too, might be saved simply by trusting the Saviour's grace. Such a method of interpreting the Scriptures makes them as much of a "crazy-quilt" patchwork as does modern radical criticism. This does not mean that we are not to recognize a progressive unfolding of a plan for the race on God's part. But this plan as progressively unfolded is a unitary plan, and its fundamental idea is salvation by grace through faith. God is not a whimsical God, jumping from one plan to another and constantly reversing himself.

Besides, if we examine the New Testament record from Pentecost on, salvation by faith is just as consistently set forth after Pentecost as before. An examination of the following passages makes that perfectly clear: Acts 10: 43; 13: 38, 39; 16: 31; Romans 1: 16; Galatians 3: 26; Ephesians 2: 8. Many others are just as decisive. The case of Cornelius and his company is decisive, as we have the record in Acts 10: 34ff. It is there made as clear as words can make it that the Holy Spirit fell on them in a great demonstration before one word was said about their being baptized (44-48).

So we maintain that the conditions of salvation have never been changed. No man was ever saved without faith; no man ever will be. It is a moral impossibility. Men have been saved without baptism, in Old Testament times and in New Testament times, before Pentecost and since, Jews and Gentile. Therefore, baptism is not a condition of salvation.

Another thing to remember is that salvation is a matter of spiritual experience; something, therefore, that one is conscious of, that one can know. It is a matter of definite, conscious experience that gives one sure evidence of acceptance with God. Thousands of men and women have known salvation apart from baptism. As a matter of spiritual experience, salvation is not tied to baptism, nor to any other external act; but salvation is inseparably connected with repentance and faith. To those who know Christianity as a vital experience of fellowship with God through faith in Christ, it is folly to argue that one cannot be saved without baptism. When one is definitely conscious in his own experience that a certain thing does take place, he is not liable to pay much attention to those who tell him that that thing cannot take place.

(2) While baptism does not save, nor is a condition of salvation, it does symbolize a salvation that comes to us by faith in Christ. This point will not need extended discussion, because much that was said on the previous point bears directly on this.

Baptism is an external washing; salvation is an inner or spiritual cleansing, a purification of the heart by faith. This inner cleansing is fittingly pictured or symbolized in the external washing of baptism. This is no doubt the significance of "washing away sins" in baptism in Acts 22: 16.

Paul sets forth the symbolic significance of baptism in Romans 6: 1ff. He speaks of the Christian as one who has died to sin and risen to walk in newness of life; as symbolized in his baptism. Baptism is a symbolical death and resurrection. It gets its meaning from an experience of dying to sin and rising to newness of life; apart from such an experience, therefore, it has no significance. To put it another way, baptism symbolizes our union with Christ. We are baptized into Christ (Rom. 6: 3). It symbolizes our remission of sins. We are baptized into the remission of sins (Acts 2: 38); i. e., baptism symbolizes or pictures our passage into a forgiven state or condition.

(3) But our death to sin and our resurrection to a new life are a death and a resurrection that come through faith in Jesus as a crucified and risen Redeemer. Paul expresses it in Galatians 2: 20 by saying that he has been crucified with Christ so that the "old man" Paul no longer lives, but Christ lives in him. He says in Romans 6: 4 that we are buried with Christ through baptism into death, but he has just said in verse three that we are baptized into Christ's death. Our baptism symbolizes our death to sin and spiritual resurrection, but it is a death and resurrection grounded in the death and resurrection of Jesus.

Our baptism, then, in symbolizing our spiritual death and resurrection commemorates the Death and Resurrection of Jesus as the fundamental facts of the gospel. Outside Christ's death for our sins and his resurrection from the dead, there is no gospel. And baptism as a gospel ordinance commemorates the Death and Resurrection of Jesus as the fundamental facts of the gospel.

(4) It is sometimes stated that baptism is also meant to point forward to the hope of the resurrection for the Christian. This hope of the resurrection is a fundamen-

tal gospel blessing for those who believe in Christ. Our hope of resurrection grows out of the resurrection of Jesus, as Paul shows in 1 Corinthians 15. And in verse 29 he says that baptism for the dead (whatever that was) would have no meaning apart from the resurrection from the dead. Paul seems to connect baptism with our hope of resurrection life beyond the grave, as well as with the death and resurrection of Jesus and with our spiritual death and resurrection with him.

2. *The act of baptism*

The question as to what constitutes the act of baptism, or, as sometimes expressed, the "mode" of baptism, is one about which there has been much discussion. We do not propose to go in any extensive way into this question. We have dwelt on the purpose or significance of baptism, believing that it is the fundamental question in regard to the ordinance and that a right understanding of its significance really settles every other question that may be raised in regard to it.

What, then, is the proper act of baptism? We maintain that immersion, and immersion only, constitutes the act of baptism. Briefly, we give a few reasons for this position.

(1) In the first place, the description of baptism, as practiced in New Testament times and given in the English translations of the New Testament, suggest immersion.

In Mark 1: 9, 10, it is said that Jesus was baptized of John into the Jordan, and that, coming straightway up out of the water, he saw the heavens opened. When Philip baptized the eunuch, they went down into the water and came up out of the water (Acts 8: 38, 39).

(2) Another argument, much more conclusive than the above, is based on the meaning of the Greek verb translated (or rather transferred, since it was not properly a translation) baptize in the New Testament and the corresponding noun translated baptism.

This word means properly to dip, or immerse, either literally or figuratively. In his New Testament Greek lexicon, Thayer defines the verb as meaning "to dip repeatedly, to immerse, submerge," and the noun as meaning "immersion, submersion." Cremer, in his *Biblico-Theological Lexicon of New Testament Greek*, defines the verb as meaning "immerse, submerse." All other meanings are secondary and derived.

Now there were words in the Greek language, in the days of the New Testament, meaning sprinkle and pour. But the New Testament writers always use the word that means to dip or immerse. If they thought of sprinkling or pouring as baptism, why is it that they never use the words that mean to sprinkle or to pour to describe the act of baptism?

(3) The strongest argument of all, however, lies in the significance of the ordinance.

Some people readily grant that the New Testament way of baptizing was by immersion, but argue that there is no necessity for adhering to the New Testament example in the matter. The Catholics hold that the church has the right to change the act of baptism since ultimate authority is vested in the church. Many Protestants maintain that it is a matter of comparative unimportance and that there is no use to divide over the question of how much water should be used in baptism. That is a very adroit and misleading way of putting the matter. Especially is this misleading to people who do not know much about the gospel of Christ and who often do not care so very much.

The fundamental question here is really this: What is the meaning and purpose of baptism? What is it for? We maintain that the fundamental facts of the gospel are the Death and Resurrection of Jesus as the ground of our salvation and that baptism is meant to set forth these facts. Consequently, we maintain that the meaning of the ordinance of baptism lies, partly at least, in the act which represents a death, burial, and resurrection.

Baptism does beautifully represent this; sprinkling or pouring does not. For this reason we maintain that no other act than immersion is baptism; it is something else substituted for baptism.

3. The candidate for baptism

Who should be baptized? Or what constitutes one a proper candidate for baptism?

If what was said about the purpose of baptism is true, then it follows that the only person properly qualified for baptism is one who has heard the gospel, accepted its message, and believed in Christ as his Saviour.

John the Baptist demanded "fruits worthy of repentance" before he would baptize those applying to him (Matt. 3: 7ff.). Jesus "made and baptized" disciples (John 4: 1), and the same was to be the order in the Great Commission (Matt. 28: 19). On the day of Pentecost they baptized those who received the Word (Acts 10: 41). Paul, in writing to the Romans, addresses them as those who have been baptized to symbolize a death to sin and resurrection to newness of life (Rom. 6: 1ff.). He usually addresses the members of the churches as "saints" or in some similar way, showing that the members of the churches to whom he wrote were adult Christians (not necessarily all grown people, but old enough to be called "saints," and so forth) (Rom. 1: 7; 1 Cor. 1: 2; 2 Cor. 1: 1; Eph. 1: 1, et al).

Against this view it is maintained that infant children should be baptized and reared in the church. This is based on various grounds. Roman Catholics and others who hold to "sacramental" salvation hold to infant baptism on the ground that children are regenerated in baptism. Evangelical Christians who repudiate baptismal regeneration have difficulty in finding grounds for infant baptism. Some defend the doctrine on the ground that the child is born in the kingdom and should, therefore, be baptized and reared in the church and thus kept in the kingdom. But this denies the New Testament teaching to the effect that no person can enter the kingdom without regeneration. It also disregards the fact that salvation is a personal transaction and that the grace of God must be personally and consciously appropriated.

Sometimes infant baptism is defended on the ground of New Testament precept and example. But there is no evidence in the New Testament in favor of the practice. Appeal is made to the household baptisms, but in most of these cases there are statements indicating that they were composed of those who could hear and believe the gospel. In the case of the jailer, Paul preached to the whole household, and they all believed and rejoiced (Acts 16:32-34). Cornelius and his whole house were saved by believing the preaching of Peter (Acts 11: 14). Paul baptized the household of Stephanus (1 Cor. 1: 16), but it might be worthy of note that the members of this household ministered to the saints (1 Cor. 16: 15). In the case of Lydia, it is to be presumed that the regular New Testament order was followed: hearing the gospel, believing the word, followed by baptism.

4. *The administrator of baptism*

A word might be said here about another phase of the ordinance of baptism. Who has the authority to baptize? Another way of putting the matter is this: Who is responsible for administering the ordinance?

In general, three answers are given to this question. One is that the "clergy," or officially recognized ministry, is responsible for the ordinance and has the authority to administer it. But this theory draws a line of distinction between "clergy" and "laity" that is foreign to the New Testament and tends toward sacerdotalism and sacramentalism. The New Testament gives no intimation that there is to be an official class who by being "ordained" are to have conferred on them the "authority to administer the ordinances" or to perform other ecclesiastical functions that other Christians cannot perform. A pastor or other "ordained minister" or official in administering the ordinances is only acting as a spokesman or representative of the congregation or church and has no other authority than that which comes by virtue of his being such a representative or spokesman.

Another view is that an individual Christian can baptize. But this would lead to all sorts of irregularities and confusion. The other view is that the responsibility for the administration of the ordinance rests with the congregation or church. This we believe to be the correct position. One reason for it is that baptism is generally recognized as the means of publicly confessing Christ and identifying oneself with the congregation or community of believers. This was clearly the case in the New Testament. If this be true, then baptism is a community affair. It is not a purely individual act. But there is a community responsibility with reference to the administration of the ordinance.

It may be objected here that the case of Philip and the eunuch does not agree with our contention, but supports the view that any Christian should be allowed to baptize. It is true that Philip baptized the eunuch. Nor is it necessary to suppose that any church had given him any special authority in the matter. Such a supposition would be a pure assumption with no ascertainable facts to justify it. Where there is no church, we believe any Christian or group of Christians could administer the ordinance. But where there is a church, the whole church is concerned, since baptism is a ceremony by which one publicly and formally identifies himself with the Christian community. What concerns the whole community of Christians the whole community has the right to regulate. Such a matter should not be left indiscriminately to any individual. When Cornelius and his household were converted, Peter consulted the group of Christians that came down with him from Jerusalem. If an individual should administer the ordinance, where there is no church, as in the case of a missionary in unevangelized territory, when the baptized person comes to a church asking for recognition and fellowship, the church can recognize the baptism by receiving him into fellowship.

This suggests the questions of "alien immersion" or "alien baptism"—i. e., an immersion performed by a minister or representative of some other denomination. Some Baptist churches receive such baptisms, while others do not. We would not favor the reception of such baptisms. We would not, however, put our objection on the ground of "church succession"—i. e., on the ground that there had been an unbroken chain or churches back to the New Testament; nor on the ground of a succession of regularly ordained ministers. Aside from the question as to whether there has been a demonstrable succession of churches back to New Testament days, if we base the validity of the ordinances on such a succession, then we could not be certain about the validity of the baptism of any particular man without tracing the succession of the church under whose auspices he was baptized. Besides, this method of validating the church and the ordinances smacks more of an episcopal ecclesiasticism than it does of a spiritual democracy. There is no "church authority" that can be handed down in any such way as that.

It is not a question of an externally conveyed authority that validates the ordinances, but rather a question of so performing the ordinances that they shall serve the spiritual purpose or function that they were intended to serve; and we do not believe that this can be done by recognizing the baptism of people who do not themselves submit to the ordinance as set forth in the New Testament—many of these bodies practicing sprinkling or pouring for baptism, many of them not requiring a profession of faith in Christ as a condition of baptism, and some of them baptizing people as a condition of receiving the remission of sins.

II. The Lord's Supper

The other ceremonial ordinance instituted by Jesus just before the crucifixion was the Lord's Supper. The principles laid down in interpreting baptism will apply to the Lord's Supper. Consequently, it will not be necessary to dwell so much at length on the Lord's Supper.

1. *The meaning of the Supper*

There are four distinct views with reference to the meaning of the Lord's Supper.

One is the Roman Catholic theory known as transubstantiation. According to this view, when the priest consecrates the bread and wine, they cease to be bread and wine (although they continue to have the appearance and apparent qualities of bread and wine) and are converted into the substance of the flesh and blood of Christ. Consequently, those who partake are not eating bread and drinking wine, but are eating the flesh and drinking the blood of Christ. This does not mean, however, that the bread and wine become merely the physical flesh and blood of Christ, but that each particle of the bread and wine becomes the whole substance of Christ—body, soul, and divinity. Any one, therefore, partaking of the least particle of the bread or wine (rather of that which was bread and wine before it was changed) receives the whole Christ. Hence it is not necessary that one should partake of both bread and wine. Consequently, the laity are given only the bread, the priesthood alone communing in both kinds.

Another theory is the Lutheran, known as consubstantiation. This theory denies that the substance of bread and wine is changed into the substance of Christ, but affirms that Christ is present "in, with, and under" the substance of bread and wine. Luther, the originator of this view, insisted on a literal interpretation of the words, "This is my body" and "This is my blood." He would not allow that this was symbolic or figurative language. His position of consubstantiation he supported on the ground of the omnipresence of Christ, which he affirmed to be true of his body as well as of his spiritual nature, after the ascension.

The Reformed or Calvinistic theology, in opposition to the Lutheran, denied the omnipresence of Christ's body. In conformity with this, it denied "consubstantiation" but affirmed the dynamic or spiritual presence of Christ in the elements of bread and wine in the Supper. This theory is not quite so clear and definite as the other two, and is hence a little more difficult to grasp. It denies, however, both the Catholic and Lutheran theories, but affirms that there is more meaning to the elements used in the Supper than simply a symbolic meaning. Christ is actually present in the elements, but only dynamically or spiritually.

Over against these three theories, we would set the view that the Supper is symbolic in its significance. These four views might be summed up with reference to their interpretation of the saying of Christ, "This is my body" (Matt. 26: 26). The Catholic view says that Jesus meant that the bread ceases to be bread and comes to be the substance of his body. The Lutheran view is that the substance of Christ's body is present "in, with, and under" the stubstance of the bread. The Reformed view is that Christ is present spiritually in the bread. The Zwinglian view is that the bread symbolizes the body of Christ broken for us.

This last view does not deny the spiritual omnipresence of Christ, but it does deny that Christ is present in the bread and wine of the Supper any more than he is present in any other material substance. And the spiritual omnipresence of Christ as expressed, for instance, in his words, "Lo, I am with you alway," is a presence that cannot be expressed or conveyed in any material substance. The bread and wine of the Supper do not contain or convey his spiritual presence; they only symbolize or picture it so that it may be real to the mind and thus strengthen faith.

We believe, then, that the Lord's Supper is symbolic in its significance. There are several phases of this general statement that might be emphasized.

The first and fundamental thing is that the Supper is a memorial of the death of Christ for our sins. He makes the bread to represent his broken body and the wine to represent his blood poured out for the remission of sins (Matt. 26: 26-28). Paul says that as often as we eat the bread and drink the wine we show forth the Lord's death. The bread and wine then constantly remind us of the broken body and shed blood of the Saviour.

While not so clearly expressed in the New Testament, it is perhaps justifiable to say that partaking of the elements symbolizes the support of our spiritual life by our appropriation by faith of Christ and his sacrifice for us. We thus symbolically eat his flesh and drink his blood in the Supper. The cup which we bless is a participation in the blood of Christ, and the bread which we break is a participation in the body of Christ (1 Cor. 10: 16, AS margin). Our repeated symbolic participation in the blood and body of Christ signifies a continuous appropriation of Christ as the once crucified Saviour, but the Saviour now living and present to the faith that appropriates him.

It has sometimes been said that the Lord's Supper is a communion with Christ, not a communion of Christians with one another. But it is clearly both. Christians commune with one another because they commune with Christ. It has also been said that in observing the Supper we are to think only of Christ. But to think of Christ always means to think of others. The Lord's Supper is not merely an individual affair; it is a community or church matter. Paul expresses this in 1 Cor. 10: 17 when he says that "we, who are many, are one bread, one body: for we all partake of the one bread." The one loaf seems to symbolize the unity of the church. He says again that because of the divisions or factions among the Corinthians they could not eat the Lord's Supper (1 Cor. 11: 18ff.). He then goes on to reprove them for their utter disregard of one another in the way in which they observed the Supper. Surely, then, in the Supper one should have some thought of his fellow Christians, and the Supper symbolizes the unity in spirit of those eating of the common loaf and drinking of the common cup.

2. *"Close communion"*

What was said in the last paragraph might throw light on another question. Among Baptists there has been some discussion of what is known as "close communion." The question is whether or not they should invite to the Lord's Supper Christians outside their denomination. Those holding the "close communion" position have been severely criticized by other people and by "open communion" Baptists for their supposed narrowness in the matter. We will try to state in a few words why we believe the "close communion" Baptist is right in his position.

In the first place, unless we are to regard the observance of the Supper as a purely individual matter, then somebody must be responsible for its administration. Naturally this would be the church under whose auspices the observance takes place. The only other alternative would be to regard the "clergy" or official class in the church as responsible for its administration. But, as pointed out in the case of baptism, that idea is foreign to a spiritual and non-sacramental religion. Paul's whole discussion of the matter shows that he regarded the church as the responsible body in the matter. (See 1 Cor. 11.) He says, "When you come together in the church." This throws the responsibility for the proper administration of the ordinance on the church or congregation. The church, then, would naturally have the prerogative of deciding who should come to the Supper.

Again, there would be general agreement that there are to be some restrictions in inviting people to the Lord's Supper. The invitation is not to the whole world. The invitation would at least be limited to Christians; otherwise the Supper would lose all significance as a Christian institution. There would be no meaning in inviting non-Christians to an observance that celebrated the event that founded Christianity. Since there are to be some restrictions in giving the invitation, it is a question as to how restricted it shall be.

Our position, then, is that the Lord's Supper is a church ordinance and not an individual matter, and that Baptists cannot consistently invite to the Lord's Supper those whom they would not admit to church membership. The stress has usually been put on the irregularity in baptism as a reason for declining to invite others to the Supper. Baptism certainly does precede the Lord's Supper, and we believe the argument that Baptists should not invite to the Supper those whom they do not regard as baptized is a valid argument. But we believe that there are other reasons. Any departure from New Testament principles in church polity or other doctrinal beliefs that would make one ineligible to church membership makes him ineligible to the Lord's Supper. We cannot consistently admit one to the Lord's Supper and then deny him the other privileges of church membership. This does not mean that Baptists do not regard members of other religious denominations as being Christians; but it does mean that they regard them as having departed from Christian principles in some respects, and, therefore, Baptists could not admit them to church fellowship. And since the Lord's Supper is a church ordinance, one of the most sacred of the privileges of church membership, no one should be admitted to this ordinance who could not be admitted to church membership.

III. The perpetuity of the Ordinances

The question is sometimes debated as to whether or not these ordinances should be perpetuated. Some seem to think that their day of usefulness is over, and that as religious forms change from age to age there is no reason for continuing to use them. Now, if we saw no more in these ordinances than some people do, we should not feel like insisting on their perpetual use. It is not simply a question of whether or not Jesus himself endorsed or commanded these. As already stated, Jesus submitted to baptism, practiced it, and gave the command in a connection that implies the perpetuity of the ordinance. He also instituted the Lord's Supper, and Paul says as often as we observe it we show the Lord's death until he come (1 Cor. 11: 26).

Why did Jesus institute or endorse these ordinances? Because they were adapted to set forth the fundamental facts of the gospel—namely: the Death and Resurrection of Jesus for the salvation of sinners. And where the gospel is kept alive in the hearts and minds of men, where they are conscious of being sinners saved by his Death and Resurrection, and where these ordinances are observed in the New Testament form and with reference to their gospel purpose of setting forth Christ's Death and Resurrection as the ground of our salvation, we do not believe that it will occur to any one that these ordinances should be abolished. It is only when men begin to lose the sense of dependence on Christ's atoning work for salvation; in other words, when Christianity begins to shade off into an indefinite religiosity, and consequently these gospel ordinances come to be regarded as only religious forms—only then do men begin to think of displacing them with something else. Gospel truth and gospel forms go together. We believe that the gospel is the only hope for a sinner to be accepted with a holy God; and as long as men are conscious of this, they should express it in these two ordinances that picture to the world man's dependence on the gospel.

THE CONSUMMATION OF SALVATION;
THE COMING OF THE KINGDOM OF GOD

CHAPTER XIV

THE CONSUMMATION OF SALVATION;
THE COMING OF THE KINGDOM OF GOD

I. MEANING AND DEVELOPMENT OF KINGDOM OF GOD

    1. Universal sovereignty of God.

    2. Theocratic kingdom of Israel

    3. Spiritual kingdom founded by Jesus

    4. Kingdom as a progressive power in the world

    5. Eternal kingdom of God

II. DEATH AND IMMORTAL GLORY

    1. Old Testament view of death

    2. Changed view in New Testament

    3. Causes for the change

    4. The Christian view

III. THE FINAL ADVENT OF CHRIST

    1. Fact of his return

    2. Purpose of his coming

        (1) To judge the world

        (2) To usher in the eternal kingdom

        (3) A cosmic significance

        (4) Creation, incarnation, consummation

    3. Time of his coming

IV. RESURRECTION

    1. Only one resurrection

    2. Nature of resurrection body

        (1) It will be a body

        (2) It will grow out of the present body

        (3) It will have higher powers than the old body

        (4) Little known about body of the wicked

V. The Judgment

  1. Certainty of judgment
  2. Purpose of judgment
    (1) To manifest character
    (2) To assign destiny in accordance with character
    (3) To consummate human history and vindicate God's
        dealings with the race
  3. Ground of judgment

VI. Heaven

  1. Intermediate state
  2. Eternal state of righteous
    (1) Place and state of character
    (2) Deliverance from sin
    (3) Fellowship with God
    (4) Freedom from natural evil
    (5) Service to God
    (6) Endless development

VII. Hell

  1. Certainty of future punishment
    (1) Taught in Bible
    (2) Required by moral order
    (3) Guaranteed by man's moral nature
    (4) Required by holiness of God
  2. Nature and extent of future punishment
    (1) May conform to nature of one's sin
    (2) Will be in proportion to one's guilt
  3. Endlessness of future punishment

CHAPTER XIV

THE CONSUMMATION OF SALVATION; THE COMING OF THE KINGDOM OF GOD

We come now to consider what is usually called eschatology, or the doctrine of last things. Christianity is a religion of redemption. It saves man from sin. The salvation that it gives is a present deliverance from the guilt and bondage of sin and the hope of complete deliverance in the life to come from the presence and from every trace of sin. Eschatology, then, is not only related to the doctrine of salvation, it is a part of that doctrine. Our salvation is consummated only in the future life. Our relation to God in the future life must be regarded as a continuation and outgrowth of our relation to him in this life. This is the way it is regarded in the New Testament. We have here the first fruits of the Spirit; the full harvest will come by and by.

I. Meaning and development of the kingdom of God

We believe that the subject of eschatology can best be understood if treated in relation to the idea of the kingdom of God, especially if we remember that this kingdom is a kingdom of redemption. As already indicated, we must keep in mind that this life is a preparation for the next, and that in some real sense of the word the next life is a continuation of this. God is working out a great purpose for the race, especially for his redeemed children. So far as the future is revealed to us, it is revealed as the development and consummation of the plan that God is working out in human history. Man's eternal destiny is to be the fruition of the moral and spiritual forces that are operative in time. This is clearly the view that is presented in the Bible. We will, therefore, treat the subject of eschatology in relation to the idea of the coming of the kingdom or consummation of God's plan of redemption.

We need first to get before our minds the meaning and development of the idea of the kingdom of God. This term is used in a number of senses in the Bible.

1. *The universal sovereignty of God*

In the first place, it is used with reference to the sovereignty of God over the whole of creation and particularly over mankind. This is expressed in many ways in the Bible. In Psalm 47: 2 we have this: "For Jehovah Most High is terrible; he is a great King over all the earth." In verse 7 of the same Psalm the thought is repeated and in verse 8 we find: "God reigneth over the nations: God sitteth upon his holy throne." In Psalm 103: 19 are these words: "Jehovah hath established his throne in the heavens; and his kingdom ruleth over all." Again in verse 22 the writer says: "Bless Jehovah, all ye his works, in all places of his dominion." This universal sovereignty or rule of God is necessarily involved in the biblical conception of God. There is only one true God, and he is sovereign over all the universe. He is everywhere present and has all power. He is infinite in wisdom and goodness. He reigns over the universe which he has created. All nations of men and individuals are subject to his moral law and must account to him for their deeds. He sends judgments on Egypt, Babylon, Phœnicia, and the other nations as well as on Israel. There is no point in space or time, no member of the human race, no part of any man's life, that is not subject to his righteous rule.

2. *The theocratic kingdom of Israel*

Then there is the kingdom of Israel in the Old Testament. God had a purpose for the race which could be best worked out by choosing one man and his descendants as his peculiar people. This he did. He selected Abraham and entered into a covenant with him by virtue of which he and his descendants should possess the land of Canaan and should be a blessing to the whole world (Gen. 12: 1-3). This people was formed into a nation, and as an organized nation became God's covenant people on the basis of God's redemptive act in delivering them from the land of Egypt under the leadership of Moses. There was a still further development when the nation became a kingdom under the leadership, but over the protest, of the Prophet Samuel. Samuel reminded the people that Jehovah was the true King of Israel and that they should be careful not to allow the human king to stand in the way of their loyalty and service to Jehovah (1 Sam. 8). The spiritual guidance of the nation came mainly from the prophets, God's specially called and Spirit-endued messengers, rather than from the worldly kings or the officially-appointed priests.

3. *The spiritual kingdom founded by Jesus*

Jehovah promised David that his descendant should ascend his throne and reign forever (2 Sam. 7: 12ff.). This promise found its fulfilment in Christ. So did the kingdom of Israel find its fulfilment in the spiritual kingdom of God founded by Jesus. The Old Testament theocracy finds its significance in relation to the spiritual kingdom for which it was a providential preparation. When Jesus came to earth, he came as a Saviour-King. The Magi from the east worshiped him (Matt. 2: 11). He was regarded as fulfilling the promise made to David (Luke 1: 32, 33; Acts 2: 25-36). The kingdom of God was instituted at his coming. This was the kingdom prophesied by Daniel (Daniel 2: 44). Jesus and John both came preaching that the kingdom was at hand (Matt. 3: 2; Mark 1: 15). This kingdom was not a political, earthly kingdom such as the Jews expected the Messiah would institute, but it was the reign of God in the hearts of men. The Jews expected that the Messiah would drop down out of the skies with such great miraculous displays of power as would overawe his enemies, break the power of the Roman yoke, and establish a great Jewish kingdom to rule over the earth.

And when Jesus came "meek, and riding upon an ass," saying that the kingdom of God did not come with outward display such as the world could see and be impressed with, but that it was an inner reality that only the twice-born could see and appreciate (Luke 17: 20, 21; John 3: 3), they rejected such a king and such a kingdom with scorn. Even the most spiritual of the disciples of Jesus did not appreciate the spiritual nature of the kingdom until after the Death and Resurrection of Jesus and the descent of the Spirit at Pentecost. Even on the occasion of the ascension of Jesus, they were still asking if he would at that time restore the kingdom to Israel (Acts 1: 6), evidently thinking of a restoration of the Davidic kingdom under the Messiah, but perhaps on a grander scale. Paul says that the kingdom of God is not eating and drinking, but righteousness and peace and joy in the Holy Spirit (Rom. 14: 17). It is an inner, spiritual experience and a present reality. John says that he is partaker with those to whom he writes in the tribulation and kingdom and patience which are in Jesus (Rev. 1: 9). John states this as a present experience of his and theirs. If the tribulation and patience belonged to John and his fellow Christians in this life, so did the kingdom. The kingdom, then, is not put off to some future age for its beginning; it begins here and now. When men submit to the authority of Christ as Saviour and Lord and by the indwelling Spirit know righteousness, peace and joy, they are in the kingdom of God.

It is sometimes said that there cannot be a kingdom without a king; and since the King is absent, the kingdom is not yet; the kingdom will not be until the King returns. It is true that there cannot be a kingdom without a king; but we do have the King present in the Spirit. He lives in the Christian (John 6: 56; Gal. 2: 20). He dwells in our hearts by faith (Eph. 3: 17). No man is a Christian who does not submit to his spiritual authority. He is now both Lord and Christ (Acts 2: 36). The promise to David that his descendant should sit upon his throne is fulfilled in the Resurrection and ascension (Acts 2: 29-34). The Jews could not reconcile a suffering Messiah with the idea of a reigning Messiah. Jesus did not announce the kingdom of God as at hand and then have to change his program because of rejection by his own nation. The kingdom of God was initiated at his coming. He ushered in a reign of peace and righteousness when he came to save men from sin. He reconciles men to God and to each other. When the angels sang about peace on earth among men of good will, they were not singing a song altogether inopportune because at least two thousand years too early.

4. *This kingdom as a progressive power in the world*

The kingdom is presented in the New Testament as having a development during the present gospel age. The gospel age and the kingdom age are not to be contrasted as two things. The coming of Christ and his gospel initiated the kingdom; the preaching of the gospel is the means of developing the kingdom. The gospel of the kingdom is the gospel of salvation by the grace of God through faith in Jesus as a crucified and risen Redeemer. There are not two gospels, but one.

In Matthew 13, Jesus gave two parables to illustrate the growth of the kingdom—the parables of the mustard seed and of the leaven (verses 31-33). Starting from insignificant beginnings, it is to become a mighty worldwide power. Some say that the parable of the leaven represents the leavening power of Christianity in the individual life, while the mustard seed teaches the spread of Christianity in the world at large. Whether this is true or not, it is true that Jesus meant to show that Christianity was to have a growth indefinitely great in the world. Just how great is to be the development, no one can tell. Evidently the kingdom of God is to become a mighty power in the world's life. Some object to taking the parable of the leaven as representing the development of the kingdom. They say that it represents the spread of evil in the "church." One reason given for this is that leaven never elsewhere represents good. Two things should be said in reply. One is that, if leaven did everywhere else represent evil, by no means would this prove that it could not represent the good here. A figurative term does not necessarily have the same meaning every time used. Another thing to remember is that leaven did not in the Old Testament always represent evil. (See Lev. 7: 13; 23: 17.) There are some passages in the Old Testament that seem to predict a universal reign of peace and righteousness, such as Psalm 46: 8, 9; Isa. 2: 2-4; 11: 6-9; Micah 4: 1-4. There are those who deride the idea that wars shall cease before the second advent of Christ. But it must be remembered that many things have come to pass that good people did not believe could come to pass. It is not a safe proposition to hold that what has not been done cannot be done, especially if we take God and his grace into the count.

But it is objected that there are predictions in the New Testament to show that the world will grow worse and worse until Christ comes. This, however, is a mistake. These passages, if examined in the light of the context, we think will usually be found to be speaking of evils arising during the writer's own day, against which he is giving warning. They are not passages that can be taken as indicating an increasing predominance of evil for the gospel age as a whole. Such an interpretation of them is contrary to the genius of the gospel and the teaching of the Scriptures as a whole. Besides, such an interpretation cannot be reconciled with two thousand years of Christian history. Even zealous Christian men may speak deridingly of what Christianity has done for human society. But in spite of that the world is a much better place in which to live than it was when Jesus was born into it. Woman has been partially liberated, childhood respected and, to some extent, protected, human personality valued more highly; and all this because of Jesus and his saving work. Political, industrial, and national ideals are being slowly, but surely, transformed. It is something that nations will now at least apologize for causing a war and try to shift the responsibility in public opinion on others. Great social evils are slowly being outlawed.

Another thing to keep in mind is that there may be in some respects a development of evil over against the development of the kingdom of God. Evil develops in opposition to the good. The subtlest and most dangerous forms of evil do not appear in the midst of heathen darkness. They appear as angels of light in the midst of gospel blessings. Evil tends to become more subtle and intense where gospel light is greatest. The Book of Revelation seems to picture the struggle between sin and righteousness as being prolonged and assuming many different forms. Sin appears in myriad forms before it is finally vanquished. When put down in one form, it reappears in another. Our aim should be to bring the whole social order of the world under the sway of the principles of the gospel and the Spirit of Christ. If it be objected that this is an ideal that is impossible of attainment in this age, it might be well to remember that, although the ideal is impossible of attainment, yet Christ has commanded us to be perfect as the Father in heaven is perfect (Matt. 5: 48). The Great Commission sets before us as high an ideal with reference to Christianizing the social order in which we live as does this command of Jesus with reference to individual Christian character. The command to pray that God's kingdom shall come and his will be done on earth as it is in heaven places before us the same high ideal and on us the same great obligation.

5. *The eternal kingdom of God*

It is made clear in the New Testament that the final stage of the kingdom is the eternal kingdom to be ushered in at the second coming of Christ. A good deal of confusion of thought appears at this point. Some insist that the kingdom age is yet to come, that it is to be ushered in at the second coming of Christ. But the New Testament makes it clear that the second coming does not usher in, but consummates, the kingdom of God on earth, and ushers in the eternal kingdom. The following passages make it clear that the word is used in this latter sense: Matthew 13: 43; 25: 34; 26: 29; 1 Corinthians 15: 24; 2 Timothy 4: 1, 18. This phase of the matter will be discussed further in connection with the second coming of Christ.

The topics that follow may be considered as steps in the establishment of the eternal kingdom or aspects of that kingdom when established. Death, the second coming of Christ, the resurrection, and the judgment are steps in the establishment of the eternal kingdom, while heaven and hell are aspects of the order of things when God's authority and power shall have been established over all things.

II. Death and immortal glory

1. *We have already considered the fact that death is viewed in the Bible as the penalty of sin*

We do not here need to treat the matter any further. But there is the fact that in the Old Testament death and the future life are generally given a rather gloomy aspect. The religion of the Hebrews was a religion mainly for this life. It is rather difficult for us to put ourselves in their place and realize that this is true, but nevertheless it is, as the Old Testament clearly shows. The promises were mainly for this life, and more largely than in the New Testament were connected with temporal good. Death at times was spoken of as the cessation of conscious communion with God and active service to him (Psalms 6: 5; 30: 9; 88: 10-12; 115: 17; Eccl. 9: 10; Isa. 38: 18). The continuance of life on earth was the mark of God's favor (Isa. 38: 18-20). At times the writer seems to look beyond death to resurrection and life with God, but even then the matter is not dwelt upon. It is simply asserted (Psalms 16: 8-11; 73: 24ff., et al). The passage in Daniel 12: 1-3 is the only undisputed one. The one in Isaiah is almost as clear. The figurative use of the expression by Ezekiel shows that the idea was not unfamiliar (Ezek. 37: 12ff.). The teachings of Peter (Acts 2: 25ff.), of Paul (Acts 13: 33), and of Jesus (Mark 12: 24ff.) show that they regarded the Old Testament as teaching the doctrine. The translation of Enoch and Elijah shows that the Old Testament writers did not regard death as the end of existence. We might sum up by saying that the Old Testament as a whole clearly does not regard death as the cessation of existence, but it does not give us much light on life beyond the grave.

2. *The remarkable thing is that in the New Testament all this is changed*

The outlook upon death is completely transformed. This does not mean that death within itself has come to be regarded as a good; it rather means that the evil of death has been overcome and death is looked upon as the entrance for God's child upon a more glorious and a fuller life. Jesus calls death a sleep (Mark 5: 39). For this he was laughed to scorn. He speaks of the death of Lazarus as a sleep (John 11: 11). This his disciples could not understand. He speaks of Abraham, Isaac, and Jacob as living, not dead (Mark 12: 26, 27). In the story of the rich man and Lazarus, Jesus shows that he does not regard death as the cessation of conscious existence, but for the righteous as the entrance upon a state of rest and peace (Luke 16: 19ff.). Stephen is said to have fallen on sleep (Acts 7: 60). Paul names death as one of the things that cannot separate us from the love of God (Rom. 8: 38), and again he includes it as among the Christian's possessions (1 Cor. 3: 21, 22). This last expression shows that Paul regards death as becoming, by God's grace, an asset rather than a liability, a blessing rather than a curse. In his own case he says that it would be far better to depart and be with the Lord; this is his desire for himself (Phil. 1: 23). Later on, when he thinks his time is about up, he quietly says that the time of his departure is at hand, henceforth there is laid up for him a crown of righteousness (2 Tim. 4: 6, 8).

3. *What are the causes that have wrought this changed view of death?*

Leaving aside the theological development of the inter-biblical period, we find in the New Testament itself the explanation. There are three primary reasons: One is the teaching of Jesus about death; another is the Resurrection of Jesus; and the third is the communion with God that came to men through faith in the crucified and risen Redeemer. He referred to death as sleep (Mark 5: 39). He said: "Whosoever liveth and believeth on me shall never die" (John 11: 26). No man had ever talked about death as he did. The disciples had seen their hopes concerning Jesus as the Messiah dashed to pieces by his cruel death upon the Cross at the hands of sinful men. But their hopes were revived by his Resurrection from the dead, and their conception of his Messiahship and the nature of his kingdom transformed. The Resurrection also wrought a transformation in their view of death. They had before them a living demonstration of the fact that death had been conquered. They interpreted the Death and Resurrection of Jesus to mean that he had dealt with the two great problems of human life. He died for our sins according to the Scriptures (1 Cor. 15: 3). In his death he met the problem of sin and solved it. He struggled with it as man's greatest enemy and conquered it. In conquering sin he conquered death, for sin and death are inseparable. The other side of the matter is that by faith in Christ men came into fellowship with the living God and thereby had conscious victory over sin and death in their own lives. They were conscious that the fellowship they had with God was one that death could not terminate. The power of sin and death had been broken in their lives by the incoming of a new power, the power of the Spirit of life in Christ Jesus (Rom. 8: 2). Christ came and took the nature of man that through death he might deliver all those who through fear of death were all their lifetime subject to bondage (Heb. 2: 14-16).

4. The Christian view

Instead, then, of death being something to be dreaded, it is the hour of deliverance for the Christian, the hour of entrance into a more glorious life.

Death is not the termination of life, it is the entrance upon a larger life. The main element in this larger life is that it is to be a life of continued fellowship with the Lord. That was the thing to which Paul looked forward with eager longing (2 Cor. 5: 1ff.; Phil. 1: 23). Death is the means, then, by which we are translated into the "upper and better kingdom."

III. The final advent of Christ

There has been, and is yet, great diversity of opinion in regard to the return of Christ to earth. A question on which there is so much difference of opinion among earnest Christian men ought to be one in which there is a tolerant spirit manifested, and one that is approached with due caution and reserve of judgment. One should not be too dogmatic where it is evidently so easy to miss the way; and when one has pronounced convictions he should have due respect for good and earnest brethren who hold opposite opinions.

We wish now to consider some of the more fundamental features of this doctrine as presented in the New Testament and set forth some conclusions which we believe can be safely held on the question.

1. The fact of his return

The New Testament teaches beyond question that Christ will return to earth. Perhaps no one who studies the New Testament would deny that the disciples ex-

pected him to return. The following references will make
it clear that the fact of Christ's return to earth is a
fundamental teaching in the New Testament: Matthew
16: 27; 24: 27, 37-39; 25: 31; Mark 8: 38; 13: 26; Luke
21: 27; John 21: 22; Acts 1: 11; 1 Corinthians 15: 23;
1 Thessalonians 1: 10; 4: 16; 2 Thessalonians 1: 7, 10;
2: 1, 8; 1 Peter 1: 7; 2 Peter 1: 16; 3: 4, 8-12; 1 John
2: 28. This list is by no means exhaustive, but it is representative. Some people might question a few of these
as referring to the final advent, but about them as a
whole there can be no question. All classes of writers
in the New Testament, early and late, evidently looked
forward to the return of Christ, and regarded this hope
as based on a promise of Christ himself, before he went
away.

2. *The purpose of his coming*

For what purpose is Christ coming back to the earth?
This question is of the greatest importance in relation
to this doctrine, and we are bound to say that we think
it is where many good people miss the way. Perhaps we
can sum the matter up in the following statements:

(1) Christ is not to return to save the world, but to
judge it.

The primary purpose of his first coming was to save
the world, not to judge it (John 3: 17; 12: 47). He came
the first time in humility; he was rejected and crucified.
But when he comes again, he comes in glory and power.
He does come on a saving mission, but it will be a saving mission only to those who have received him before
he comes. He will raise the dead and transform the living Christians, and thus complete their salvation (1 Cor.
15: 50ff.; 1 Thess. 4: 13ff.). But no sinner will repent
after he comes. His coming to judge the world is a motive to repentance now, but it will offer no opportunity
for repentance after he comes (Acts 17: 30ff.). To hold
that Christ is now saving a small remnant of the race,
the elect, the church, the bride of Christ, and that he

will save the great majority of mankind after he returns and overawes the world with a manifestation of his majesty and power—this is practically to give us two plans of salvation: One is the plan of salvation by moral suasion, spiritual power, and gospel influences; the other is the plan of so impressing the world with an outward demonstration of majesty and power that the world will be compelled to submit. There is no such plan as the latter. No amount of outward manifestation of power will change the will of man. This might lead him to give external and professed submission as a matter of slavish fear, but it would not renew the moral nature of the sinner. The weapon by which the world is to be subdued is the gospel of Christ, preached by sinners saved by God's grace and endued by his Spirit for their task. If that plan fails, God has no other that he has revealed to man. It is the Christ out of whose mouth proceeds the sharp, two-edged sword of the Word of God that goes forth to make war on sin and unrighteousness and drive them from the earth (Rev. 1: 16).

Paul gives us to understand that Christ is to stay on the throne of his mediatorial kingdom until all his enemies are put beneath his feet (1 Cor. 15: 25). When he leaves that throne, his mediatorial work, so far as saving sinners is concerned, will be ended. Then comes judgment, not salvation, for the sinner. Peter seems to teach that the reason the Lord delays his coming is because he does not wish that any should perish, but that all should come to repentance (2 Peter 3: 9). He delays that men may have an opportunity to repent.

(2) He comes, not to establish a temporal kingdom on earth, but to consummate the mediatorial kingdom and usher in the eternal kingdom of God.

As the incarnation of God and as the One who had wrought redemption for man by his Death and Resurrection, Christ was given supreme authority over the human race (Matt. 28: 18). This authority had special reference to the salvation of men and looked toward that end (John 17: 2). This authority is one day to be universally recognized and owned (Phil. 2: 10, 11). It will continue until the last enemy of his in the world is subdued, which is to be death (1 Cor. 15: 24-26). This conquering of death will take place at the second coming, when Christ will raise his people from the dead (1 Cor. 15: 23). Then he will deliver up the kingdom to the Father (1 Cor. 15: 24). Perhaps this last statement means that the work of redemption is now accomplished, and so far as that work is concerned, he gives the kingdom back to the Father. He brings the redeemed race with himself back into submission to God, and, since his work in that respect is finished, he surrenders his commission and authority back to God who gave them. But the fact that the conquering of death in the raising of his people at his coming is expressly stated here to be the last enemy to be conquered—this shows that the resurrection of the saints at Christ's coming to earth is the consummation, not the initiation, of his kingdom, and is the ushering in of the eternal kingdom of God.

(3) The fact that Christ comes to raise the dead and judge the world has been referred to. Both of these will be discussed later on. But there are certain passages that seem to give a cosmic significance to Christ's coming. Peter indicates that the present order will pass away and there will be new heavens and a new earth (2 Peter 3: 12, 13). John saw new heavens and a new earth (Rev. 21: 1). Paul indicates that the creation was subjected to vanity, perhaps because of man's sin. Man groans within himself waiting for his adoption, the redemption of his body. So does the whole creation groan waiting to share the liberty of the glory of the sons of God (Rom. 8: 19-23). This would be the counterpart of what is said in Genesis 3: 17-19 about a curse coming upon nature because of man's sin. Some of these statements may be figurative and symbolical of moral and spiritual realities, but they indicate at least the possi-

bility of the renewal of the physical world along with the redemption of man.

(4) There seem to be three outstanding points in God's dealings with humanity in Christ: The first was creation, when human history began; the second was the incarnation, when the recreation of the race in Christ as the head of a redeemed humanity began; the third will be the second coming, when the history of the race in time comes to an end, when redemption is consummated and the eternal order of things is ushered in.

We can see why it is in the New Testament, then, that the coming of Christ is the one outstanding event of the future toward which everything else points, just as in the Old Testament the first coming of the Messiah was the great event looked forward to. The second coming of Christ is the glorious hope for the Christian.

3. *The time of his coming*

There is no place where greater wisdom is needed than in discussing this phase of the second coming.

There are two things it seems clear that we cannot do. One is to fix the time for the second coming of Christ. Jesus said that he himself did not know the time and that no one did know except the Father (Mark 13: 32). Paul rejected the inference from his own teaching that he was fixing the time as immediately at hand (2 Thess. 2: 1ff.). Jesus warns us against those who would point out the time and place of the appearance of the Messiah (Matt. 24: 23ff.). He says that his appearing will be sudden and unexpected like a flash of lightning (Matt. 24: 27). He will come unexpectedly on the world like the flood in the days of Noah (Matt. 24: 37ff.). This is the point, and the only point, in his illustration of the flood. It has no reference to the moral condition of the world at the time of his coming.

This brings us to the other thing we cannot do— namely: to fix plans and programs of human history. The Bible is not intended to give us such a foresight of the

development of history. All such efforts are in vain.
It does seem to be made fairly clear in the New Testament that the second coming of Christ will wind up the
affairs of human history; so that we seem to be safe
in saying that whatever is to come in the way of the
conversion of the Jews, the revelation of the man of sin
(more than has already taken place), the triumphs of
Christianity in the world—all this will be before the final
advent, not after. It is because the writer does not
believe any scheme of history can be made out beforehand that he leaves to one side the question of the millennium. The Bible refers to the millennium in only
one obscure passage, and nobody seems to know what it
means (Rev. 20: 1-10). It is also to be noted that
nothing is said in the passage about the second coming
of Christ. The writer does believe that whatever triumphs
of Christianity are to come must come before the final
advent, and that there will probably be great triumphs
of the gospel and its principles in human history. To
that extent he is a postmillennialist.

IV. Resurrection

1. *Only one resurrection*

The teaching of the Bible seems to be that there will
be one general resurrection, at the time of the second
coming of Christ, including the righteous and unrighteous. The statement of Daniel is that "many of them
that sleep in the dust of the earth shall awake, some to
everlasting life, and some to shame and everlasting con-
tempt" (Dan. 12: 2). Here both the righteous and the
wicked are included in the resurrection. Jesus says that
the hour comes in which all that are in the tombs shall
hear the voice of the Son of God and shall come forth;
they that have done good, unto the resurrection of life;
and they that have done evil, unto the resurrection of
judgment or condemnation (John 5: 28, 29). Luke re-
ports Paul as saying that there shall be a resurrection

both of the just and the unjust (Acts 24: 15). In the account of the judgment found in Revelation 20: 11ff., it is said that the sea gave up the dead that were in it; and death and Hades gave up the dead that were in them (verse 13). While not spoken of as a resurrection, this evidently means a resurrection of all the dead. The biblical conception of the resurrection is that it will be a universal resurrection, including the righteous and the wicked. The impression from these passages is that all the dead are raised at the same time. There is not a suggestion in any of them that there is to be an interval of time between the resurrection of the righteous and of the wicked.

2. *Nature of the resurrection body*

Not a great deal is said in the New Testament about the nature of the resurrection body. Some light is thrown upon the subject, however, from two sources: One is the Resurrection and appearances of Jesus; the other is such teachings as we find in 1 Corinthians 15 and in Jesus' teaching in his controversy with the Sadducees on this question (Mark 12: 18-27). With these as a basis, we feel safe in taking the following positions:

(1) It will be a body.

The Resurrection does not stand simply for the immortality of man's spiritual nature or soul. It carries with it the fact of immortality, but means more than that. The fact that Jesus ate before the disciples after the resurrection, that he walked and talked with them, shows that he was more than a spirit. In fact, Jesus repudiated the idea that he was such a spirit, saying that he had flesh and bones (Luke 24: 39). On another occasion they took hold of his feet and worshiped him (Matt. 28: 9). Besides, the body of Jesus came out of the tomb. The tomb was found empty (John 20: 11, 12). When Paul speaks of a spiritual body (1 Cor. 15: 44), he does not mean a body that is simply spirit in essence. Such would not be a body at all. Our eternal state will not be that of a disembodied spirit, but our spirits will be clothed and objectified in a body.

(2) It will grow out of, and be a continuation of, the present body.

As already pointed out, Paul teaches in 1 Corinthians 15 that the body that is planted in the grave will rise again. It was the body of Jesus that was laid in Joseph's tomb which rose and in which he appeared to his disciples.

It is sometimes objected to this that it will be impossible to gather together all the particles of matter that belong to the present body and reunite them in the resurrection body. Sometimes a particle of matter may belong to more than one human body. The answer to this objection is that the continuous identity of the body does not depend on its possessing the same particles of matter continuously. Every particle of matter in one's body is supposed to change every few years; yet there is continuous identity. The body of the mature man is continuous with the body of the infant; yet the particles of matter have changed. So have the size, features, and other characteristics changed to such an extent that no one who has not known the person during the intervening period would recognize the body of the man as having any identity with that of the child. The principle of continuity does not seem to reside in the particles of matter composing the body; it is probably in the life that animates the body. This may suggest the appropriateness of Paul's figure of the grain of wheat that is planted in the ground and dies. So the body is planted, and out of the old body comes a new one with higher powers, and yet it is continuous with the old.

(3) The new body has higher powers than the old.

This is evident in the case of the body of Jesus. He seemed to come through closed doors at will (John 20: 26). At the time of the ascension his body moved through space. Possibly our resurrection bodies will largely transcend the limitations of space, as those limitations belong to matter as we now know it. Paul calls the resurrection body a spiritual body. As pointed out already, this does not mean a body composed of spirit, but one perfectly adapted to the ends and uses of our glorified spirits. Paul says that flesh and blood shall not inherit the kingdom of God (1 Cor. 15: 50). Some interpret this to mean that the resurrection body will not be composed of matter but spirit. This would not agree with the statement of Jesus that his resurrection body was flesh and bone. Paul rather means flesh and blood as we now know them, subject to corruption and decay. Corruption, decay, and death will be done away with, and our resurrection bodies will be immortal, incorruptible, and glorious. As to the definite respects in which its powers will transcend those of the present body we are not told.

(4) As to the nature of the resurrection body of the wicked, we are left almost entirely in the dark.

About all that we learn is the fact that the wicked are raised and that they rise to a resurrection of shame and condemnation. Possibly in some ways their bodies will conform to their depraved and deformed spirits, but we are not told; and where nothing is revealed and we have no suggestions in experience as to which way to go, we had better practice a reverent silence.

V. The Judgment

1. *The certainty of judgment*

The principle of judgment in God's dealings with man runs all the way through the Bible and through human experience and history. The fact of judgment is involved in man's moral freedom and in his responsibility to God. Judgment is not wholly deferred to the future. No man can do either good or evil without reaping immediately a reward of good or evil in accordance with his deed. Perhaps it could not be otherwise under a reign of moral law. And yet we can see that it would probably interfere with man's freedom, at least to some extent, if every deed were immediately followed by its due reward, especially if such a result were open and manifest. Man would follow the right course then, not so much because he loved the right and hated the wrong, as because he feared to do the wrong. Such an arrangement would hardly be one of moral freedom and discipline, but rather one of coercion. Much of our moral discipline and spiritual development we now get out of loyalty to right in face of the fact that right often seems to go unrewarded and sin unpunished. Such rewards as do follow the doing of right or wrong are often of such a nature as not to be evident to the world. Many times they consist in the approval or the disapproval of our own consciences. The full reward of our deeds does not follow immediately upon the commission of a deed right or wrong, nor is such reward as does follow immediately fully evident to the world. Such an arrangement as we have in this life seems to be necessary in a world designed as a place of moral discipline and probation.

The Scriptures are full of examples showing how God bestows his blessing upon the individual or nation that does right or his curse upon the one that does evil. This is especially evident in such periods of judgment as the flood, the destruction of Sodom and Gomorrah, the deliverance of Israel from Egypt with judgments upon Egypt, and the Babylonian captivity of the Jews. In the history of the Jews we have another outstanding example in the destruction of Jerusalem in A.D. 70. We have the prophecy of this in the New Testament but not the record of its fulfilment. Jesus foretold this coming destruction upon the Jewish nation as a judgment for their rejection of him as the Messiah and God's Son.

In the Old Testament, the emphasis is upon judgment in this life; in the New Testament, final judgment is postponed until the next life. Final judgment does not come until the final advent of Christ. This is clearly shown in Matthew 25. It may be that final judgment is postponed until the end of human history in order that our deeds of good and evil may have time to work themselves out in human history to their final consequences. All our deeds will then have had plenty of time to manifest themselves in their moral quality in their effects upon the lives of others. Every man will then be judged, not as an isolated individual, but as a member of the race. The race in its unity and totality, as well as the individual units of the race, will be judged. God will be vindicated in his work of creating the race and in his providential direction and redemption of it. The judgment comes at the end of the history of the race on earth and as the consummation of that history.

There is no contradiction, then, between the idea of partial judgment in God's dealings with individuals, with nations and the race during the course of history, and the idea of a final judgment at the end of human history. The latter comes as the completion and vindication of the former. Each implies the other, and neither would be complete without the other.

2. *The purpose of the judgment*

The purpose of the judgment is not to institute an investigation to determine whether or not the individual will be saved or lost. The God of infinite wisdom and knowledge needs no such court of investigation. Known unto him are all man's ways, man's character, man's destiny, without any such court of inquiry. Nor is it necessary in order that the man himself shall know what his destiny is. This is known to each man at death, if not sooner. Death itself is doubtless a great crisis of judgment in which character is manifested and crystallized, when one comes into the immediate presence of God. But in spite of this, it seems that there is still necessity for a final judgment at the end of human history.

What, then, is the purpose of the judgment? We might sum it up as follows:

(1) To bring out into the light each man's character as revealed in his words and deeds in relation to his fellow man, and in the effects of his deeds upon the lives of others.

Perhaps this is the reason final judgment does not come until the end of human history at the second coming of Christ. The purpose of the judgment is not to weigh over against each other a man's good and bad deeds and determine his destiny according as the good or the bad preponderates. But his words and deeds are brought into the judgment as indicating his character. Character determines destiny, and character is indicated and determined by deeds.

(2) To assign one a destiny in accordance with his character.

As just stated, this does not mean that one must wait until the judgment to know whether he is saved or lost. Nor does it mean that one does not enter upon the enjoyment of the fruits of a good life or the suffering of the evil consequences of a bad life immediately upon death. The teaching of the New Testament is to the contrary. But it does mean that the final and complete possession of such rewards for good or evil does not come until the end of time and the consummation of the historical order. Man does not come to his final destiny this side of the second coming of Christ and the judgment. Each man comes to his final destiny along with every other member of the race.

(3) It is, then, to bring the affairs of human history to completion and vindicate God's dealings with the race as well as his dealings with the individual.

If it were only to assign the individual strictly speaking as an individual, his destiny in accordance with character, then the judgment might possibly not be a necessity. But God created man as a race, not as isolated individuals; the race as a race fell in the sin of the first man; God provided redemption for the race in the last Adam; he preserves and governs the race in him; and he will judge the race at his final manifestation. It is especially stressed in the New Testament that the judgment is to be universal (Matt. 25: 32; Rom. 14: 10; Rev. 20: 13). All men will be there, and the affairs of the race in its history in time on the earth will be consummated. God's ways with man will be vindicated.

3. The ground of the judgment

The ground of the judgment is the fact that man is responsible to God as the Author of the world and of man's being. Man is responsible to God, because God creates and preserves him in existence and gives him all that he has in life. He lives in God's world. God is the ground and support of our being. "In him we live, and move, and have our being" (Acts 17: 28). As free, man can choose or reject God and his service. To him, therefore, we are accountable for our lives. The New Testament nowhere regards salvation by grace as delivering man from responsibility and accountability to God. This is why Paul repudiates the idea that justification by faith abrogates or nullifies the law. He says rather that it establishes law (Rom. 3: 31). Salvation by grace does away with the law as a method of salvation, but it does not do away with man's responsibility to moral law and his accountability to God. The opposite view is the antinomian view of salvation by grace and would undermine the moral order. It has been urged from New Testament days as an objection to salvation by grace (see Rom. 6: 1ff.), but it is based on a misunderstanding of what salvation by grace means. Man is not saved by being delivered from obligation to keep the righteous requirements of the moral law; he is saved by being freely forgiven on the basis of Christ's atoning blood and so reenforced by the power of God's renewing grace that he can meet the requirements of the law (Rom. 8: 1-4).

The gift of God's grace to sinful man does not deliver man from responsibility to God; it increases his responsibility. Since God has dealt with man in grace, certainly

God's gracious dealings with man will be taken into account in the judgment. This may give a suggestion of what Paul means when he says that God will judge the secrets of men according to his gospel (Rom. 2: 16). The judgment will be the vindication of God's past dealings with the race and with the individual members of the race. And since all God's dealings with man have been in and through Christ, Christ will be the judge of mankind. In Christ the race was created, preserved, and redeemed; in Christ the race will be judged (Matt. 25: 31ff.; Acts 17: 31; Rom. 2: 16).

VI. Heaven

By heaven we mean the final state of the righteous. This state of final blessedness does not come until after the judgment. This is shown by Matthew 25: 34ff., and by Revelation 20: 11-15; followed by chapter 21. It is also shown by such scriptures as 1 Corinthians 15, in which the possession of the resurrection body is placed at the second coming of Christ.

1. *The intermediate state*

But what about the intermediate state, as it is called; that is, the Christian's condition between death and the resurrection? It is made clear that this state is not one of unconsciousness, or "soul sleeping," so-called; it is a state of consciousness both for the wicked and the righteous. The parable of Dives and Lazarus shows this. Jesus speaks of death as a sleep, but this is not meant to teach that it is a state of unconsciousness, but a state of rest and peace as compared with the turmoil and strife of this life. Lazarus was seen in a position of rest in Abraham's bosom (Luke 16: 19ff.). This intermediate state is a state of conscious fellowship with the Lord. Paul, in speaking about death, as compared with continuing in this life, says that it is "very far better." Why does he think so? Because it means to "depart and be with Christ" (Phil. 1: 23). While the intermediate state, then, is not the final state of the Christian, it is made clear that it is a condition of conscious and immediate fellowship with Christ and is, therefore, more glorious and blessed than the present life.

2. *The eternal state of the righteous*

More properly speaking, heaven denotes the eternal state of the righteous, or their state after the resurrection and the judgment. Yet it has to be recognized that there is no very clear line of demarcation made in the Bible between the state upon which the righteous enter immediately after death and their condition after the judgment. Perhaps systems of theology have made more of a distinction than the teachings of the New Testament would justify. The fact, however, that the resurrection and final judgment are placed at the second coming does justify the position that the Christian does not come to his final state this side of the eternal order ushered in at the general judgment. The Christian does not come to the full and final enjoyment of the blessings of redemption until the recreation of a new humanity in Jesus Christ is completed. Our salvation is a part of a plan that a redeeming God has in mind for a new race now being created in the image of Jesus Christ. The individual Christian comes to his final destiny as a member of this new redeemed race of which Christ is the head. Apart from those who come after and those who have preceded us, we shall not be made perfect. We have a foretaste of the blessedness of redemption in this life; we enter upon a fuller possession of that blessedness at death; we come into full possession of it after judgment. What is said here, however, about the eternal blessedness of the redeemed will apply very largely to their condition between death and the resurrection.

(1) Where is heaven?

Heaven is not primarily a place but a state of character. It is freedom from sin and fulness of fellowship with God. A man with sin in his heart could not be happy anywhere in God's universe; he would convert any paradise into a hell. Character is more than environment. A perfect environment will not make perfect character. Some modern soap-box orators seem to think a full dinner pail is all that is needed to turn sinners into saints and the world into a paradise. But experience rather indicates that, without the regenerating grace of God, the easier conditions are for the sinner the more perverse he will likely become.

On the other hand, salvation would not be complete without a change of environment as well as a change in character. We have seen that there will perhaps be a renovation of the physical universe along with the deliverance of the children of God from the bondage of sin and corruption (Rom. 8: 19ff.; 2 Peter 3: 13). There will be new heavens and a new earth for a new humanity to inhabit. This will be true whether Peter's statement refers to the renovation of the physical universe or is a figure for the regeneration of the moral universe. The fact that we are to inhabit bodies will probably call for a "local habitation and a name." Heaven will doubtless be a location as well as a state of character. Will it be on this earth? Nobody knows, and there is no use to speculate about the matter. Our glorified bodies may have the power to move through space at the behest of our glorified wills. We do feel safe in holding that, while the primary thing about heaven is a state of character, it will also include a perfect environment.

(2) Our eternal state will be complete deliverance from sin.

Or, to state the matter affirmatively, it will be holiness of character. To be like Christ will be heaven. We know that when he shall appear we shall be like him (1 John 3: 2). To make us like Christ in character is the thing that God has had in mind for us from eternity. He predestinated us to be conformed to the image of his Son (Rom. 8: 29). Nothing grieves the heart of the Christian so in this life as his own sins and moral lapses; he longs with unutterable longing for complete deliverance. This comes to him in the next life. To be free from sin will be one of the chief elements in the Christian's blessedness in the coming age. Not only will sin be taken out of us, but also out of the whole social order of which we shall be a part. The dogs, the sorcerers, the fornicators, the murderers, the idolaters, and every one that loveth and maketh a lie—these shall all be left outside the Holy City (Rev. 22: 15).

(3) Our eternal state will be a life of unhindered fellowship with God in Christ.

The Christian's fellowship with God is his chief joy in this life. It is this that brings joy and hope and conquering power. It is for a fuller fellowship with the Lord that the Christian longs in the next life. Paul says that it would be very far better to depart in death and be with the Lord (Phil. 1: 23). This is the explanation of the eager looking toward the second coming that we find in the New Testament. While Jesus was on earth, his disciples had fellowship with him in the flesh. In this life our fellowship with God is hindered by our sins and spiritual blindness. When we see the Lord face to face and are completely transformed into his image, then our fellowship with him will be full and complete. This carries with it the idea that heaven is the complete realization of the life of fellowship that man has with God here and now.

Fellowship with God carries with it fellowship with his people. Those we have known on earth we will probably know there, as well as the host of the redeemed. Earthly relations, however, will be swallowed up in a higher relationship. That is true to some extent here; it will be more completely true there. The fundamental relation there will be our relation to God. If family relationships are remembered, they will be subordinated to the higher. There will be no marrying and giving in marriage (Mark 12: 25). There will be social relations in heaven, but they will be subordinate to the religious. God will be first, our fellows second.

(4) The eternal order is one of freedom from natural evil, such as sorrow, sickness, and death.

There are abundant indications in the New Testament that all forms of natural evil will be transcended in the glorified life of the Christian during the coming age. God will wipe away all tears from the eyes of his people (Isa. 25: 8; Rev. 7: 17; 21: 4), and sorrow and sighing shall flee away (Isa. 51: 11). The complete conquering of sin carries with it complete transcendence of all other forms of evil. When man is entirely right with God and in complete harmony with his will, then all is bound to come right for man. "There shall be no curse any more: and the throne of God and of the Lamb shall be therein" (Rev. 22: 3). And the reason there shall be no curse is because the throne of God and of the Lamb is there. God's authority and rule will have abolished all evil and everything that is accursed. This is relatively true for this life, but comes to full realization in the life to come.

This complete transcendence of evil is beautifully pictured in Revelation 21 and 22 under the figure of the new Jerusalem come down out of heaven to men. In the Book of Revelation, we do not get out of the atmosphere of turmoil and strife until we get past the judgment in chapter 20 and come to the new Jerusalem in chapter 21. But when we get to chapter 21, we seem to have come into an altogether new atmosphere, one of eternal calm and joy. The strife and disappointments of this earth-life are past. We come into a perfected social life in which love to God and one's fellows reigns. God is supreme. All his enemies and ours are vanquished. Life abundant is the portion of God's people and eternal peace is theirs.

(5) There will be ceaseless service to God.

His servants shall serve him in the eternal order (Rev. 22: 3). Heaven is no place for inactivity; it is no lazy man's paradise. It is a place of abundant life—and life means activity. In the very nature of the case, created beings would serve the God who created them. What forms our service will take we are not told. It is enough that we are assured that we shall serve God. Doubtless praise and adoration will forever be given to the God who has redeemed us (Rev. 12: 10). But doubtless also we will do something more than sing and praise. Even singing might grow monotonous if it were not mixed with other forms of activity.

(6) Heaven will also doubtless be a place or state of endless development.

It will be at once asked, "Is not heaven a state of perfection, and does not perfection exclude the idea of growth?" Heaven is a state of perfection; it is freedom from sin and its total curse. But a perfect state for man is not a state in which there is no growth. This is shown in the case of Jesus. He was sinless, but he grew. A state of perfection for a created being is rather a state in which everything that hinders growth is removed. The great hindrance to growth in this life is sin. When sin is taken out of us and we are placed in an environment in which sin as an obstruction to growth is removed, we will then be in a condition to begin to grow as we should.

In 1 Corinthians 13: 9-12, Paul indicates that there will be a great change in the method and character of our knowledge. He is here perhaps referring to the eternal order. Doubtless our knowledge then will be more direct and intuitive than now. We shall then see face to face and know fully as we are known. But we cannot interpret this to mean omniscience. Only God is omniscient. For a being who is not omniscient there is always room for growth. And when we come into face-to-face communion with God, there will doubtless be such a renovation and readjustment of our rational powers as to make it possible for us to grow in knowledge as we do not now dream possible.

Again, Paul indicates that faith, hope, and love are the abiding virtues of the Christian life (1 Cor. 13: 13).

Knowledge passes away in that it is swallowed up in fuller knowledge, as the knowledge of the child is swallowed up in that of the man (1 Cor. 13: 8-11). Faith, hope, and love do not pass away; they abide forever. But hope looks to the future; it looks for something not yet realized. This indicates that even in heaven there will always be before us possibilities toward which we are moving that we have not yet attained. And Paul's statement indicates that faith and hope are just as eternal as love. This would seem almost to necessitate the idea that the future life for the Christian will be a life of eternal growth. Boundless possibilities of development in knowledge, power, and holiness are our inheritance in Christ Jesus, and endless ages are ours in which to attain our possibilities.

VII. Hell

1. *The certainty of future punishment*

As pointed out in connection with the Judgment, the idea of judgment runs through the whole Bible. The ideas of divine judgment and punishment for sin are inseparable. What was said, therefore, about the certainty of judgment will apply to punishment for sin.

Men are punished in this life for their sins. That is made clear in the examples and teachings of the Bible. It is also verified in experience. But men do not get the full punishment for their sins in this life. The full punishment for sin, therefore, must come in the next life. We maintain that men will be punished in the future life for the following reasons:

(1) It is distinctly taught in the Bible.

Punishment for sin is emphasized in the Old Testament, but it is mainly punishment in this life. In the New Testament punishment for sin in the future life is clearly taught. Nobody teaches this more clearly and emphatically than does Jesus. He solemnly and repeatedly warns men against the dangers of a hell of fire in which God will destroy both soul and body (Matt. 5: 22, 29; 10: 28; 18: 9; Mark 9: 43, 45; Luke 12: 5, et al). The teaching of Jesus is set forth with special clearness in connection with what he says on the Judgment (Matt. 25: 41-46). The Book of Revelation speaks of the lake of fire into which the wicked will be cast after the Judgment and identifies it with the second death (Rev. 20: 10, 14, 15; 21: 8).

(2) The very existence of a moral order requires that sinners shall be punished.

The reason there is a hell is because there is sin in the world. In a moral world there must be a difference between the righteous and the wicked. If the righteous and wicked were treated alike, there would be no moral order; it would be non-moral. The very existence of sin, then, demands the punishment of sin. The man who lives in sin can never be made happy. Sin and punishment cannot be separated. Christ saves men first from sin, then from punishment. He cannot save from punishment except as he saves from sin. The same word in the Old Testament may be translated iniquity or punishment. (See Gen. 4: 13.) This shows that in Hebrew thought punishment could not be separated from sin. Sin carries its own punishment. Many men think that if they can just stay out of the fire after they die they will be all right. What they need to see is that they must get the fire of sin out of their souls. Man cannot be made happy while he remains in sin. The moral order of the world makes it impossible. Looked at from this viewpoint, man makes his own hell. He reaps what he sows. His violence comes down upon his own pate. His feet are ensnared in the gin that he sets for others. He digs a ditch and falls into it himself. (See Psalms 7: 15, 16; 9: 15, 16; 57: 6, et al.)

(3) The sinner's moral nature is a guarantee that sin will be punished.

Because man is what he is, he will suffer for sin. He cannot escape from punishment for sin, because he cannot escape from himself. The lashings of conscience and memory, the vain regrets and remorse that follow in the wake of a misspent life will make a hot enough hell for any man. "Myself am hell." So many a man finds out. He thinks, at first, that, if he can escape the law and public reproach, he will be all right. But he finds at last that he cannot have peace anywhere until he comes to be at peace in his own mind and heart.

(4) Sin must be punished because it is opposed to the holy nature of God.

Sin violates the moral order of the world; but that order is a revelation of the holy nature of God. This is God's world. The very nature of sin is such that it would dethrone God. God must punish sin or abdicate his throne. As already stated, man brings down destruction upon himself. But it does not follow from this that his punishment is not from God. God instituted and sustains the moral order under which the sinner suffers. That moral order is so made that man cannot sin without suffering, and the reason it is that way is because God wills that it should be. It may be truly said, then, either that the sinner destroys himself, or that God destroys him.

2. *The nature and extent of future punishment*

(1) Such expressions as those spoken of—"the hell of fire," "the lake of fire," and "the second death"—indicate the awfulness of the fate of the impenitent.

There are those who insist that the fire spoken of must be literal fire. Some insist on this with great strenuousness and seem to think that to interpret the language as figurative means to do away with the reality of future punishment. But one could maintain this position only on the assumption that a figure of speech does not represent a reality. Jesus speaks of the place of punishment as a place of outer darkness (Matt. 8: 12; 22: 13; 25: 30). It could not be a place of both literal fire and of literal darkness. But there is no more reason for taking one expression as literal than there is for taking the other as literal. Besides, literal fire would destroy a body cast into it. Some would say that it is a literal fire, but not the kind of fire we are used to. But this is equivalent to saying that it is not literal fire. Moreover, to inflict purely physical pain on the sinner would not be to adapt his punishment to the nature of his sin. The sinner's punishment in this life is adapted to the nature of his sin, and there is no good reason why the same should not be true in the next world. Since we reap the final reward of our deeds in the next life, it would seem that the conformity of punishment to sin in its nature would probably be closer even than in this. Physical suffering would not be an adequate punishment for spiritual sins. It is entirely possible, then, that the nature of the punishment in the next life will depend on the nature of the sin for which it is a punishment, and that there will be as much variety in the kinds of punishment inflicted as there is variety in the kinds of sinners punished.

(2) It is made clear in the New Testament that punishment will be in proportion to the greatness of one's guilt.

Jesus recognizes this when he says that it will be more tolerable in the day of judgment for Tyre and Sidon than it will be for the cities that have rejected him and his message (Matt. 11: 22). Paul also manifests a belief in this principle. He says: "As many as have sinned without the law shall also perish without the law: and as many as have sinned under the law shall be judged by the law" (Rom. 2: 12). He says also that those who do not have the law are a law unto themselves in that they show the work of the law written in their hearts, their consciences bearing witness therewith (Rom. 2: 14, 15). This principle clearly commends itself to man's sense of justice. There is nothing in either reason or the Scriptures to justify the idea that all the impenitent will be punished to the same extent in the next life.

3. The endlessness of future punishment

It seems to be made clear in the Bible that the future punishment of the wicked is endless. In the parable of the rich man and Lazarus, in answer to the rich man's request that Lazarus dip his finger in water and cool the rich man's tongue, Jesus represents Abraham as saying, "And besides all this, between us and you there is a great gulf fixed, that they that would pass from hence to you may not be able, and that none may cross over from thence to us" (Luke 16: 26). Here Jesus seems to be expressly teaching that, if a man dies unrepentant, there is no hope of mercy in the next life. His condition is unchangeable. There is no crossing from one place to the other. Another passage that seems to be decisive on this point is on the judgment in Matthew 25. Jesus says: "These go away into eternal punishment: but the righteous into eternal life" (Matt. 25: 46). Here the Lord uses the same word to describe the endurance of the punishment of the wicked that he uses to describe the endurance of the blessedness of the righteous. If it means never ending, in the case of the righteous, why should it not mean the same thing as applied in the same context to the punishment of the wicked?

In general, there are two views that deny the endlessness of future punishment. One is the view of restorationism or universalism. This holds in different forms to the idea that man will suffer in the future life for his sins, but that this suffering will be remedial in its nature, and that through his sufferings he will be purified from sin and finally delivered from it. There is no evidence in the Scriptures, however, that suffering in the future life will be remedial in its nature, and positive teaching to the contrary. Suffering is remedial in this life, but not wholly so. There is no teaching in the New Testament that the next life will be redemptive in its purpose. All that we have on the subject is in the contrary direction.

Then, it is held by some that sin and its punishment are destructive in the sense that the soul and its powers are blotted out of existence. It is pointed out that sin here tends to dissipate and destroy. This destructive tendency of sin is the punishment for sin, and the second death is the complete annihilation of man's existence. But this would lead to the conclusion that the greater sinner one became, the sooner would his conscious existence come to an end and, therefore, the less his punishment. Besides, sin does not always tend to destroy one's conscious powers in this life. And when it does so, it may be due to the fact that man's soul inhabits an organism of "flesh and blood." This may not be true of the soul during the intermediate state nor after the resurrection of the body.

So the only hope of deliverance from sin and its awful consequences held out in the gospel of Christ is in this life, and the evidence indicates that no man will be saved after he departs this world. This does not mean, as sometimes held, that evangelical theology teaches that the great mass of mankind is damned to an eternal hell, since only a small portion of the race has professedly accepted Christ. It means that it is made clear in the New Testament that the man who consciously and definitely accepts Christ as Saviour and Lord is assured of eternal blessedness with him in the next world; and that the man who consciously and wilfully rejects God's mercy manifested in Christ and dies in impenitence is solemnly warned that he will be eternally punished for his sins. The great mass of mankind lying in between these two classes we can safely leave in the hands of God, being assured that he will do what is right with reference to every son of man and that he knows to which of these two classes each man belongs.

How much moral light and spiritual knowledge one must have before he can so commit sin as to seal his destiny for evil, we perhaps cannot determine; nor is it our business to do so. To decide this question is God's prerogative. It is ours to give every man we possibly can the full light of the gospel, so that he may have conscious salvation through faith in Christ or be left without excuse because of the rejected grace of God.

GENERAL INDEX

Absoluteness of God, 80.

Accountability, ground of judgment, 319.

Administrator of baptism, 283.

Adoption, 113, 160, 210.

Advent, final, 307.

Advocate, Jesus Christ as, 180.

Alien immersion, 285.

Apostles as Church Officers, 263.

Appearances of Jesus, 53, 179.

Annihilation, 330.

Answered prayer, 236.

Anthropomorphism, 79.

Ascension of Jesus Christ, 65, 179.

Assurance, 113, 220; conditions of, 221.

Atheism, 145.

Atonement, 99, 169; motive of, 174; relation to law, 175; relation to righteousness, 175; objections to, 176; and love, 176; and faith, 177.

Authority: and freedom, 42; of Jesus, 66.

Baptism: of Spirit, 114; of Jesus, 170; and church membership, 261; ordinance of, 273; mode of, 280; candidates for, 282; infant, 282; administrator of, 283.

Baptismal regeneration, 274.

Bible: and revelation, 35; Gospels, heart of, 36; human agency, 40; inspiration of, 40f; as authoritative, 41; means of grace, 250.

Blasphemy, against Holy Spirit, 111, 136.

Body, nature of resurrection, 313.

Bunyan, John, 142.

Calvin, view of Lord's Supper, 286.

Catholic, Roman, 193, 221; church government of, 266; sacraments of, 273; on baptism, 273ff; Lord's Supper, 285ff.

Character, goal of, 254.

Christ, see Jesus Christ.

Christian Doctrine: definition of, 11; purpose of, 11; need of, 11.

Christian effort and election, 165.

Christian experience: and Person of Christ, 55; and election, 162; as regeneration, 213; normal, 219; related to church government, 267.

Christian life: 227; growth of, 246.

Church: the Spirit and, 110, 115; as means of grace, 250; doctrine of, 259; founding of, 259; membership of, 259; officers of, 262; government, 265; presbyterial, 266; episcopal, 266; monarchial, 266; democracy, 266; mission of, 269; co-operation, 270; ordinances, 273.

Clarke, W. N., 92.

Clergy, 283.

Close Communion, 289.

Communion of Lord's Supper, 288.

Communion with God, 78, 219; spiritual experience, 79; in prayer, 233; in death, 306.

Confession: of sin, 201; prayer of, 233.

Conscience, 93; and revelation, 133.

Consubstantiation, 286.

Consummation of salvation, 113

INDEX OF SCRIPTURE REFERENCES